LEARNING THROUGH GEORGE WASHINGTON

FROM PAMPHLETS TO PODCASTS

An Institute for Thomas Paine Studies Series

Nora Slonimsky and Mark Boonshoft, Editors

LEARNING THROUGH GEORGE WASHINGTON

A Guide for Educators, Students, and Citizens

EDITED BY KATE ELIZABETH BROWN
AND LORRI GLOVER

UNIVERSITY OF VIRGINIA PRESS
Charlottesville and London

Published in association with the Institute for
Thomas Paine Studies at Iona University

The University of Virginia Press is situated on the traditional lands of the Monacan Nation, and the Commonwealth of Virginia was and is home to many other Indigenous people. We pay our respect to all of them, past and present. We also honor the enslaved African and African American people who built the University of Virginia, and we recognize their descendants. We commit to fostering voices from these communities through our publications and to deepening our collective understanding of their histories and contributions.

University of Virginia Press

Printed in the United States of America on acid-free paper

First published 2026

1 3 5 7 9 8 6 4 2

ISBN 978-0-8139-5584-1 (hardback)
ISBN 978-0-8139-5585-8 (paperback)
ISBN 978-0-8139-5586-5 (ebook)

Library of Congress Cataloging-in-Publication Data is available for this title.

Cover art: Duncan1890/iStock
Cover design: Joel W. Coggins

For Mom, Dad, and the late Mike Miranda

&

For Dan

CONTENTS

Part III. Enslaved Americans and Slavery in the Revolutionary Era

Part IV. Martha Washington's World

Part V. Sharing George Washington and the Founding Era with Varied Audiences

Part VI. Eighteenth-Century Society and Culture

FOREWORD

I am thrilled to be a part of this innovative collection of essays that traces its origins to the George Washington Teacher Institute (GWTI). My role at George Washington's Mount Vernon is to ensure that our education programs connect people to the Mount Vernon Ladies' Association's mission in vibrant and vital ways. The GWTI residential program is at the heart of this effort. Each summer we work to bring together passionate, learned, and dynamic experts to help teachers and their students engage with the life and world of George Washington in resonant and powerful ways.

Now, for the first time, those expert voices have been collected in a single volume. When the editors, Kate Elizabeth Brown and Lorri Glover, brought this concept to me, I got giddy. I have the privileged joy, each (hot) summer, of attending sessions led by these individuals, but it is a joy I can only share with 150 other people each year. Now anyone can experience this diverse collection of perspectives on teaching about George Washington that we share with educators. The strategies and perspectives the authors provide come from a diverse range of teaching environments, from research universities to elementary school libraries to public history sites. The authors shape rural communities and urban enclaves. They teach sometimes-distracted middle school students, curious fifth graders, driven AP students, historic site visitors, college students, kindergarteners, and pundits in the public eye. This book is not primarily about what we know about George Washington and his world, though leading scholars who research his life and times certainly cover a great deal. Readers will learn about Washington's influences in politics, economy, and civic and family life from Kate Elizabeth Brown, Denver Brunsman, and Lynn Price Robbins; about Native American perspectives on the creation of the American republic from David J. Silverman; and about the lives of enslaved people in the eighteenth century from Kathryn M. Silva. *Learning Through George Washington* is, however, principally about how we teach what we know about George Washington and his world. It is in this civic act of classroom instruction that educators share the knowledge and tools for democracy with their students, who, in turn, form our shared future.

Yikes, yes. I went there! Teaching about George Washington is vital for the nation's future. After a decade at Mount Vernon, I have come to appreciate how closely tied our success in educating young people about the founding era is to their success in engaging in present-day civic decisions. George Washington is so inextricably intertwined with the founding of the United States that his biography can provide a blueprint for civic values. His biography can also bear the weight of the accolades and the critiques of the founding era, with compelling narratives and evidentiary sources that number more than any other figure in that time. The authors explore all facets of his leadership and legacies in his lifetime and beyond, and they connect his life to their students in meaningful and valuable ways. Giving students these historical insights and tools for learning also offers them the opportunity to reflect on what it means to be an American, to shape their practice in reflective patriotism, and to become conscientious contributors to civic communities. Okay, I'm getting too far into the future . . . back to the pages in front of you.

In this volume, you will find deep dives into primary source analysis, techniques for grappling with disengaged students, tools to help put Washington's achievements in the context of his time and ours, methods for illuminating underrepresented voices from the eighteenth century, and strategies for tackling the complexities of Washington's actions. In response to our teachers' needs, we have brought a special focus to teaching through the tensions and critiques they report hearing from their classrooms and communities. Some of the key strategies we share come from the public history world. The links between classroom practice, academic scholarship, and public history interpretation methods shine through these essays to benefit educators from all three of these disparate worlds.

As I have had the opportunity to work with each of this volume's authors, I can hear their voices and envision their animated faces as they talk through each of these topics with a small group of teachers each summer. I hope you can hear Scott E. Casper's "HUH?!?!" as he voices student confusion with eighteenth-century language when you read it in the text of his essay. Sarah J. Purcell's in-person rapid-fire delivery rockets Washington's military career, with vitality and urgency, through a reinvention for the twenty-first-century classroom. Lorri Glover's essay on George Washington puts the reader at ease by showing how his biography illuminates the distant and sometimes unreachable eighteenth-century cultural world that confuses and befuddles those of us living in a very different era. Laura J. Ping's exploration of comparative sources from across centuries and class divisions illuminates Martha Washington's experiences in her own time and helps students see the impact of the romanticization of her in the nineteenth century.

The essays by the K–12 educators and administrators center the teaching and learning experience in the classroom in ways that open instructional doors on George Washington through self-reflection (Eric Louérs-Phillips), collaboration (John Clinton Walsh), case study design (Bonnie A. Belshe), storytelling (Shawnel Padilla), and cultural sensitivity (Morgan Smith). I love the fact that so many of these education experts first attended one of our workshops and then proceeded to share their brilliance with other attendees each summer—and now, in this volume, with you.

Some contributors are my current and former colleagues here at Mount Vernon who, for every summer of their Mount Vernon experience, were critical to the success of GWTI, handling the day-to-day details, program design, visionary leadership, and public history research and interpretation that shape what we offer in the sessions and in this volume. Their essays on integrating object-based learning (Lucy Smith), elevating humanity through multiple perspectives (Jessie MacLeod), measuring tone and balance to navigate critique (Lindsay M. Chervinsky), and supporting teacher needs in programming (Alissa Oginsky) can fuel innovative approaches in any classroom, school, cultural site, or museum.

In my time here, I have seen how the connections people make to George Washington and his world change, but the strategies to make those connections are resilient and sturdy, making this volume both timely and timeless. So whether you dog-ear one section (or whatever the digital equivalent is to dog-earing) or find greater value in reading the essays as a collective whole, I look forward to welcoming you back to the book each time.

K. Allison Wickens

INTRODUCTION

The Revolutionary era and creation of the American republic laid the foundation for the rest of American history. Across generations, Americans worked to expand—and sometimes constrain—who belonged in "we, the people" and to build their often-clashing visions of "a more perfect union." Leaders of the founding generation—homogenized as the "Founding Fathers"—are often invoked but not well understood by policymakers and citizens. Despite (or perhaps because of) the tendency to misunderstand and misrepresent the founders, they loom large in popular imagination.

Americans seem to perpetually cling to an imagined past that never existed. That mythology is vividly captured in the iconic, romanticized paintings by John Trumbull displayed in the US Capitol Rotunda: Thomas Jefferson and his committee presenting the Declaration of Independence to the Second Continental Congress, the members in their velvet knee-breeches, orderly, dignified, resolute; Lord Cornwallis, surrendering at Yorktown before an array of elegantly clad, unscathed soldiers; George Washington, bathed in light and the very embodiment of civic virtue, resigning his command of the Continental Army. Many Americans weigh present-day civic culture against those impossible measuring sticks. We often think that if only we did what the founders did, all would be right in the United States. A deep dive into the life and world of George Washington affords a critical corrective to that mythology, an entry into a fascinating, still resonant history, and a powerful example of leadership that recognizes the complexity and contingency of the nation's past.

Learning Through George Washington offers that deep dive through the experiences of those who teach George Washington and his world. United by a love for early American history and a commitment to studying the nation's first wartime commander and first president under the Constitution, the contributors to this volume are scholars of early American history, Advanced Placement US history teachers, librarians, curriculum specialists, museum curators, civics and government instructors, administrators, and middle and elementary school teachers. Each author offers unique insights, strategies, and lessons for teaching about George Washington and the eighteenth century. Their essays all address the complexity, nuance, and "tough history" that arise from an honest assessment of America's past, informed by historiographical debates and based on primary sources. The collection reflects what we have learned, together, about and through George Washington.

This collection focuses on George Washington and his world, which included colonial British America, the Revolutionary era, and the early American republic, but the lessons offered in the following pages can be applied to other periods as well. *Learning Through George Washington* presents an approach to learning and teaching that can be employed to study the Lowell mills and early industrialization, Abraham Lincoln and the Civil War era, women in the Civil Rights Movement, and Ronald Reagan and the Cold War, to name a few examples. So why focus on George Washington?

Washington is the first person in American history whom many schoolchildren meet, and he remains today, as he was in late eighteenth-century America, nearly universally known. He is arguably the most important individual in US history; certainly, he would make anyone's top ten influencer list. Perhaps one could argue for Abraham Lincoln or Martin Luther King Jr. as exerting greater significance in the long arc of the nation's history. But their achievements were to a degree shaped by Washington's life and legacy, the unfinished business of the founding era. And both, along with many other transformational leaders, invoked Washington and his world.

George Washington's model of leadership and republican values was of singular importance to securing the survival of the young country. He commanded the Continental Army for eight long years, ultimately prevailing against all odds. He worked during the war and in the early years after peace to build a strong national government and identity, eventually chairing the Philadelphia Convention of 1787, which produced the US Constitution. Washington exerted tremendous influence in the closely contested ratification debates. Then he served as the first president of the yet unproven experiment in representative democracy, establishing models of executive branch conduct and leadership that persist into the third century after his presidency. In perhaps the most important action of his extensive career of service, Washington resigned his command of the Continental Army in 1783. It was an act completely unprecedented in world history, one so significant that even King George III reportedly said, "If he does that, he will be the greatest man in the world." Washington repeated that sacrifice of power when he declined to serve a third term as president in 1796 and retired to Mount Vernon.

Though lacking in formal education when compared to contemporaries such as Alexander Hamilton, James Madison, Thomas Jefferson, and John Adams, Washington was a prolific writer and a careful preserver of the records of his extraordinary life and the new country he helped build. His papers—including diaries, farm logs, correspondence, and a myriad of other written materials—have proven immeasurably important for historians. For generations, scholars compiled and studied his writings, and today students of all ages and across the country and world can access more than fifty thousand documents, transcribed and annotated to the highest of professional standards by skilled documentary editors, on Founders Online. We reference this National Archives–sponsored website across essays, making it easy for readers to go directly to the sources and explore topics that capture their attention.[1]

This rich repository includes Washington's papers, along with documents from and about his wife, Martha Dandridge Custis Washington, and their extended family; his friends and rivals; leaders of Native American and European nations; the people Washington enslaved; and individuals from across the Atlantic world. Students of history can use those materials to learn about eighteenth-century cultures and economy, the Revolutionary War and Revolutionary era, the origins of the Constitution and the office of the president, civic leadership and republican values, the experiences of enslaved people and the institution of slavery, Native nations and peoples, medical innovations, gender and family values, diplomacy—the list goes on and on! Other innovative digital repositories, starting with the Mount Vernon website, enable widespread access to a myriad of other kinds of sources: art and architecture, archaeological finds, clothing, farming tools, and foodways, to name just a few. People unable to visit Virginia can tour Mount Vernon virtually. For anyone, anywhere, interested in learning more about any part of eighteenth-century life, George Washington provides an unparalleled number and range of sources.[2]

The bountiful evidence documenting Washington's accomplishments also makes clear that he remained a lifelong enslaver, one whose exceptional service to his country was enabled by enslaved laborers. Adults and children labored at Mount Vernon throughout the Revolutionary War, during Washington's presidency, and as he lay dying in 1799. No part of his life and legacy can be separated from those facts. The house, wealth, clothing, time to serve the nation and to curate all those records—enslaved labor subsidized all of it. Washington also built large parts of his wealth and the financial security of the young country from seized Native American lands in the interior of North America. It is impossible to understand the early American republic absent the systematic dispossession and displacement of Native peoples.

Being a good student of history requires seeing and accepting the interconnections between the achievements of people in the past, including George Washington, and the terrible costs of those achievements. Thus, the essays in this volume interpret the ways in which Washington's life and leadership were inextricably linked to racial slavery and Indigenous dispossession. Readers will see that while authors foreground varying themes and methods, those topics are not separated across our essays, for they were not separate in Washington's life and world. The historical ways of thinking and the critical thinking skills emphasized by authors in this collection provide a road map for readers, helping them avoid the seduction of celebration versus condemnation and move instead to thoughtful historical understanding.[3]

This volume represents the collective work of the scholars and teachers who annually gather at the George Washington Teacher Institute (GWTI). Since the summer of 1999, early American historians, museum and educational experts, and K–12 educators from across the nation have worked together at George Washington's Mount Vernon in these residential professional development programs. Currently organized around weekly themes exploring the important and overlapping endeavors of Washington's life, the GWTI aims to further the study of Washington and his world by bringing together those who teach the youngest generation of Americans with those whose scholarly research and public history projects shape our understanding of America's past. During the five-day GWTI programs, public and private school teachers from all disciplines explore the Mount Vernon estate, discuss lesson plans and classroom activities, participate in museum and other site-based learning projects, and engage with the latest developments in historiography and scholarship relating to George Washington's life, the eighteenth century, and Washington's legacy. The GWTI invites historians to present innovative research as guest scholars, speaking about topics relevant to the theme of the week. Lead scholars and teacher facilitators provide intellectual and pedagogical continuity. The George Washington Presidential Library at Mount Vernon is the site of much GWTI programming, and the library's holdings and the Papers of George Washington projects (print and digital) form the foundations for GWTI participants' scholarship and teaching.

The K–12 participants selected for the institutes, as well as the academic scholars and public historians invited to speak on Washington and early American history, are all teachers; they operate on the front lines of history education and are responsible for providing students vital lessons about civics and engaging them in honest conversations about America's past. To facilitate their work, the GWTI emphasizes historical scholarship, primary source–based historical inquiry, and inclusive engagement with the people, ideas, and events of the colonial period, American Revolutionary era, and early republic. The learning communities created by the GWTI engage in a constant pedagogical dialogue about topics such as how to help students better engage with sources and use technology, how to teach with material culture artifacts, and how to discuss controversial topics respectfully and accurately.

Mirroring the collaboration between scholars and teachers that defines the GWTI program, this volume brings together essays from academic historians, public historians, and K–12 historian-educators. We asked each author to lean into their own expertise and voice. Unlike most traditional multiauthored collections, these essays are not uniform in length or tone—by design. The best historical inquiries are deeply personal, driven by individual curiosity, and, therefore, often generative of innovative questions and answers. This applies equally to experienced students of history and beginning learners and is reflected in the essays. Some authors provide more narrative detail, particularly for topics central to understanding Washington's world but less familiar than his wartime or presidential leadership, including African American history, women's history, and Indigenous cultures and US Indian policy. Some authors center their essays around objects—Washington's dentures or children's books or a museum exhibition—while others concentrate on educational challenges and innovations. For readers pursuing further study, we weave throughout the essays signposts for primary sources and first-rate online resources such as those provided by Mount Vernon, the Museum of the American Revolution, and the National Council for the Social Studies (NCSS). We also discuss pedagogies including Reacting to the Past and learning games such as those created by iCivics.[4]

The contributors have a wide range of experiences with archives, classrooms, and historical sites. We teach in varied venues and for different audiences, study a broad expanse of topics, and use diverse approaches. But we share a common commitment to fostering greater understanding of Washington and eighteenth-century America—and of how to learn from that world in the twenty-first century. We all seek to answer the call to action that George Washington made in his 1796 Farewell Address: "Promote then, as an object of primary importance, institutions for the general diffusion of knowledge."[5]

We hope that learners of all ages and levels of experience will benefit from studying George Washington alongside the historian-teachers in this collection. We crafted our essays not only for classroom teachers and students of eighteenth-century history and American civics but also for all readers eager to learn more about the "Father of His Country"—leaving behind the ripped-from-history, larger-than-life, mythologized hero for the real-life man and the fascinating, enduring, flawed American republic he led.

The essays in *Learning Through George Washington* are grouped around themes related to Washington's life as well as how these experienced teachers present eighteenth-century American history. The first section, "Entering George Washington's World," provides two rich overviews, one about studying Washington through primary sources and the other about the GWTI. Part II introduces four quite different and compelling approaches to understanding and teaching Washington's leadership: as he envisioned himself; during the Revolutionary War; through encounters with and perspectives of Indigenous nations in the longer Revolutionary era; and in twenty-first-century middle school classrooms. The next section, "Enslaved Americans and Slavery in the Revolutionary Era," presents groundbreaking approaches to recovering perspectives of enslaved people through a museum exhibition, in classrooms, and from academic historical scholarship. Part IV pivots to the life of Martha Washington and offers innovative methods and sources for learning about her experiences, including within the wider context of eighteenth-century gender expectations. In Part V, author-educators share how they present Washington and the founding era in divergent venues and for varied groups of learners: university classrooms, elementary school libraries, public audiences, and communities of educators. The last section, "Eighteenth-Century Society and Culture," illuminates ways to better understand the wider eighteenth century, with essays centering the values Washington sought to exemplify, the economic innovations he advanced, and material and medical culture during his lifetime.

Across all the essays, authors have tried to be mindful of the language they use to describe the past, and their word choices reflect recent (and still evolving) scholarly conventions. In recent years, for example, historians began using the term "enslaved people" rather than "slaves" when referring to Black people kidnapped, sold, and born into slavery. This linguistic shift aims to separate the degraded status of slavery from the person experiencing it and to refrain from defining the person subjugated into slavery by that imposed status. Similarly, when referring to the Native peoples of North America, writers use, when possible, the specific nation—Haudenosaunee or Shawnee, for example. (Likewise, when practical, we adopt "England" or "France" rather than "Europe.") When such specific usages are not possible or practical, writers use "Indian," "Native American," and "Indigenous."[6] One of George Washington's first encounters with Native American nations occurred in 1754 in the Ohio River Valley, when a young Lieutenant Colonel Washington inadvertently sparked an international war. Americans often refer to the subsequent fighting as the French and Indian War. We instead use the term "Seven Years' War" to acknowledge the broader, global scope of the conflict. And although Americans today know the wife of the sitting president as the First Lady, this language was not yet in use when Martha Washington served in that role. To avoid anachronism, essayists in this volume resist referring to Martha Washington as First Lady, instead identifying her by her own name or as the wife to the nation's first president.[7]

Finally, we use the term "American Revolution" to designate the opposition to British imperial policy, break from the British Empire, and creation of the nation under the Constitution, roughly the period between 1763 and 1789. That political transformation propelled but was not the same thing as the Revolutionary War or War for Independence (1775–1783). And the terms "Revolutionary era" and "founding era" are broader still, used by authors to capture, in the first case, the wider social, cultural, and political transformations unfolding between the 1750s and 1790s and, with the latter, the continuing struggle to secure the nation-state, running from the 1770s to the 1800s.

Learning Through George Washington seeks to connect to educators who teach about George Washington in what contributor Denver Brunsman calls our "dysfunctional" times. (This perceived and real dysfunctionality, alas, we share with people who lived in the founding era.) The volume is also meant for readers who admire George Washington, who want to learn more about him and his era, who may be puzzled or troubled by the ways in which Washington's life and legacy are discussed, or who seek a deeper understanding of the country's origins to more thoughtfully engage in civic life today. The authors featured in this volume offer ways to learn, teach, and think about America's past through source-based, straightforward, innovative approaches. The skills they employ provide models for navigating divisive contemporary politics to faithfully, rigorously pursue historical knowledge, to holistically continue learning through George Washington.

Notes

1. The essays containing citations for Founders Online documents do not include individual links, as each source can be found by searching the site at https://founders.archives.gov/.
2. George Washington's Mount Vernon, https://www.mountvernon.org/; virtual tours of Mount Vernon are available at the George Washington's Mount Vernon website, https://virtualtour.mountvernon.org/. Other exceptional digital resources for the era include the Museum of the American Revolution, https://www.amrevmuseum.org/; the National Constitution Center, https://constitutioncenter.org/; Thomas Jefferson's Monticello, https://www.monticello.org; and the Yale Law School Avalon Project, https://avalon.law.yale.edu/subject_menus/18th.asp, which provides a wealth of documents running from ancient history to the twenty-first century.
3. The National Council for History Education provides extensive and valuable resources, including History's Habits of Mind, https://ncheteach.org/resources/historys-habits-of-mind/.
4. Learn about NCSS, RTTP, and iCivics at https://www.socialstudies.org/, https://reacting.barnard.edu/, and https://ed.icivics.org. The National

Archives and Library of Congress both offer excellent resources for teaching and learning though primary sources: see https://www.archives.gov/education/lessons/worksheets and https://www.loc.gov/programs/teachers/getting-started-with-primary-sources/.

5. See Farewell Address, September 19, 1796, Founders Online, for the full text. To learn more, see Shira Lurie, "George Washington's Farewell Address," in *The Digital Encyclopedia of George Washington,* George Washington's Mount Vernon, https://www.mountvernon.org/library/digitalhistory/digital-encyclopedia/article/george-washington-s-farewell-address.
6. For context, see Brooke Bauer and Elizabeth Ellis, "Indigenous, Native America, or American Indian? The Limitations of Broad Terms," *Journal of the Early Republic* 43, no. 1 (2023): 61–74.
7. For context, see Matthew Costello, "The Origins of the American 'First Lady,'" White House Historical Association, https://www.whitehousehistory.org/the-origins-of-the-american-first-lady.

PART I

ENTERING GEORGE WASHINGTON'S WORLD

GEORGE WASHINGTON IN TWO PORTRAITS AND TWO FAREWELLS

SCOTT E. CASPER

George Washington's likeness has been the most familiar American face for more than 250 years. We carry him in our pockets on the dollar bill and the quarter. His portrait, reproduced in the thousands, hung for generations on classroom walls across the United States. We know—or think we know—that he crossed the Delaware, chopped down a cherry tree, prayed in the snow at Valley Forge, and ascended to heaven and immortality, all because nineteenth-century artists depicted these scenes with no small dose of imagination. In our own time, Lin-Manuel Miranda's musical *Hamilton* has given us yet another imaginary Washington, the stoic statesman who teaches his countrymen how to say goodbye.[1]

George Washington's words are less well known today. This has not always been the case: his 1796 Farewell Address was standard fare in nineteenth- and twentieth-century schoolbooks, almanacs, and compilations of significant national documents. Portions of it, especially his warnings against political parties and permanent alliances with other nations, remain perpetually potent for those dissatisfied with elements of contemporary politics or policy. (Snippets of it feature in *Hamilton*'s "One Last Time," too.) Washington's 1790 letter to the Hebrew congregation of Newport, Rhode Island, endures as a touchstone expression of religious freedom and toleration. However, for all his voluminous correspondence, diaries, and state papers, now seventy-eight volumes and counting in *The Papers of George Washington,* Washington is not mostly remembered as a man of words—certainly not as Thomas Jefferson and Thomas Paine are.

Since 2000, the second year of the George Washington Teacher Institute

(GWTI), I've offered lessons on using primary sources—images and words—in the classroom. Analyzing visual images of Washington produced in his own lifetime renders his world more tangible. Digging deeply into a few of his writings elucidates his ideas and his expressive style. Just as important, reading these kinds of sources together can equip educators and students with questions and tools to apply to countless other materials in different historical eras and across social studies, English language arts, and other subjects.

In the following pages we will look at two of those images and two written documents and ask the questions that fuel my GWTI sessions, questions about *content* and *context*. What do we notice within the source itself, whether visual or verbal? How might we explain what is here, why someone made it the way they did? What else do we need to know to understand it? Or—to use language I learned years ago from a GWTI participant and again more recently from a contributor to this volume, Morgan Smith—"I see. I think. I wonder."[2]

George Washington's first portrait (see fig. 1) predated both his global fame and the United States itself. Painted by thirty-one-year-old artist Charles Willson Peale in 1772, it is a far cry from the Gilbert Stuart images most familiar today. At forty years old, George Washington was a gentleman farmer, his Seven Years' War service more than a decade behind him. But we are getting ahead of ourselves, because the first question is: What do we see?

Teaching with visual images, I try to keep students focused on that basic question before we move on to "why" questions. This method engages every student in observation, offering a low-stakes way for them to participate in the discussion. Going around the classroom, each identifies exactly one thing they notice, with two stipulations. First, it must be something within the picture itself (not "I see the future greatness of America"). Second, it cannot be something another student has already identified. With this approach, we collectively observe as much as possible before we jump into why it is there. Typically, once every student has taken a turn, I ask the question once more: Is there anything else that nobody has mentioned?

Washington's body dominates this portrait, centered from left to right, surrounded by landscape on both sides and above. It is a three-quarter-length portrait, head to thighs. Gazing upward and apparently beyond the frame, Washington holds his left hand behind him and conceals his right inside his vest. His mouth is closed, without obvious expression; his face is smooth,

FIGURE 1. *George Washington as Colonel in the Virginia Regiment,* Charles Willson Peale, 1772. (Washington-Custis-Lee Collection, Washington and Lee University, Lexington, Virginia)

devoid of wrinkles, his cheeks slightly ruddy. Dark hair appears from beneath his hat. Light, seemingly entering from the left, illuminates his youthful face and bright costume—blue coat, red waistcoat (vest) and trousers, trimmed in silver with silver buttons. Four buttonholes up from the bottom of his amply filled vest, he is missing a button. Flourishes in his costume include a lavender sash from his left shoulder across his torso, a white cloth at his neck, a ruffled sleeve, an engraved silver gorget hanging from his neck, and a silver medallion on his hat. A silver hilt at his left hip suggests a sword; a longarm is visible at his left side. In his vest pocket, he carries a small book or pamphlet titled "Orders of March." The landscape above and to his left (the viewer's right) is shadowed by trees. In the background to his right (the viewer's left) appear an encampment of tents, a waterfall, and forested mountains beneath a blue sky clouded with white and gray.

You will notice additional details as you closely examine the portrait. Be as specific as possible, because we are amassing the evidence from which to develop hypotheses and questions. Notice, too, the different categories of detail: the artist's use of color, light, and shadow (what is and is not illuminated and where the light originates); foreground and background; body and facial position, including the direction of the subject's gaze (people); costume and objects (things); landscape features (places).

Next, "I think": Based on this evidence, what is going on here? What did Washington himself and artist Charles Willson Peale wish to convey, and why? At this stage, it can be difficult to separate content (what we see) from context (what we know, or think we know, about Washington's life and times), which is fine. The key is to ground our ideas in the painting and to figure out what else we need to know (for "I wonder"). Most obviously, Peale portrays Washington as a military man, his large frame dwarfing all around him. His unlined face suggests a young man, younger than his forty years. The background landscape—definitely not Mount Vernon—connects him with the American backcountry, perhaps the Ohio River Valley, where he had served in the Seven Years' War and where he possessed thousands of acres of land. Even ostensibly militaristic objects connote other pursuits. For example, the longarm at Washington's side is not a military musket (officers in the Virginia Regiment typically did not carry longarms) but a fowler, the gun that landowning planters employed to hunt birds on their estates.[3]

As we move toward "I wonder," the central question is *why:* Why did Peale paint this portrait, in this way, at this moment in Washington's life? Who would have seen it, and what story would it have told? For context, Peale knew Jonathan Boucher, the Annapolis-based Anglican priest who was also the tutor of Jacky Custis, Martha Washington's son and George Washington's stepson. When Jacky returned home to Mount Vernon in 1772, Peale accompanied him, perhaps hoping for a commission.[4] Martha Washington likely provided the impetus, because her portrait and another of Jacky and his sister Patsy Custis had hung at Mount Vernon since the late 1750s. Those images, by the artist John Wollaston, came from Martha's first marriage, and she desired a companion portrait of George for Mount Vernon's walls. Typical among the Anglo-American gentry, his-and-her portraits asserted wealth and standing for anyone who visited their estates.

George and Martha Washington surely imagined that this would be the *only* portrait ever painted of George. Nobody in 1772 clamored to place his likeness in public settings: the walls of Mount Vernon were its only home. Moreover, George may not have expected to live much longer. Washington men tended to die young: his father at forty-eight or forty-nine, his beloved half brother Lawrence at thirty-three or thirty-four, his other elder half brother Augustine at forty-one or forty-two. If this was to be George's single opportunity to define himself visually, what would be his story?

Posing in uniform, George reminded visitors to Mount Vernon of the defining episode of his public life, his service in the Virginia Regiment during the Seven Years' War. Closer examination reveals the coat of arms of King George II on the silver gorget. This Washington was proudly an English subject, a paragon of the Anglo-American, not yet solely "American," gentry class. The fowler reflects the life of a country gentleman; the landscape, his western landholdings. Although he had had the uniform tailored in the 1760s to the prevailing style, its missing button and his full midsection suggest the thirteen years that had elapsed since he resigned his commission. This was George Washington in 1772: seemingly at ease in domestic pleasures, his most exciting days behind him.

Consider, too, what Peale's image does not reveal. By 1772, Washington shared other Virginia planters' restiveness about the financial arrangements binding him to English factors, the moneymen who bought and marketed Virginians' agricultural products—and typically kept the Virginians in long-term debt. By 1772, he owned dozens of enslaved people in his own right and managed the larger number of Custis "dower slaves" who had come with Martha to the Washingtons' marriage. The western lands Washington possessed, and the lands he had known since his teenaged surveying days, were the tribal homelands of Native Americans—as he knew well from encounters during the Seven Years' War. Peale's portrait implies none of these simmering tensions, all of which would soon surface in the revolutionary crisis.

Washington would sit for Peale six more times over the next two decades. Unlike the 1772 portrait, the later paintings were commissioned for public settings. On January 18, 1779, with the Revolutionary War raging, Pennsylvania's Supreme Executive Council resolved to commission a portrait for its chamber (see fig. 2).[5]

Notice the differences between Peale's original painting and this wartime image. One key difference is not evident on the internet or in books. The 1772 portrait, meant for a parlor wall, measures 50½ inches high by 41½ inches wide. Painted for a public building, *George Washington at Princeton* towers over the viewer at 93 inches high by 58½ inches wide. The full-length image captures the general from head to foot. Resolutely patriotic, it depicts Washington in his Continental Army uniform—a dark blue, gold-trimmed coat, gold

FIGURE 2. *George Washington at Princeton,* Charles Willson Peale, 1779. (Pennsylvania Academy of the Fine Arts, Philadelphia)

waistcoat, buff-colored trousers—holding his hat beside him. Still wearing his spurs, ostensibly fresh from battle, this Washington stands fully in command, resolute yet at ease despite the dark clouds above. His left hand rests on a cannon, and he crosses his feet—a relaxed pose. He gazes directly at the viewer. Behind Washington, a young attendant holds a horse's reins, another symbol of control. Accoutrements of war surround the general, including his commander-in-chief flag, a ring of thirteen stars on a field of blue, and captured British and Hessian standards at his feet and before him. In the left background appears the scene of the 1777 Battle of Princeton, with the college's Nassau Hall distinctly visible and prisoners of war being marched by American troops; a leafless tree serves as a reminder that the battle occurred in January.

Once more, context helps explain what we see. Commissioned for public view, this portrait of a now-public Washington served as a form of propaganda for the ongoing Revolutionary War. Peale, himself serving as a soldier in Washington's army (he spent the 1777–1778 winter at Valley Forge), presented his commander as a profile in confidence. But when Peale painted this image, in 1779, American victory was far from assured. The Continental Army had won battles at Princeton, Saratoga, and elsewhere, and France had allied with the new United States, but British troops occupied New York City, and Britain still had the world's strongest army and navy. Peale's painting was as much a rallying cry as a portrayal of historical fact.

George Washington at Princeton (1779) became Peale's most famous likeness, because he and his sons made numerous copies for other patrons and other venues in the United States and Europe. Some featured different battle scenes, notably Trenton.[6] The details might change slightly; for example, the flag might fly higher than Washington's head. But the essence was constant, a paragon of assured command.

In 1783, the United States secured its independence through the Treaty of Paris. Headquartered with his officers at Newburgh, New York, Washington prepared to resign his commission as commander in chief and return home to Mount Vernon as a private citizen. First, though, he wrote a letter to the governors of the thirteen states—which he knew would be printed in newspapers across the new nation. Today this document is known as his Circular Letter to the States, with "circular" meaning designed for simultaneous circulation to multiple recipients or audiences.[7] We can think of this as Washington's first farewell address. Much as he imagined his first portrait eleven years earlier, he surely figured that this would be his *only* farewell, his last (and lasting) message to the country he had labored to bring into existence. With the benefit of hindsight, we know he would write a more famous farewell address in 1796. But neither he nor his fellow citizens could have predicted that in 1783.

Before we examine Washington's Circular Letter to the States, let's consider some approaches to teaching written primary sources, especially documents in language unfamiliar to twenty-first-century students. No matter what the source, historians always read for *content* and *context*. *Content* embraces everything the author did inside the document itself: its themes, its arguments, and the evidence to back them up; its larger structure, the flow from paragraph to paragraph, the order of ideas; specific language, word choices, and figures of speech; and rhetorical strategies deployed to appeal to readers' reason, emotions, shared values, or other pressure points. As we did with Peale's

1772 portrait, we should start by closely examining the work itself. The crucial question with eighteenth-century documents, given their antiquated language, is frequently "HUH?" What, exactly, is the author saying?

How we teach the content depends on what we want students to learn. Is one idea particularly important, and therefore we focus attention on just a few key sentences or paragraphs? Do we want to understand how the author thought and wrote, requiring closer examination of more of the document? For a brief document—a single letter or short newspaper article—it may be possible to give students time to read it whole and summarize it together. Longer or more complex documents, including the Circular Letter, with its twenty-two paragraphs and more than four thousand words, call for other approaches: select a few paragraphs for analysis; provide framing questions or graphic organizers; or use a jigsaw approach, in which different students read and explain different passages.

Context includes everything outside the source that might help explain why the author wrote it that way, at that moment. *Historical* contexts can be political, social, economic, cultural, environmental, ideological, and more—anything about the period and place that influenced the creation of the document. *Biographical* contexts home in on the author: How do their life history and experience help explain what and how they wrote? *Textual* contexts include the specifics of the source's production, circulation, and reception. Did anyone besides the author have a hand in creating it, such as a secretary, coauthor, printer, publisher? Who was the intended audience, those whom the author expected to consume this source? In what form(s) did it reach that audience: private correspondence, public circulation (e.g., newspaper or pamphlet), reading aloud, or some other medium?

For the Circular Letter to the States, let's start with the document's structure and key ideas. Washington's first five paragraphs set the stage, detailing his own situation and the position of the United States at war's end. Then he listed "four things . . . essential to the well being" and even "the existence, of the United States as an independent Power":

—an "indissoluble Union of the States under one federal Head";
—a "sacred regard to public justice," by which he meant the nation and states honoring their debts to other countries and especially to the officers and soldiers;

—the "adoption of a proper Peace Establishment," that is, a national, uniformly equipped standing army; and
—a disposition among the people to put the national interest above "their local prejudices and policies."

The big middle section elaborated on the first three of these, leaving the fourth "to the good sense and serious consideration of those immediately concerned." Finally, in the last four paragraphs, Washington harkened back to his own Revolutionary War experience and offered a prayer for the nation and its citizens' happiness. His big idea was simple: for all its favorable conditions, the United States required stronger central authority *and* states' and citizens' adherence to that authority if their hard-won independence was to endure. Notice my use of the plural in the previous sentence to describe the country—which is how Washington and his contemporaries wrote and thought. "The United States" meant the multiple states. The "union" or "confederation" or "confederated states" described the singular entity they constituted, which Washington deemed necessary to maintain independence.

Now let's look at *how* Washington presented himself and his argument, because his rhetorical strategies matter. The first paragraph, two very long sentences, tugged at his audience's heartstrings. He indicates his intention to "return to that domestic retirement," which he had left behind "with the greatest reluctance" and for which he "never ceased to sigh through a long and painful absence." (Ah, Mount Vernon.) Then he emphasized the finality of this message: "my last official communication"; "to take my leave . . . as a public Character"; "to give my final blessing to that Country, in whose service I have spent the prime of my life, for whose sake I have consumed so many anxious days and watchful nights, and whose happiness, being extremely dear to me, will always constitute no inconsiderable part of my own." (I've given my country—you—the best days of my life, and I'll always desire its happiness.) The second paragraph continued the theme of happiness. The end of the war is a "pleasing occasion" and "the greatest possible reason for gratitude and rejoycing," given "the magnitude of the prize": independence. Every "benevolent & liberal Mind" could take "infinite delight" in contemplating America's present and future.

In the third paragraph Washington described the ways Providence and history favored the American republic and its citizens: an enormous continent far from European conflicts and possessing all the necessary resources for happiness; the age of Enlightenment, in which the collected wisdom of "Philosophers, Sages, and Legislators . . . may be happily applied in the establishment of our forms of Government." We live in an age of reason, Washington wrote, and what better time to come into existence as a nation? But notice how he ended that third paragraph: "At this Auspicious period the United States came into existence as a Nation, and if their Citizens should not be completely free & happy, the fault will be entirely their own."

Wait! Those last words signal a change in tone, raising the specter of failure. This brings us to Washington's fourth paragraph, which deserves scrutiny:

> Such is our situation, and such are our prospects: but notwithstanding the Cup of blessing is thus reached out to us, notwithstanding happiness is ours if we have a disposition to seize the occasion and make it our own, yet it appears to me there is an option still left to the United States of America: that it is in their choice and depends upon their conduct, whether they will be respectable and prosperous or contemptible and miserable as a Nation. This is the time of their political probation: this is the moment when the eyes of the whole World are turned upon them.— This is the moment to establish or ruin their National Character for ever.—This is the favorable moment to give such a tone to our federal Government, as will enable it to answer the ends of its institution—or this may be the ill fated moment for relaxing the powers of the Union, annihilating the cement of the Confederation and exposing us to become the sport of European Politicks, which may play one State against another, to prevent their growing importance and to serve their own interested purposes; for according to the System of Policy the States shall adopt at this moment, they will stand or fall, and by their confirmation or lapse, it is yet to be decided whether the Revolution must ultimately be considered as a blessing or a curse: a blessing or a curse, not to the present Age alone, for with our fate will the destiny of unborn Millions be involved.

HUH? Let's acknowledge, first, that this reads like a wall of words. It consists of only four sentences, the first running 81 words and the fourth 142. How can we and our students make sense of all this prose? Start with the same question we used to look at the paintings: What do we see? Watch for—and even mark—where Washington repeated words, phrases, and ideas. Look for words that seem especially strong or powerful. Use specific tools, like color-coding or underlining and circling, to highlight what you observe.

You might see that Washington began by turning happiness on its head, using the contrast words "but" and "notwithstanding." The future might be bright, but he perceived another possibility. Washington used the first-person plural pronouns "we," "us," "our," and "ours" nine times. He used the third-person plurals "they," "their," and "them" ten times. The conjunction "or" appeared seven times, always to contrast opposing outcomes: "establish or ruin," "stand or fall," "a blessing or a curse," and so on. Similarly, Washington deployed words suggesting contingency: "if," "option," "choice," "depends." And he referred six times to the momentous prospect facing Americans: "This is the time," "This is the moment," "This is the favorable moment," "this may be the ill fated moment," "at this moment," and "not to the present Age alone." The country's choices carried enormous consequences. The confederation could be annihilated (literally, made into nothingness), and "the destiny of unborn Millions" was in "our" hands.

Here is how the same paragraph might look, marked up with those observations:

> Such is our situation, and such are our prospects: BUT NOTWITHSTANDING the Cup of blessing is thus reached out to us, NOTWITHSTANDING happiness is ours *if* we have a disposition to seize the occasion and make it our own, YET it appears to me there is an *option* still left to the United States of America: that it is in *their choice* and *depends* upon *their* conduct, whether *they* will be respectable and prosperous *or* contemptible and miserable as a Nation. THIS IS THE TIME of *their* political probation: this is the moment when the eyes of the whole World are turned upon *them.*—THIS IS THE MOMENT to establish *or* ruin *their* National Character for ever.—THIS IS THE FAVORABLE MOMENT to give such a tone to our federal Government, as will enable it to answer the ends of its institution—*or* THIS MAY BE THE ILL FATED MOMENT for relaxing the powers of the Union, annihilating the cement of the Confederation and exposing us to become the sport of European Politicks, which may play one State against another, to prevent *their* growing importance and to serve *their* own interested purposes; for according to the System of Policy the States shall adopt AT THIS

> MOMENT, *they* will stand *or* fall, and by *their* confirmation *or* lapse, it is yet to be decided whether the Revolution must ultimately be considered as a blessing *or* a curse: a blessing *or* a curse, NOT TO THE PRESENT AGE ALONE, for with our fate will the destiny of unborn Millions be involved.

Through such an exercise, we can see what Washington was doing with language; next, let's think and wonder. What was he up to, and why? Begin with his deceptively simple use of first- and third-person pronouns ("our" versus "their"). "Our" and "we" refer to people, possibly the governors to whom he addressed the letter, but more likely all the fellow citizens who would read it in their newspapers or even hear someone else read it aloud. Washington used words to create a nation of common feeling, a shared "we." "Their" referred to the states or to the United States collectively—whose "National Character" could be established or ruined, whose conflicting interests could make them "the sport of European Politicks," and so on. In other words, it was up to the citizens ("we") as well as their governments ("they") to sustain the republic so hard won and dearly treasured.

Despite favorable circumstances, all was not well in the new nation—the context for Washington's Circular Letter to the States. He knew the threats firsthand. In March 1783, three months earlier, Washington had faced down what came to be known as the "Newburgh Conspiracy," an attempt by some of his officers to issue an ultimatum to Congress: pay us our back wages, or we might overthrow the government. Washington quelled this potential mutiny by emphasizing his own personal sacrifice ("Gentlemen, you will permit me to put on my spectacles, for I have not only grown gray but almost blind in the service of my country").[8] But he knew the officers had a point. The Confederation Congress had not fulfilled its duty to those who served in the Continental Army, because the states had not met their financial obligations to support the central government. Throughout the war, states had failed to provide resources requested by Washington and requisitioned by Congress. Washington summarized that problem in the last section of the Circular Letter, where he reminded readers about his own wartime experience: if the states had put the common good first, the war might have been shorter and less expensive. With the fighting over, he witnessed state governments already reverting to their own self-interest (for example, establishing trade barriers with one another) and citizens at odds over whether to obey their states' authority (a tendency that would culminate in the so-called Shays's Rebellion in 1786).

Washington employed emotional appeal, carefully chosen words, and the value of his own experience to raise the stakes. If his fellow citizens and their state governments would not allow the general government to use the powers granted to the Confederation Congress, "every thing must very rapidly tend to Anarchy and confusion." To realize the happiness everyone desired, "there must be lodged somewhere a supreme power to regulate and govern the general concerns of the confederated Republic, without which the Union cannot be of long duration." Six months later, after the Treaty of Paris ended the war and British troops left New York City, Washington appeared before Congress at Annapolis on December 23 to resign his commission and get back to Mount Vernon for Christmas.

If the themes of Washington's Circular Letter to the States sound familiar, they should. They are the same arguments that self-styled Federalists used in 1787–1788 to advocate for ratifying the Constitution with enhanced central government powers. Throughout his "retirement" at Mount Vernon in the mid-1780s, Washington corresponded frequently with friends and compatriots who shared his views on the need for a stronger, national government and maneuvered behind the scenes to bring the states into greater dialogue about revising the Articles of Confederation. Ultimately, he agreed to attend the Philadelphia Convention in the spring of 1787, was elected its presiding officer, and conveyed his personal prestige to the proposed Constitution.

The ideas in Washington's Circular Letter also resembled key points in the more famous Farewell Address, thirteen years later, which announced his second "resignation"—his intention not to seek a third term as president. The two most famous sections of the document (he never called it the Farewell Address) are the ones that seem perpetually relevant to our own day, even if we tend to oversimplify his meaning and ignore his context. He warned fellow citizens about "the danger of Parties" and "the baneful effects of the Spirit of Party, generally." Partisan feeling, he wrote, rendered fellow citizens alien to one another and opened the door to scheming demagogues and "foreign influence and corruption." President Washington also cautioned the United States "to steer clear of permanent Alliances, with any portion of the foreign World." Contrary to some later uses of the Farewell Address, he did not encourage isolation. Rather, he argued for commercial relations without perpetual political alliances that would embroil the still-fledgling United States in other countries' conflicts. These two warnings shared a common root: Washington's concern for the new nation's survival as an independent republic, exactly the point of his Circular Letter to the States.[9]

In the George Washington Teacher Institute, I teach the Farewell Address using two strategies. First, we read the opening nine paragraphs together. This section both mirrored and diverged from the 1783 Circular Letter. Both were written with an eye to newspaper publication. (The "Farewell Address" was not a speech.) But Washington addressed this later one directly to "Friends and Fellow Citizens," not state governors, and he used the second-person pronouns "you" and "your" throughout. He again reminded readers of his sacrifices for the country's good, including accepting a second term as president despite his wish to retire four years earlier. Now, "every day the increasing weight of years admonishes me more and more, that the shade of retirement is as necessary to me as it will be welcome." (Ah, Mount Vernon.) He performed the same rhetorical maneuver as in 1783, offering the "disinterested warnings of a parting friend, who can possibly have no personal motive to bias his counsel." (My only concern is for you, not myself.) He even referred to the Circular Letter: "Nor can I forget . . . your indulgence of my sentiments on a former and not dissimilar occasion."

This all led to his crucial ninth paragraph, which we unpack together: "The unity of government which constitutes you one people is also now dear to you." Washington loaded this paragraph with sixteen instances of "you," "your," and "yourselves." He also used a series of architectural metaphors. National unity was "a pillar in the edifice of your real independence," "the palladium of your political safety and prosperity." (Derived from Greece, a palladium was a building or statue that afforded protection or security: think of the famous cartoon from the late 1780s of the new nation being erected and stabilized, column by column, as each state ratified the Constitution.) The danger of disunity, Washington wrote, was "the point in your political fortress"—another architectural term—"against which the batteries of internal and external enemies will be most constantly and actively (though often covertly and insidiously) directed." He beseeched his countrymen to frown upon "the first dawning of every attempt to alienate any portion of our country from the rest, or to enfeeble the sacred ties which now link together the various parts."

As a second learning strategy, GWTI participants perform a gigantic jigsaw exercise. Everybody gets a printed copy of the Farewell Address. In every copy, I have marked a different paragraph (roughly eight to fifteen lines) with a Magic Marker—and I shuffle the copies. For five minutes everyone quietly reads only their own marked paragraph, figuring out what Washington is saying. Then we move through the entire Farewell Address, with every participant summarizing their paragraph. Since the printed copies are shuffled, people speak up from different places in the classroom. We might pause to note the context for a particular section if it connects to something we already learned, but we avoid getting bogged down in any single paragraph. The exercise is empowering. In less than an hour, we have read and comprehended a long, challenging document and learned much more than the two-sentence summary in most history textbooks.

Through this careful and collaborative engagement with the whole Farewell Address, we learn that political parties and foreign entanglements were not Washington's primary concern. They were merely the most potent "batteries of internal and external enemies" that would target the United States at the nation's weakest point, the all-too-human tendencies toward self-interest and disunity. As president, Washington saw this problem (from his political perspective) over and over: in the Whiskey Rebellion, in the fierce debates over his 1793 Neutrality Proclamation, and in the Democratic-Republican clubs and newspapers that attacked his policies and motives and bedeviled his second term. He witnessed foreign threats at the nation's western borders, and he knew the dangers slavery posed to the union of northern and southern states. He alluded to all this in the Farewell Address. Reading the whole thing, not just the famous parts, unearths those references—as well as his well-wrought rhetorical strategies.

As he had done in 1783, Washington closed his 1796 letter to his countrymen by evoking his own selfless labors on behalf of the nation. Surely, he acknowledged, he had "committed many errors" (humility, or a bit of false modesty?). But he hoped that "my Country will never cease to view them with indulgence; and that, after forty-five years of my life dedicated to its service with an upright zeal, the faults of incompetent abilities will be consigned to oblivion, as myself must soon be to the mansions of rest" (Mount Vernon, or heaven?). Soon, he concluded, he would "realize, without alloy, the sweet enjoyment of partaking, in the midst of my fellow-citizens, the benign influence of good laws under a free government, the ever favorite object of my heart, and the happy reward, as I trust, of our mutual cares, labors, and dangers." As Washington imagined himself among his fellow citizens, "you" gave way to "our" at last.

History textbooks necessarily boil documents down to one or two key points and treat visual images as illustrations to accompany the textbook-writers' words. But every primary source tells its own story. Somebody *created* it, at a specific moment in time, for an audience of one, a few, or thousands. For more than twenty-five years, the George Washington Teacher Institute has offered opportunities for participants to understand sources more deeply—and with approaches and skills that apply far beyond Washington and the eighteenth-century world. The simple questions we have asked here can be applied to any primary source. What do we see? What do we think the artist or author was up to? What else do we need to know, especially about the contexts behind the source? From this foundation, teachers and students can expand their methods and hone their skills. Many historic sites and institutions, notably the National Archives and Records Administration, have created outstanding guides and worksheets for exploring specific kinds of primary sources.[10]

Visual and written sources related to George Washington are too numerous to count. He sat for scores of portraits in the last quarter-century of his life.[11] Artists who never met him also depicted him long after he died in 1799, sometimes to illustrate scenes from his life but often to teach lessons about American identity, civics, or morality, comment on issues of the day, or advertise products. Do a Google image search for "Crossing the Delaware" and you'll find takeoffs on Emanuel Leutze's renowned painting: Klingons, superheroes, Peanuts characters, and more have been in that boat. Serious artists have used that iconic image to make more profound statements, such as Robert Colescott's 1975 painting *George Washington Carver Crossing the Delaware: Page from an American History Textbook,* in which the pathbreaking scientist is surrounded by racist images of Black Americans derived from nineteenth- and early twentieth-century textbooks, media, and commercial packaging (see fig. 3).[12]

Washington's words are also widely accessible, especially through Founders Online, a comprehensive website of the papers of Revolutionary-era US leaders. Letters by and to Washington, not written as public documents, offer revealing windows on his and his colleagues' perspectives on an incredible range of topics, and they are much briefer than the Circular Letter or the Farewell Address. Mount Vernon's own website, especially *The Digital Encyclopedia*

FIGURE 3. *George Washington Carver Crossing the Delaware: Page from an American History Textbook*, Robert Colescott, 1975. (Lucas Museum of Narrative Art, Los Angeles, 2021.45.1)

of George Washington, includes full texts of some documents and helpful essays about specific sources, both visual and written.[13]

Approached in a spirit of inquiry, primary sources bring the past alive. They restore human beings—complicated, opinionated, accomplished, and flawed—to the story. What could be more rewarding, or more fun?

Notes

Citations of Founders Online documents do not include individual links, as each source can be found by searching the site at https://founders.archives.gov/.

1. Lin-Manuel Miranda's *Hamilton: An American Musical* opened in 2015.
2. For this approach, see "See, Think, Wonder," Facing History and Ourselves, https://www.facinghistory.org/resource-library/see-think-wonder. I derived my version, especially for visual sources, from Jules David Prown, "Mind in

Matter: An Introduction to Material Culture Theory and Method," *Winterthur Portfolio* 17, no. 1 (1982): 1–19. Prown distinguishes three steps of analysis, roughly consistent with "see/think/wonder": description, deduction ("what would it be like to use or interact with the object, or, in the case of a representational object, to be transported empathetically into the depicted world"), and speculation (theories, hypotheses, and research in external evidence).

3. For detailed descriptions of the 1772 portrait, see William M. S. Rasmussen and Robert S. Tilton, *George Washington: The Man Behind the Myths* (Charlottesville: University Press of Virginia, 1999), 37–45; "George Washington Portrait by Charles Willson Peale," George Washington's Mount Vernon, https://www.mountvernon.org/george-washington/artwork/george-washington-portrait-by-charles-willson-peale.
4. Hugh Howard, *The Painter's Chair: George Washington and the Making of American Art* (New York: Bloomsbury Press, 2009), 37–46, details Peale's first encounter with Washington. Howard's book introduces several of the artists who painted Washington from life, including Peale, his son Rembrandt Peale, John Trumbull, Gilbert Stuart, and Edward Savage, as well as the sculptor Jean-Antoine Houdon, whose bust Washington considered the most accurate likeness. According to Howard, "Washington sat for at least twenty-eight different portraitists" (14), some for miniatures or pastels rather than oil paintings. For the best explanations of Washington in visual art during and beyond his lifetime, see Rasmussen and Tilton, *George Washington.*
5. Charles Willson Peale, *George Washington at Princeton,* 1779, Pennsylvania Academy of Fine Arts, https://www.pafa.org/museum/collection/item/george-washington-princeton.
6. Charles Willson Peale, *George Washington,* ca. 1779–81, Metropolitan Museum of Art, https://www.metmuseum.org/art/collection/search/11707.
7. George Washington to the States, June 8, 1783, Founders Online. For a concise summary, see Shira Lurie, "Circular Letter to the States," in *The Digital Encyclopedia of George Washington,* George Washington's Mount Vernon, https://www.mountvernon.org/library/digitalhistory/digital-encyclopedia/article/circular-letter-to-the-states.
8. Michael Hattem, "Newburgh Conspiracy," in *The Digital Encyclopedia of George Washington,* https://www.mountvernon.org/library/digitalhistory/digital-encyclopedia/article/newburgh-conspiracy.
9. Mount Vernon produced an excellent teaching resource for the Farewell Address, including an image of its first appearance in print on September 23, 1796; a full transcript; and classroom tips. See "Washington's Farewell Address, 1796," George Washington's Mount Vernon, https://www.mountvernon

.org/education/primary-source-collections/primary-source-collections/article/washington-s-farewell-address-1796.

10. See "Document Analysis," National Archives and Records Administration, https://www.archives.gov/education/lessons/worksheets. This site includes worksheets for artworks, photographs, maps, cartoons, written documents, videos, sound recordings, and more, with distinct worksheets for novice and intermediate students.
11. Excellent interactive museum websites include "George Washington: Reading the *Lansdowne Portrait*," Smithsonian Institution, https://learninglab.si.edu/resources/view/1411, and "Can a Painting Tell More Than One Story?" (resources for Leutze's *Washington Crossing the Delaware*), Metropolitan Museum of Art, https://www.metmuseum.org/articles/washington-crosses-delaware-leutze-lawrence.
12. In addition to Colescott's *George Washington Carver Crossing the Delaware*, 1975 (acrylic on canvas, Lucas Museum of Narrative Art, https://www.lucasmuseum.org/news/the-lucas-museum-of-narrative-art-acquires-robert-colescotts-landmark-painting-george-washington-carver-crossing-the-delaware), see Roger Shimomura's *Shimomura Crossing the Delaware*, 2010 (acrylic on canvas, National Portrait Gallery, Smithsonian Institution), which reinterprets Leutze's canvas from the perspective of Japanese American immigrants, replacing the Continental soldiers with samurai and echoing the composition of a Hokusai woodblock landscape print. The National Portrait Gallery has created a classroom resource for Shimomura's painting: see *Shimomura Crossing the Delaware*, National Portrait Gallery, https://npg.si.edu/learn/classroom-resource/shimomura-crossing-delaware.
13. *The Digital Encyclopedia of George Washington* can be accessed at https://www.mountvernon.org/library/digitalhistory/digital-encyclopedia.

INSIDE THE GEORGE WASHINGTON TEACHER INSTITUTE

Teacher Training About the Founding Era for the Twenty-First Century

ALISSA OGINSKY

In 2024, as the United States neared the 250th anniversary of the Declaration of Independence, the George Washington Teacher Institute (GWTI) celebrated its twenty-fifth year of supporting educators (and their students) in exploring the life and legacies of George Washington. The GWTI is one of the leading professional development (PD) programs for social studies teachers in the United States today. As the museum educator and former classroom teacher who has had the distinct pleasure and responsibility of managing GWTI since 2018—equating to about one-quarter of the Institute's history—I am excited to share the outcomes and strategies that have led to many areas of positive and impactful growth.

The GWTI is six weeks of immersive, five-day residential programs, open to K–12 educators from across the United States, hosted on-site at George Washington's Mount Vernon each summer. It is important to note that the GWTI is part of a wide variety of PD programs offered by Mount Vernon, including those that serve national, regional, and local audiences, are offered virtually and on-site (including three-week teacher-in-residence fellowships), and are hosted in partnership with other historic sites and museums.[1]

Before I take you "inside" the GWTI, let us zoom out. The GWTI does not exist in a vacuum. Its goals and outcomes were born out of the mission of our founding organization, the Mount Vernon Ladies' Association (MVLA). For more than 150 years, the MVLA has protected and preserved George Washington's Mount Vernon for the public. In addition to restoring and maintaining the estate to the highest standards of historic preservation, the MVLA's mission also centers on education, so that Washington's example of character and leadership can continue to inform and inspire future generations. More than 500 employees and 250 volunteers contribute to this mission. And the GWTI is one of the programs advancing these goals.

The success and popularity of the GWTI over the last twenty-five years derive from our focus on the teachers who spend their summers in our immersive program. Every day, the K–12 team at Mount Vernon asks, *What do teachers need?* We then strive to deliver it. As Christine Baron, principal of Baron Consulting and former assistant professor of social studies and education at Columbia University's Teachers College, reminds us, "Supporting teachers as they work . . . requires an understanding and appreciation for the complexity of the professional problem-solving in which teachers are engaged . . . this means working with teachers to find out what they need, if possible before they come on-site."[2] Second to Mount Vernon's mission, the GWTI prioritizes understanding the complexity of teachers' needs and the diverse sets of challenges they face across the country, as well as current trends in history pedagogy, in order to provide meaningful and relevant programs for its participants.

This commitment to understanding our audience is demonstrated through providing dedicated time for teachers to share their needs with staff and with each other. During each GWTI program, this takes the form of structured activities and reflections, focused one-on-one conversations and group discussions, and informal and formal evaluations. Further feedback is obtained by maintaining a national teacher advisory group; some of its members are new to the GWTI, and others are already familiar with it. The group meets regularly to discuss the state of education in their respective school districts and subject specialties and what support they seek through PD and classroom resources.

GWTI staff members also participate in national social studies and history education associations and exhibits, attending annual conferences and presenting their work. Exhibiting affords the GWTI the opportunity to share our commitment to supporting educators; presenting allows us to model the inquiry-based learning opportunities we offer through our programs; and attending sessions offers us a way to learn alongside teachers and hear firsthand what their needs are.

Additionally, by keeping in close contact with past participants (our "alumni network"), we develop a more nuanced understanding of teachers' evolving

PD needs. To this end, we use strategies such as communicating with alumni several times during the school year following our summer programming, writing to the full network quarterly, featuring alumni within each edition of the *Mount Vernon Magazine*, and responding to individual alumni requests. Mount Vernon's vice president for education, K. Allison Wickens, explains that maintaining the GWTI alumni network "demonstrates your support [of alumni] in the long run, and with the safety net, they are more likely to take risks and try new techniques included in your training . . . it's a great opportunity to build a sustained relationship with that teacher and his or her school and district."[3]

We also try to create opportunities for more engaged, trusted alumni to serve as teacher leaders through paid roles, such as GWTI program facilitators or regional outreach ambassadors, and through volunteer opportunities, such as joining staff as exhibitors or co-presenters at PD sessions.[4] My first shout-out goes to the fantastic alumni you will meet in this volume.

Each year, the GWTI staff seeks to better understand our teacher audience by building relationships with practicing teachers, and this provides a foundation through which we can continually improve and develop successful PD programs each year. Having over two decades of opportunities to F.A.I.L. (I am not sure which motivational poster I got this from, but it stands for "First Attempt in Learning") and meticulously reviewing evaluation data help, too.

In 2024, through all the means outlined above, we learned that teachers today need PD support in a range of areas. Many reflect not only our politically contentious times but also the important civic work teachers are doing within their communities every day. They include:

—teaching civics and inspiring students, the future citizenry, to be more civically engaged in analyzing primary sources to draw conclusions about the past;
—investigating the ideals of the Revolutionary and founding eras in politically charged and divisive environments, including their school communities and classrooms;
—sharing an inclusive history of the United States that honors the diverse voices and contributions of individuals and groups within historically marginalized and underrepresented groups of the past; and
—exploring the duality and the many facets of individuals such as George Washington, whose leadership and legacies provide value to

the nation and its residents' lives today and whose legacy also includes active participation in the institution of slavery throughout his lifetime.

With great knowledge comes great responsibility, or so the saying goes. Once we understand what teachers need, the difficult work begins. Because GWTI is engaged in proactively seeking ways to support teachers year-round (and not just during programming), we constantly evaluate decision-making throughout the year to be sure we are applying and implementing our most recent understandings into all that we do. That is, we are doing the "So what? Now what?" work.

To this end, the GWTI constantly asks what we can do now to better provide teachers with PD experiences that combine public history, academic scholarship, and state curriculum requirements. Not only do we seek to build programs at this challenging intersection but we also aim to provide teachers with the professional support that they may need to implement new lessons into their classrooms. Through intentional choices along the way, we can offer collaborative spaces for teachers to participate in the creation of their own extended and lasting professional learning communities.

GWTI program outcomes produce the strongest evidence of our successful integration of formal and informal education spaces. Bringing together our organization's mission and teachers' needs, we focus on diving into George Washington's social and cultural influence across the eighteenth century. Washington continues to be relevant to our teachers' and students' worlds today, and so our program outcomes affirm that participants will:

—gain knowledge of George Washington and the world he shaped in the Revolutionary era;
—examine political, social, ideological, and economic histories and concepts;
—analyze primary sources in order to investigate Washington's leadership and legacies;
—address inclusive histories that reflect the diversity of the eighteenth century;
—create and utilize strategies for the classroom that encourage discussion and inquiry;
—explore how the eighteenth century is relevant to today's world; and
—apply new knowledge in the civic act of instruction.

Another programmatic decision in support of the GWTI's mission-based work and teacher needs is to use six different weekly themes related to George Washington's biography rather than offer a single "George Washington 101" catchall program (which GWTI did in its earliest years). Participants have the opportunity to apply for one or all of the following programs:

—"George Washington and the Economy of a New Nation"
—"George Washington at War: From Soldier to Commander in Chief"
—"The Great Experiment: George Washington and the Founding of the U.S. Government"
—"Leadership and Legacy: Lessons from George Washington"
—"Lives Bound Together: Enslavement in George Washington's World"
—"The Worlds of Martha Washington and the Women of the Eighteenth Century"

Using these different themes, the GWTI team at Mount Vernon, in consultation with lead scholars and teacher facilitators, designs each program to focus on more specific historical content. This, in turn, allows for a more comprehensive investigation of George Washington's life and legacies. Within all these themes, we also analyze the lives of men and women involved in Washington's life and the larger topics related to the founding of the new nation. Our thematic programming provides relevant examples of how historical actors lived in and led the American republic—and how their actions and words can illustrate values that Americans share today. The philosophy of choice-based, student-centered learning is one that many teachers use in their classrooms to help motivate students.[5] With these strategies in mind, we offer common foundational information about George Washington across each program while giving teachers the chance to pursue their own path of more in-depth exploration.

Additionally, the GWTI is committed to providing opportunities for teachers to learn from the experts who become part of the GWTI faculty each year. This faculty includes a mix of leaders in both K–12 and museum education, academic scholars, guest speakers, and estate experts. All GWTI experts are expected to present accurate, inclusive, and up-to-date historical narratives that reflect curricula around the country and are supported by primary sources and educational resources that can be accessed digitally in the classroom. The University of San Diego's Division of Professional and Continuing Education explains that teachers "are tasked with responding to ever-changing social, political, and cultural landscapes. There are always new developments and innovations in education, meaning new trends, skills and strategies to keep up with in the classroom."[6] This is why we require all GWTI speakers to be engaging, make their message relevant, and communicate the respect that professional teachers deserve. Faculty must also be willing to participate fully, with curiosity, learning alongside the teachers. This is no small feat—and often why we share our experts with teachers across multiple programs and bring them back again each year. (A shout-out here to all the expert presenters in this volume!)

Diversity in the methodologies presented and the types of learning opportunities planned throughout the program are equally important. For "classroom-application" sessions, the focus is on exploring history content while modeling teaching strategies, including partner and group activities, whole group discussions and discussion panels, and the use of historical thinking and analysis practices. For example, Morgan Smith, in her essay in this volume, describes the teaching strategies she presents to our teachers during the GWTI each year. Scott E. Casper, in his essay, walks through strategies to approach close readings of primary source documents. These sessions are the ideal time to model the use of Mount Vernon's digital classroom resources, including *Be Washington,* an interactive leadership game that allows students of all ages to "come face to face with challenges that George Washington confronted as commander in chief or president."[7] Teachers have the opportunity to play the game, and the staff provides time to explore the various modes and features of the game to further support student inquiry. Through these instructional sessions, the GWTI strives to create spaces to learn and grow, to explore ideas and have difficult conversations, in an environment that respects individual voices, feelings, and perspectives. We also understand that teachers can attend our "history nerd camp" for their own enjoyment and edification, which is one of the reasons why our program accepts teachers outside history or social studies as well.

Indeed, the GWTI is not only for history lovers. For example, STEAM concepts are evident throughout the estate, particularly in locations in the historic area, like the kitchen, blacksmith shop, gristmill, and farm, and through the work of the different Historic Preservation and History Interpretation departments. Take, for example, one of Mount Vernon's most important archaeological finds to date: thirty-five glass bottles of berries found in the Mansion cellar during restoration. Analysis has determined that these bottles have not seen the light of day since prior to the American Revolution, and as Mount Vernon's principal archaeologist, Jason Boroughs, explains, they provide a "rare opportunity to contribute to our knowledge of the eighteenth-century environment, plantation foodways, and the origins of American cuisine. The bottles and contents are a testament to the knowledge and skill of the enslaved people who managed the food preparations from tree to table, including Doll, the cook brought to Mount Vernon by Martha Washington in 1759 and charged with oversight of the estate's kitchen."[8]

The layers of stories behind the objects and documents within our museum and archaeology collections, like these glass jars, and in the George Washington Presidential Library at Mount Vernon can easily be incorporated into the English language arts curricula as well, meeting a call to action (or an actual mandate) for most social studies educators to incorporate literacy standards into their lesson planning.[9] As Zara Anishanslin, one of GWTI's guest scholars, often shares, material culture—the "things" of history—is relevant to all of us, "because we all live in a material world in which our past shapes our present... they'll tell you something about yourself and your world."[10] In addition, by accepting teachers of non-history subjects, we invite a larger variety of voices into our GWTI classroom, which means more opportunities for interdisciplinary connections (administrators love that!) and, hopefully, a catalyst for studying or implementing history in classrooms across the curriculum.

GWTI adopts an approach to place-based education that echoes what Ethan Lowenstein and his colleagues describe in their study of place-based teacher training as "a hands-on, inquiry-based, contextually embedded... approach to teaching and learning that occurs *in and with* a place or community, is *about* a place or community, and *yields benefits for* a place or community."[11] The "in and with" of GWTI is Mount Vernon, the "about" is the life and legacies of George Washington, and the "yields benefits for" refers to a powerful experience for our teacher-participants (and, ultimately, their students). All of this aligns with Mount Vernon's mission.

GWTI incorporates site-based sessions with the goal of using place as a primary source. These sessions include a variety of experiences, such as guided tours of the eighteenth-century spaces everyday visitors might encounter, like the mansion, farm site, and outbuildings in the historic area. As a bonus, when teachers return to the classroom, they can guide their students through primary analysis of these same places using Mount Vernon's Virtual Tour and the related classroom resources created by the K–12 team.[12] However, VIP opportunities for teachers to go behind the scenes with estate experts into spaces used to better understand how we know what we know—such as examining documents in the Special Collections Suite at the Washington Library, working to identify objects in the archaeology lab, or venturing down into the collections facility to view the fine and decorative art objects, all the while being able to interact with preservation experts—are, hands down, some of the most meaningful learning moments for the teachers. Like those immersive or experiential activities students experience in their classrooms, these sessions keep the teachers engaged and invested in their learning. Time and again, teachers report to us that this rare access to on-site spaces not available to the daily visitor sparks curiosity and engagement in an impactful way.

The GWTI also values reflection as a crucial component of learning.[13] Reflection is built into the GWTI in a variety of ways, including breaks between sessions for conversation, individual free writing, anonymous digital polling, inquiry prompts for engaging in conversation with a partner, various group activities, and full group discussion. Intentional planning for reflection is incorporated into the GWTI's formal schedule, though reflection prompts often vary according to the content and goals of the session or set of sessions. For example, during our themed program dedicated to exploring enslavement on the Mount Vernon estate, content and discussion sessions can raise intense, conflicted feelings in participants; as a consequence, we offer even more moments of reflection each day, including extra breaks and activities like a sound bath or mindfulness yoga practices. Jay T. Johnson, Indigenous studies professor at the University of Kansas, acknowledges that "people relate to, interpret, and make meaning of the world around them in a multitude of ways."[14] With this in mind, the GWTI takes on the responsibility of creating time and space for choice-based self-reflection, with the option to step in and out of all sessions and activities across our programs.

As K. Allison Wickens acknowledges, "History is volatile and personal, and every time your program delves into the past, you create potential routes to both joy and trauma for your participants."[15] Because Mount Vernon was a site of enslavement and therefore a site of trauma, where intergenerational, race-based chattel slavery happened, the GWTI strives to keep this perspective top of mind. When exploring the community of people enslaved at Mount Vernon, for example, we are intentional about sharing stories of resistance and resilience, agency, and joy, despite slavery's violent circumstances. This includes sessions dedicated to exploring the biographies of individuals such as Ona Judge, who successfully sought her freedom during Washington's presidency; lectures on the economy of the enslaved community; discussion panels with members of the League of Descendants of the Enslaved at Mount Vernon, who share the oral histories of their families; and wreath-laying ceremonies at the on-site memorial for the enslaved.

In the summer of 2024, we welcomed GWTI alumna Rachael Rudis back to observe programming as part of her doctoral work at Michigan State University, which explored "place-based professional learning . . . [and] museums as sites of potential racial literacy development." As Rudis shared with participants, "When I attended the GWTI in June 2022, I was struck by the program's commitment to supporting teachers in teaching inclusive history. Institutional commitment towards inclusivity and racial justice is essential for historic site-based PD to be effective in developing racial literacy skills. The GWTI's focus on this work makes it a fruitful site for this research."[16]

We also draw from a critical pedagogy of place when investigating the Indigenous history of the Piscataway and the Dogue people who inhabited the land on which the present-day Mount Vernon sits. Jay T. Johnson recognizes this as "the concrete experiences of communities grounded in shared histories, stories and challenges based within a politics of a place . . . [and] seeks to decolonize and reinhabit the storied landscape through 'reading' the way in which Indigenous peoples' places and environment have been injured and exploited."[17] Throughout the week, we seek to honor these nations in many ways, including acknowledging the land and its caretakers who have come before, sharing the archaeological evidence we have to support their history on the site, using thinking routines to model classroom application using artifacts, and inviting scholars of Indigenous history and tribal members to share content and multiple perspectives. We end each week by making connections to the agency and diversity of North American Native peoples' experiences by returning to discussions of multiple perspectives, hidden narratives, and place-based learning and by asking teachers to investigate and then honor the nations that shaped their communities.

Nonnegotiable elements of the GWTI experience include providing teachers with the opportunity to connect with peers and treating teachers as the professionals they are. Research from *Bringing Teachers to the History Museum* supports this prioritization as well. Editor Lora Cooper reminds us that "teachers are excellent translators and scavengers, especially when collaborating with one another," and that they are choosing "to attend site-based TPD [teacher professional development] because they want to be there and are passionate history lovers."[18] Unlike required PD programs organized by school districts, which are designed to meet the district's specific goals, the GWTI offers voluntary opportunities for PD, which is often much more meaningful. And since GWTI seeks to invite a diverse set of teachers to each program every summer, participants are likely to meet professional peers from different regions, school communities, grade levels, and subject areas.

One of the many ways we recognize teachers' personal commitments to finishing the lengthy GWTI application, getting on planes and trains (and automobiles), leaving their families and the comforts of home behind, forfeiting extra pay for teaching summer school classes, rearranging vacations, and/or sharing lodgings and meals with new friends for a week is through welcoming and thanking our teacher-participants for making room in their lives for a week of voluntary learning. This public recognition not only signifies our gratitude for choosing the GWTI but also helps build the foundation for their new community of practice. Sarah Jenks, principal and founder of Every Museum a Civic Museum, writes, "Cultivating community is crucial to making a learning space that acknowledges the experience and wisdom that participants bring to it." Learning is enhanced by "asking participants to bring their full selves into the rooms where we learn . . . [and] encouraging them to learn from one another as much as from the group leaders and scholars."[19] The GWTI expresses at the start of each program that the goal is to include teachers as partners in our shared learning. Each cohort of teachers is made up of a unique set of individuals, offering new ideas, experiences, and values through which we can all learn. This community of learning is critical to forming deeper relationships among participants, especially for teachers who do not have strong support in their own professional networks. It connects back to the GWTI's goal of maintaining deeper relationships with program alumni to better understand teachers' evolving needs.

The GWTI also depends on the dedication and support of "lead scholars" and "teacher facilitators," who are contracted to provide guidance on up-to-date scholarship and current best practices in education during the planning of the six themed programs and are critical to the goal setting, community building, facilitation, and overall mission and success of each program. A lead scholar's main responsibility is to provide historical content and context through multiple foundational core sessions while making the content relatable and applicable to their teacher audiences—and to do so in an accessible and engaging way. No big deal! In addition, "leads" are asked to fully participate throughout all program sessions and experiences to assist in answering questions and to join discussions, providing an academic bridge between different presenters and experts across program days. Lead scholars make a lasting impression on teacher participants. Take, for example, this remark about Kate Elizabeth Brown, editor of this collection and the lead scholar of the economy-themed program in 2024, from one of the participants: "I feel I learned so much from her. She provided information that challenged me to think and consider new ideas, plus she presented in such a passionate way that I was completely engaged in her sessions. Beyond the lectures, she was involved and interacted with us outside of the classroom . . . she really listened and was truly with us."[20]

Teacher facilitators are likewise invaluable contributors to GWTI. The teacher facilitator's role as expert educator, staff representative, and group leader is key to creating a community among participants. Teacher facilitators lead methodology sessions like "Teaching History and Civics in a Divisive Environment . . . the Classroom," model the use of Mount Vernon's resources like those built for the *Lives Bound Together: Slavery at Mount Vernon Virtual Exhibit,* and share their relevant experiences as classroom teachers and educational leaders in their schools and districts.[21] As staff representatives, they serve as a point of contact for participant needs and act as liaisons between staff and participants at all hours of the day. As group leaders, they help expose teachers to the culture of GWTI and create a sense of community and camaraderie, including goal- and norm-setting and providing guidance to participants on how to navigate program content and logistics. Zooming in again to look at the evaluation data from 2024, this time for our women-themed program, one participant offered this insight into the efforts of our longest-serving GWTI teacher facilitator and a contributor to this volume, Bonnie A. Belshe: "Bonnie's ability to offer relevant examples for how to connect content to classrooms for a variety of grade levels was awesome! She also helped everyone connect and develop a sense of voice and community."[22]

However, the magic of GWTI is in the logistics behind caring for these professionals in the short time they are with us. This includes everything from giving GWTI participants the option to share their pronouns (and using them), providing a golf cart to those individuals who might need it (who oftentimes forget to disclose this until the last minute), and covering lodging expenses (including the night before the program, to rest from travel) to providing three meals a day and copious amounts of snacks (chips at 9:00 a.m.—you got it!). I must acknowledge that many of these "thoughtful details" come with a price tag, and much of this magic-making would not be possible without a commitment to staffing, the generosity of donors, and the hard work of our dedicated colleagues from across the institution from year to year. Detailing the history of GWTI's inception, development, and evolving processes would need to be its own essay.

The use of a very intentional and detailed "Participant Experience Form" gives teachers the opportunity to share information that helps GWTI staff better meet their more basic needs, which helps set the stage for learning. This thinking is based loosely on Abraham Maslow's motivational theory of a "hierarchy of needs," the same theory that most, if not all, of the teacher participants explored in their undergraduate or graduate studies on fostering effective learning environments. When attending GWTI, the teachers are the students, and we prioritize the lowest levels of physiological and safety needs first, knowing that to reach the higher levels of belonging and self-actualization, which are the needs inherently more difficult to satisfy, we must first provide a foundation from which to do so.[23] This set of internal standards guides GWTI decision-making regarding the types of vendors we use for lodging, catering, and shuttle services, how and when to communicate via forms, emails, or program websites, and the balance of lectures, hands-on or place-based experiences, and scheduled breaks. We prioritize the "T" for "Teacher" in GWTI in all that we do: we continually and proactively seek to understand teachers' professional needs throughout the year, and we address, to the best of our ability, their basic needs while they're on-site.

I'm not sure George Washington had providing teachers "breakfast Doritos" (a favorite on the snack table each summer) in mind when he commented on the value of education in his 1796 Farewell Address, but we believe that snacks at all times of the day, along with everything else I have described, honors his sentiment.[24] Washington stated that education was essential in a government based on the will of the people and that it was vital that the people be informed and knowledgeable. The George Washington Teacher Institute is proud to be a part of how we, as a nation, support the growing and diverse needs of US educators—the essential workers, frontline soldiers, and civic activists who educate the future citizenry—just as Washington hoped when he urged Americans to "[p]romote then, as an object of primary importance, institutions for the general diffusion of knowledge."[25]

Notes

Citations of Founders Online documents do not include individual links, as each source can be found by searching the site at https://founders.archives.gov/.

1. For insights into how educational programs such as the GWTI get started, find donors, create and review applications, organize programming, undertake evaluations, and more, I suggest digging into Lora Cooper, Linnea Grim, and Gary Sandling, eds., *Bringing Teachers to the History Museum: A Guide to Facilitating Teacher Professional Development* (Lanham, MD: Rowman & Littlefield, 2022). Mount Vernon was part of the research study used to inform this book, and approximately twenty museum educators from various sites and museums contributed to the ideas and strategies presented in it.
2. Christine Baron, "Translating Content into Pedagogical Content Knowledge," in Cooper, Grim, and Sandling, *Bringing Teachers to the History Museum,* 27.
3. K. Allison Wickens, "Effective Teacher Professional Development Program Design," in Cooper, Grim, and Sandling, *Bringing Teachers to the History Museum,* 89.
4. Wickens, "Effective Teacher Professional Development," 83.
5. James Fester, "4 Simple Steps to Providing Free-Choice Learning," Edutopia, https://www.edutopia.org/article/4-simple-steps-providing-free-choice-learning/.
6. "5 Reasons Why Continuing Education Matters for Educators," University of San Diego, https://pce.sandiego.edu/wp-content/uploads/2022/03/5-Reasons-Why-Continuing-Education-Matters-for-Educators.pdf.
7. *Be Washington,* George Washington's Mount Vernon, https://www.mountvernon.org/education/interactive-tools/be-washington.
8. "Archaeologists Unearth 35 Glass Bottles from the 18th Century at George Washington's Mount Vernon During Mansion Revitalization, Most Containing Perfectly Preserved Cherries and Berries," Mount Vernon, June 13, 2024, https://www.mountvernon.org/about/news/article/archaeologists-unearth-35-glass-bottles-from-the-18th-century-at-george-washington-s-mount-vernon-during-mansion-revitalization-most-containing-perfectly-preserved-cherries-and-berries.
9. Primary sources can be accessed here: "Primary Source Collections," George Washington's Mount Vernon, https://www.mountvernon.org/education/primary-source-collections.
10. *Thing4Things: The History Podcast Where Things Happen and Stuff Matters,* https://podcasts.apple.com/us/podcast/thing4things/id1820157131.
11. Ethan Lowenstein, Imandeep Kaur Grewal, Nigora Erkaeva, Rebecca Nielsen, and Lisa Voelker, "Place-Based Teacher Education: A Model Whose Time Has Come," *Issues in Teacher Education* 27, no. 2 (2018): 39.
12. "Mount Vernon Virtual Tour," George Washington's Mount Vernon, https://virtualtour.mountvernon.org/.

13. Wickens, "Effective Teacher Professional Development," 84–89.
14. Jay T. Johnson, "Place-Based Learning and Knowing: Critical Pedagogies Grounded in Indigeneity," *GeoJournal* 77, no. 6 (2012): 833.
15. Wickens, "Effective Teacher Professional Development," 87.
16. Rachael Rudis, unpublished manuscript, June 2024, in author's possession.
17. Johnson, "Place-Based Learning," 829.
18. Lora Cooper, "Introduction," in Cooper, Grim, and Sandling, *Bringing Teachers to the History Museum,* 2.
19. Sarah Jenks, "Evaluation," in Cooper, Grim, and Sandling, *Bringing Teachers to the History Museum,* 122.
20. Participant evaluation, June 2024, in author's possession.
21. *Lives Bound Together: Slavery at Mount Vernon Exhibit,* George Washington's Mount Vernon, https://www.mountvernon.org/education/interactive-tools/lives-bound-together-resources.
22. Participant evaluation, July 2024, in author's possession.
23. Saul McLeod, "Maslow's Hierarchy of Needs," Simply Psychology, https://www.simplypsychology.org/maslow.html.
24. To learn more about the Farewell Address, see "The Farewell Address," George Washington's Mount Vernon, https://www.mountvernon.org/george-washington/the-first-president/the-farewell-address.
25. For the full text of the address, see George Washington Farewell Address, September 19, 1796, Founders Online.

PART II

GEORGE WASHINGTON'S CIVIC LEADERSHIP AND CONTESTED LEGACIES

GEORGE WASHINGTON'S TALENTS

The First President's Leadership Lessons for Today

DENVER BRUNSMAN

Since its inception in 2016, I have had the privilege of serving as the lead scholar for the weeklong George Washington Teacher Institute (GWTI) session titled "Leadership and Legacy: Lessons from George Washington." During that time, I have noticed two seemingly contradictory trends related to the week's twin themes of leadership and legacy. First, George Washington's leadership accomplishments, steering both a successful revolution and the formation of a new government, become even more impressive through the lens of modern leadership styles. Second, it has grown increasingly difficult to impart Washington's leadership lessons to K–12 students because of American society's extreme partisanship and overall distrust of its institutions and leaders. Indeed, in America's current "history wars," a subset of its culture wars, few historical giants have escaped critical examination—including Washington, the country's indispensable founder.[1]

As in the GWTI week on "Leadership and Legacy," this essay seeks to turn the dysfunction of our current historical moment to a productive end: identifying elements of Washington's conduct not suited for our times as well as the characteristics that we still want to embrace. Put another way, there lies a fertile path between rash dismissal and uncritical celebration, and any hope of imparting Washington's positive leadership legacies to future generations requires educators to find this middle ground. To help in translating Washington's leadership qualities for today, we can draw inspiration from an unlikely source: the first vice president and occasional Washington critic, John Adams.

In attempting to salvage Washington from unfair critiques, we must first acknowledge the educational and historiographical benefits that have come from

America's national reckoning on race. It was not long ago that leading historians went to illogical lengths to explain away Washington's enslaving or even include his approach to slavery among his leadership qualities. In an essay titled "The Greatness of George Washington" (2006), the eminent early American historian Gordon S. Wood described Washington as a "good master, constantly concerned with the health and welfare of his slaves."[2] Aside from discrediting the characterization of any enslaver as "good," more recent works have shown that Washington does not deserve a pass on slavery simply because his will provided for the emancipation of the people he enslaved after his death. Historian Erica Armstrong Dunbar has profiled George Washington's zealous and ultimately unsuccessful efforts in the last years of his life to recover Martha Washington's freedom-seeking enslaved seamstress Ona Judge. In addition, Bruce A. Ragsdale has demonstrated how Washington's growing opposition to slavery after the American Revolution was driven as much by economic as moral concerns.[3]

In recent years, scholars have also started to reckon with Washington's record on Native Americans. As David J. Silverman explains in his essay in this collection, here there is also much to reject, particularly Washington's call to exterminate entire Haudenosaunee (Iroquois) villages during the Revolutionary War. The Sullivan Expedition of 1779 led the Senecas to reprise a Native name attached to Washington through his male ancestors, "Conotocarious," which he embraced in his youth; the name translates roughly to "Town Destroyer."[4] As with slavery, rather than see Washington's relations with Indigenous peoples as somehow exceptional, scholars increasingly interpret his conduct as consistent with the larger historical processes that devastated Native nations and communities in the colonial era and early republic.[5]

When taken seriously, the transgressions committed by Washington against African Americans and Native Americans make dismissing him seem wholly rational. The problem is that neglecting Washington is bad history by the simple criterion that it ignores a great deal of the past, and particularly his other, more positive legacies. While Washington shared enslaving in common with nineteenth-century Confederates, he differed significantly from them—as even they recognized—by helping create a society and government committed to human equality, even if the promise of that society went unfulfilled in his lifetime.[6]

As we turn to identify Washington's redeeming characteristics, a surprising voice provides a model for approaching him in a critical yet fair manner. In

November 1807, John Adams shared with his friend and fellow revolutionary Benjamin Rush, a Philadelphia physician, what Adams called Washington's ten "talents," traits that allowed for his greatness. Rush had pondered how someone with so little formal education could rise to such heights. "Self taught or Book learned in the Arts, our Hero, was much indebted to his Talents," Adams responded. "Talents? You will Say, what Talents? I answer." Adams's irreverent approach to Washington reminds us that the founders did not see themselves as above criticism. For the sake of concision, here is a summary of Adams's list of Washington's talents in the original order and language:

1. An handsome Face
2. A tall Stature
3. An elegant Form
4. graceful Attitudes and Movements
5. a large imposing Fortune
6. Washington was a Virginian
7. Washington was proceeded by favourable Anecdotes
8. He possessed the Gift of Silence
9. He had great Self Command
10. Whenever he lost his temper as he did Sometimes, either Love or fear in those about him induced them to conceal his Weakness from the World.[7]

Adams's list focuses heavily on superficial qualities. Washington was handsome, tall, and a Virginian, where the "Geese are all Swans," according to Adams. But the listing reflected more than Adams's usual snark. It captured, too, his continued frustrations with Washington's conduct during Adams's presidency. Washington accepted the second president's offer to lead American forces in the Quasi-War (1798–1800) against France but then turned over effective control of the army to Adams's rival, the increasingly paranoid Alexander Hamilton, rather than the loyal Henry Knox.[8]

Adams also knew about efforts to draft Washington to replace him in the presidential election of 1800. Washington strongly resisted the overtures, at least in part from frustration with the rise of partisan and democratic politics in the country, for which he blamed Thomas Jefferson's Democratic-Republicans. "Let that party set up a broomstick, and call it a true son of Liberty, a Democrat, or give it any other epithet that will suit their purpose, and it will command their votes in toto," Washington complained. The campaign to draft

Washington lasted literally until his death. Almost ten years after first encouraging Washington to accept the presidency in 1789, Gouverneur Morris wrote another letter lobbying the first president to pursue the office again in 1800. The letter arrived at Mount Vernon a few days after Washington died on December 14, 1799.[9]

At the same time, Adams softened while penning his list of Washington's attributes. The eighth and ninth talents ("Gift of Silence" and "great Self Command") recognized leadership qualities in Washington that Adams did not possess. Further, Adams's willingness to criticize Washington gave credibility to the positive recollections that he shared with Rush. For these reasons, Adams's approach provides a fresh way to capture Washington's most appealing talents, or qualities, for our times and connect them to modern leadership styles. Like Adams's list, the list I have compiled grows in seriousness, except by following the more modern convention of reversing the numbering, to create a countdown:

10. "Repository for dung"
9. pet lover
8. master of the humblebrag
7. knowing when to cut one's losses
6. recognizing genius
5. Photoshop not required
4. giving people the hits
3. uncling
2. "to bigotry no sanction"
1. "Washington however did not deceive them"

As with Adams's list, some explanation is in order. The tenth and ninth talents, "Repository for dung" and pet lover, both reflect Washington's ethic of servant leadership, or advancing the well-being of others and one's community before oneself. Of course, Washington's service in the Revolutionary War, when the notorious homebody stayed away from Mount Vernon for eight years (except for a brief visit on the way to the Battle of Yorktown), provides a classic example of servant leadership. But in appealing to young people, we must present Washington as fully human, with passions that are relatable and, at times, a bit eccentric. The dung repository is a structure still standing at Mount Vernon, where, as its name suggests, Washington collected different types of animal excrement to discover the perfect fertilizer. The practice points to Washington's status as an Enlightenment figure committed to using science and his privileged place to develop agricultural practices that could benefit the entire nation.[10]

Lest students think that Washington only appreciated animals for their waste, his ninth talent reflects his passion for breeding animals. Recognized as the father of both the American mule and the foxhound, he considered each animal a superior breed and, with evangelical zeal, sought to spread them across the growing country. Washington also clearly found joy in his animals, especially his dogs. He gave them such names as Sweet Lips, Venus, Trulove, and Madame Moose, just as one would beloved pets today.[11]

With talents eight (master of the humblebrag), seven (knowing when to cut one's losses), and six (recognizing genius), Washington displayed authentic leadership. This leadership style is inherently collaborative: it emphasizes honest relationships with followers by valuing their input. Again, we could draw on any number of famous examples of Washington's working collaboratively with partners, from allying with the French in the Revolutionary War to bringing the concept of his war councils into the presidency to create the cabinet.[12] But students will relate to Washington's mastery of the humblebrag, the modern cultural practice of pointing out one's own strengths in a self-deprecating way. In accepting command of American forces in the Revolutionary War in June 1775, Washington claimed to "feel great distress . . . that my abilities & Military experience may not be equal to the extensive & important Trust" placed in him by Congress. Yet Washington famously arrived at the Second Continental Congress wearing his Fairfax militia uniform, a reminder that he was, in fact, the most militarily experienced colonist, based on his service in the Seven Years' War. With this humblebrag, Washington established a long pattern of exuding modesty in depicting American common causes as larger than himself.[13]

As talent seven highlights, Washington was a master of exits. He knew when to cut his losses, whether in war or politics, starting with his dramatic escape from the British in New York in 1776.[14] To cut one's losses often requires compromise, a key tenet of authentic leadership. Washington's most difficult political compromise arguably came at the Philadelphia Convention in 1787. A leading nationalist, in the eighteenth-century sense of simply wanting a stronger national government, he initially balked at the Connecticut ("Great") Compromise as it came together in July 1787. In granting states equal representation in the Senate, he worried that the convention was repeating the mistake of the Articles of Confederation in honoring provincial interests at the expense of the national common good. "In a word," Washington wrote to Hamilton, "I almost despair of seeing a favourable issue to the proceedings of the Convention, and do therefore repent having had any agency in the business." Washington might have regretted attending the convention, but he decided to trust his fellow delegates and helped broker the final compromise. As a result, the US Constitution came into being with Washington as its public face.[15]

While attending the Philadelphia Convention in 1787, Washington joined other delegates in meeting regularly in the home of Elizabeth Willing Powel. Reflecting his sixth talent, he appreciated the genius of Powel and other talented women, including the African American poet Phillis Wheatley and the English historian Catharine Macaulay Graham. Washington's perceptions of women's abilities possibly derived from the influence of his strong mother, Mary Ball Washington, and his limited formal education. Washington so valued the genius and input of women, a function of his authentic leadership, that during the Philadelphia Convention, he joined other delegates in attending a lecture by the pioneering female educator Eliza Harriot Barons O'Connor. According to the scholar Mary Sarah Bilder, O'Connor's influence likely contributed to the mostly gender-neutral language in the Constitution, in which various offices and rights are not limited to men but instead given to "citizens," "inhabitants," and "persons."[16]

Talents five (Photoshop not required) and four (giving people the hits) come closest in spirit to the superficial qualities that Adams emphasized, but they also represent examples of Washington's inspirational leadership. He did not require Photoshop, because he took an active role in crafting his own image, including by working closely with portraitists such as Gilbert Stuart. Even when suffering discomfort with his dentures, as Washington did while sitting for Stuart's "Athenaeum" portrait (1796), he projected an inspiring masculine ideal for early American society. The image is so iconic that it persists to this day on the dollar bill.[17]

We are so accustomed to seeing the stately Washington that it can be jarring to see the alternative. The exception that proves the rule in Washington portraiture is his official masonic portrait, completed by William J. Williams in 1794 (see fig. 1). With Washington in masonic regalia, the painting includes a scar below his left eye, smallpox scars on his cheeks and nose, and a mole below his right earlobe. The "mole and all" portrait was no accident: Washington sat for Williams thirteen times over nearly a year. Sometimes Photoshop *is* required.[18]

FIGURE 1. *George Washington,* William J. Williams, 1794. (Alexandria-Washington Lodge No. 22, Free and Accepted Masons of Virginia)

President Washington further inspired the American people during his tours of the northern states in 1789 and the southern states in 1791. Early in the northern tour, he discovered—much like an aging rock band today—that the people mostly wanted his greatest hits. Therefore, before entering individual towns, Washington changed into his Continental Army uniform and mounted a white charger. He gave the people the hits. Still, audiences were demanding. After his visit to Charleston, South Carolina, in May 1791, the townspeople were so moved that the city council commissioned a portrait of the president by John Trumbull. When Trumbull presented *George Washington at Trenton* (1792; see fig. 2), South Carolina leaders disapproved because they wanted a painting of the president at Charleston in his Continental Army uniform. Washington had never been in Charleston during the Revolutionary War, but Trumbull reluctantly complied, adding a playful prank. The artist produced *George Washington at Charleston* (1792; see fig. 3) but, given the prominence of the horse's backside in the painting, it could just as easily be called "Trumbull's Revenge."[19]

As with Adams's list, my list grows more serious with Washington's last three modern talents. Number three (uncling), two ("to bigotry no sanction"), and one ("Washington however did not deceive them") all reflect his character-based leadership. In leading with integrity and model behavior, rather than merely relying on a title or official position, character-based leadership transfers more easily than any leadership style between the eighteenth and twenty-first

FIGURE 2. *General George Washington at Trenton,* John Trumbull, 1792. (Yale University Art Gallery, New Haven, Connecticut)

centuries. Honesty never goes out of style. Uncling—"the art of unclehood," per *Urban Dictionary*—refers to Washington's generosity in providing various means of support, including character instruction, for his nephews, nieces, and other young people. Washington served as a stepfather and step-grandfather to Custis offspring but had no children of his own, possibly due to being sterile from having had smallpox as a young man (the scars from which apparently lasted his entire life, as depicted in the 1794 Williams painting). While Washington will likely always be known as America's Father, we might also think of him as the country's uncle.[20]

Washington took his role as an uncle seriously, as is evident by his frequent advice to his nephews and nieces. He had notable successes, including in his nephew Bushrod Washington, who thrived in his studies and eventually became a US Supreme Court Justice. George Washington also faced challenges as an uncle, not least with his nephew George Steptoe Washington. In March 1789, he wrote to George Steptoe (as he was known) as the young man

FIGURE 3. *Washington at the City of Charleston,* John Trumbull, 1792. (City of Charleston, South Carolina)

prepared to enter the Georgetown Academy (today Georgetown University). Much of the avuncular advice concerned striking the right balance between industry and idleness, the perpetual challenge of all college freshmen. George Washington pleaded with George Steptoe to keep upstanding friends, for "good Company will always be found much less expensive than bad." Sometimes even the best advice goes unheeded. George Steptoe, like several other Washington and Custis men, struggled with his studies, cycling through multiple schools, before becoming a plantation owner and dying young. Not all nephews could be Bushrod.[21]

Washington's second-greatest talent ("to bigotry no sanction") relates to his commitment to religious liberty and reflects his character-based leadership. During his 1789 visit to the northern states, Washington skipped Rhode Island because it had not yet ratified the Constitution. After the state ratified it in May 1790, Washington made a special trip there in August 1790. While in Newport, he visited the Touro Synagogue, the oldest synagogue in the United States, whose congregants asked Washington in writing if their Jewish faith would be tolerated under the new government. He used language in the original letter from the synagogue in pledging more than toleration. "For happily the Government of the United States," Washington wrote, "which gives to bigotry no sanction, to persecution no assistance requires only that they who live under its protection should demean themselves as good citizens." Although Washington never overcame the barrier of race, his unwavering support for religious liberty is important to share with students, particularly given the current resurgence of antisemitism and other forms of religious persecution in the United States and much of the world.[22]

For Washington's No. 1 talent, we consider a final example of character-based leadership by drawing words from Adams's letter to Benjamin Rush in November 1807: "Washington however did not deceive them." When discussing Washington's large fortune, Adams stated that many rich people claimed to be disinterested—that is, committed to the common good and not self-interested—but they actually sought personal gain. Adams distinguished Washington from other financial elites by stressing that Washington maintained his word by staying truly disinterested. Although Washington was human and no doubt pursued his self-interest, examples also abound of his selfless service, particularly the decision to resign his commission as commander of American forces at the end of the Revolutionary War. It was enough to impress another George, King George III, who predicted that if Washington retired from public life and returned to his farm, "he will be the greatest man in the world." Again, our recent history, namely, the attack on the Capitol on January 6, 2021, has given new relevance to Washington's republican virtue.[23]

Taken together, this list of Washington's talents can help convey his leadership lessons for the current generation. In combining multiple approaches to leadership, Washington defied today's conventional wisdom that leaders need to identify a particular leadership style. Instead, as the longtime dean of leadership studies, James MacGregor Burns, showed, Washington achieved a higher, multifaceted leadership that Burns called "transformational." For Burns, such leadership is creative and visionary rather than simply transactional. Put another way, transformational leadership involves much more than simply getting a job done. Washington did not merely carry out the duties of the presidency; he used all his leadership talents to invent the office. It may seem obvious that Washington, as the first president, heavily shaped the office, but consider the US Supreme Court. John Jay might have been the first chief justice, but it was the fourth, John Marshall, who became the transformational leader of the Court.[24]

The focus of career coaching today also often centers on discovering an individual's special strength or unique calling. Again, the scale of Washington's accomplishments could not have been realized without his diverse collection of talents. John Kotter's insights into leading organizational change offer another modern leadership framework that places Washington's record in perspective. Kotter argues that transforming an organization, such as a business or agency, takes eight steps, ranging from creating a sense of urgency to communicating a change vision. Washington followed these steps, and more, in leading change for a much larger entity: the US government. Washington marshalled his many leadership skills to help launch the new national government under the Constitution—one of the most significant organizational "makeovers" in world history.[25]

Of course, in sharing these leadership triumphs with students, we do not want to move so far that we replicate the mistake of the nineteenth century in turning Washington into a mythical, godlike figure. Sound pedagogy demands that we leave the cherry tree undisturbed in the Ferry Farm orchard. To return to the question posed at the start, then, How do we present a balanced perspective on Washington? In addition to John Adams's model of not taking "our Hero" so seriously, we can also benefit by following the lead of two other individuals with privileged, unique insights into Washington: Abigail Adams, a contemporary, and Christopher Jackson, who played the first president in the original Broadway production of the musical *Hamilton.*

Like her husband, Abigail Adams felt great admiration for Washington throughout the Revolutionary War and first presidency. Moreover, Abigail Adams remains among our most valuable sources on Martha Washington's talents, particularly her earthy charm, that so well compensated for George Washington's more staid personality. Yet Adams grew disillusioned by the almost immediate deification of George Washington following his death in December 1799. She had known the full, complex person, faults and all, and hence wrote that "Simple Truth is his best his greatest Eulogy."[26] "Simple truth" has never been very simple when it comes to Washington. Rarely in the more than two hundred years since his passing has he been treated simply as he was, a flawed human being who also did extraordinary things.

No one understood these flaws better than George Washington himself—at least the Washington for our times, Christopher Jackson. As numerous films and musicals demonstrate, portraying Washington is extremely difficult owing to his practiced diffidence, his "Gift of Silence," in John Adams's memorable words. Jackson succeeded by capturing Washington's gravitas while also finding an emotional core missing in other portrayals. Scholars have rightly critiqued *Hamilton,* despite its diverse casting, for not including a person of color from the eighteenth century. Yet, as an African American man, Jackson provided a constant reminder of Washington's enslaving. He also spoke eloquently about his challenges in playing a White enslaver. His personal resolution of Washington's contradictions, to present the full person in all his flawed humanity and greatness, followed the similar approaches left by John and Abigail Adams.[27]

Teaching Washington's leadership lessons demands more humanity, nuance, and skill today than at any other point in American history. The same man who owned other human beings and decimated Indigenous populations also guided America's republican experiment, with its commitment to representative government, social equality, and personal liberty. To impart this "simple truth" will require that educators fully realize their own leadership potential in the classroom. The alternative—to either uncritically malign or reflexively glorify Washington—would require us to submit to the worst impulses in our fractured politics and public discourse. More than a myth or villain, the human Washington is what the United States, and especially its young people, most needs now.

Notes

Citations of Founders Online documents do not include individual links, as each source can be found by searching the site at https://founders.archives.gov/.

1. For earlier works on Washington and leadership, see James C. Rees with Stephen Spignesi, *George Washington's Leadership Lessons: What the Father of Our Country Can Teach Us About Effective Leadership and Character* (Hoboken, NJ: John Wiley & Sons, 2007); Richard Brookhiser, *George Washington on Leadership* (New York: Basic Books, 2008). For an introduction to recent debates over American history and memory, see David W. Blight, "The Fog of History Wars," *The New Yorker,* June 9, 2021, https://www.newyorker.com/news/daily-comment/the-fog-of-history-wars.
2. Gordon S. Wood, "The Greatness of George Washington," in *Revolutionary Characters: What Made the Founders Different* (New York: Penguin, 2006), 39. The essay expands on Wood's article of the same name in *Virginia Quarterly Review* 68 (Spring 1992): 189–207.

3. Erica Armstrong Dunbar, *Never Caught: The Washingtons' Relentless Pursuit of Their Runaway Slave, Ona Judge* (New York: Atria, 2017); Bruce A. Ragsdale, *Washington at the Plow: The Founding Farmer and the Question of Slavery* (Cambridge, MA: Harvard University Press, 2021). For Washington's broader relationship with the enslaved community of Mount Vernon, see Mary V. Thompson, *"The Only Unavoidable Subject of Regret": George Washington, Slavery, and the Enslaved Community at Mount Vernon* (Charlottesville: University of Virginia Press, 2019).
4. Seneca Chiefs to George Washington, December 1, 1790, Founders Online; Colin G. Calloway, *The Indian World of George Washington: The First President, the First Americans, and the Birth of the Nation* (New York: Oxford University Press, 2018), 69–70, 256–57.
5. This is the broad lesson of Calloway, *Indian World.*
6. Alexander H. Stephens, "Cornerstone Speech, March 21, 1861," in *The Civil War and Reconstruction: A Documentary Reader,* ed. Stanley Harrold (Malden, MA: Blackwell, 2008), 59–64; Gary W. Gallagher, *The Enduring Civil War: Reflections on the Great American Crisis* (Baton Rouge: Louisiana State University Press, 2020), 101–3.
7. John Adams to Benjamin Rush, November 11, 1807, Founders Online.
8. Lindsay M. Chervinsky, *Making the Presidency: John Adams and the Precedents That Forged the Republic* (New York: Oxford University Press, 2024), 140–47, 152–60; Peter R. Henriques, *First and Always: A New Portrait of George Washington* (Charlottesville: University of Virginia Press, 2020), 134–41; James Rogers Sharp, *American Politics in the Early Republic: The New Nation in Crisis* (New Haven, CT: Yale University Press, 1993), 181–82, 208–25.
9. George Washington to Jonathan Trumbull Jr., July 21, 1799, Founders Online (quotation); Gouverneur Morris to George Washington, December 9, 1799, Founders Online. For efforts to draft Washington in the election of 1800, see Jonathan Horn, *Washington's End: The Final Years and Forgotten Struggle* (New York: Scribner, 2020), 182–85, 207–8; Henriques, *First and Always,* 142–43.
10. Ragsdale, *Washington at the Plow,* esp. 171–201. For servant leadership, see Robert K. Greenleaf, *Servant Leadership: A Journey into the Nature of Legitimate Power and Greatness,* 25th anniversary ed. (Mahwah, NJ: Paulist Press, 2022).
11. Philip G. Smucker, *Riding with George: Sportsmanship and Chivalry in the Making of America's First President* (Chicago: Chicago Review Press, 2017), 8–9; "Dogs," in *The Digital Encyclopedia of George Washington,* George Washington's Mount Vernon, https://www.mountvernon.org/library/digitalhistory/digital-encyclopedia/article/dogs.
12. Lindsay M. Chervinsky, *The Cabinet: George Washington and the Creation of an American Institution* (Cambridge, MA: Harvard University Press, 2020),

13–55. For authentic leadership, see Bill George, *Authentic Leadership: Rediscovering the Secrets to Creating Lasting Value* (Hoboken, NJ: Jossey-Bass, 2003).

13. George Washington, Address to the Continental Congress, June 16, 1775, Founders Online.
14. Rick Atkinson, *The British Are Coming: The War for America, Lexington to Princeton, 1775–1777* (New York: Henry Holt, 2019), 374–79.
15. George Washington to Alexander Hamilton, July 10, 1787, Founders Online; Edward J. Larson, *The Return of George Washington, 1783–1789* (New York: HarperCollins, 2014), 150–52. See also Larson, *George Washington, Nationalist* (Charlottesville: University of Virginia Press, 2016).
16. Charlene M. Boyer Lewis and George W. Boudreau, eds., *Women in George Washington's World* (Charlottesville: University of Virginia Press, 2022); Mary Sarah Bilder, *Female Genius: Eliza Harriot and George Washington at the Dawn of the Constitution* (Charlottesville: University of Virginia Press, 2022).
17. Hugh Howard, *The Painter's Chair: George Washington and the Making of American Art* (New York: Bloomsbury Press, 2009), 192–96; Scott E. Casper, "The Washington Image in American Culture," in *A Companion to George Washington*, ed. Edward G. Lengel (Malden, MA: Blackwell, 2012), 593–95. For the complexities of Washington's masculinity and its representation, see Maurizio Valsania, *First Among Men: George Washington and the Myth of American Masculinity* (Baltimore: Johns Hopkins University Press, 2022). For inspirational leadership, see Kristi Hedges, *The Inspiration Code: How the Best Leaders Energize People Every Day* (New York: AMACOM, 2017).
18. Mark A. Tabbert, *A Deserving Brother: George Washington and Freemasonry* (Charlottesville: University of Virginia Press, 2022); Ron Chernow, *Washington: A Life* (New York: Penguin, 2010), 720–21.
19. T. H. Breen, *George Washington's Journey: The President Forges a New Nation* (New York: Simon & Schuster, 2016), 73, 113–17.
20. "Uncling," *Urban Dictionary*, https://www.urbandictionary.com/define.php?term=Uncling. For Washington's commitment to supporting family members, particularly with education, see Paul K. Longmore, *The Invention of George Washington* (Charlottesville: University of Virginia Press, 1999), 213–15, 295n10; Lorri Glover, *Founders as Fathers: The Private Lives and Politics of the American Revolutionaries* (New Haven, CT: Yale University Press, 2014), esp. 29–31, 103–5, 122–25, 137, 144; Kevin J. Hayes, *George Washington: A Life in Books* (New York: Oxford University Press, 2017), 125–42; Cassandra A. Good, *First Family: George Washington's Heirs and the Making of America* (Toronto: Hanover Square Press, 2023), 25–116. For character-based leadership, see Lead Change Group, *The Character-Based Leader: Instigating a Leadership*

Revolution . . . One Person at a Time (Carmel, IN: Dog Ear Publishing, 2012); David Brooks, *The Road to Character* (New York: Random House, 2015).

21. George Washington to George Steptoe Washington, March 23, 1789, Founders Online; Glover, *Founders as Fathers*, 103–5, 111, 122, 124–25, 209.
22. George Washington to the Hebrew Congregation in Newport, Rhode Island, August 18, 1790, Founders Online. For the legacy of Washington's letter, see Walter Russell Mead, *The Arc of a Covenant: The United States, Israel, and the Fate of the Jewish People* (New York: Alfred A. Knopf, 2022).
23. Gary Wills, *Cincinnatus: George Washington and the Enlightenment* (New York: Doubleday, 1984), remains the definitive study of Washington's resignation and its legacy.
24. For the classic definition of transformational leadership, see James MacGregor Burns, *Leadership* (New York: Harper & Row, 1978), 141–254. For the concept applied to Washington, see James MacGregor Burns and Susan Dunn, *George Washington* (New York: Times Books, 2004).
25. John P. Kotter, *Leading Change* (Cambridge, MA: Harvard Business School Press, 1996). For the concept of leading change applied to Washington, see Denver Brunsman and George R. Goethals, *Leading Change: George Washington and Establishing the Presidency* (Mount Vernon, VA: George Washington Leadership Institute, 2017).
26. Abigail Adams to Mary Smith Cranch, January 28, 1800, Founders Online. See also Chervinsky, *Making the Presidency*, 235–36.
27. Lin-Manuel Miranda and Jeremy McCarter, *Hamilton: The Revolution* (New York: Hachette, 2016), 58–59; *Great Performances*, season 44, episode 4, *Hamilton's America*, dir. Alex Horwitz, premiere October 21, 2016, PBS. For critiques, see Renee C. Romano and Claire Bond Potter, eds., *Historians on Hamilton: How a Blockbuster Musical Is Restaging America's Past* (New Brunswick, NJ: Rutgers University Press, 2018).

GEORGE WASHINGTON AT WAR IN THE TWENTY-FIRST CENTURY

SARAH J. PURCELL

In the preface to his 1804–1807 biography of George Washington, Chief Justice John Marshall wrote, "The history of General Washington, during his military command [was] . . . that of his country."[1] Marshall was right in more ways than he knew. The history of George Washington at war, especially his years as the commander in chief of the Continental Army during the Revolutionary War, furnishes an excellent way to examine the history of the United States. Teaching in the twenty-first century about Washington at war gives us a chance to reinforce and complicate US history for students of all ages while offering them a deep and meaningful engagement not only with Washington himself but also with the complexity of the eighteenth century and the military conflict that brought the United States into being.

John Marshall wrote Washington's biography from documents provided to him by Washington and his family and from lifelong memories of working with Washington in Virginia while serving as a colonel in the Virginia militia during the Revolutionary War. The biography was no impartial history, even though it was based on some sound historical principles and primary sources; it was largely hagiographic in tone. Marshall intended Washington's life to serve as a series of usable history lessons to the still-forming United States, which Marshall emphasized at times in the language of hyperbolic providential millennialism, proclaiming that Washington was "the chosen instrument of Heaven" in creating the country itself.[2] For Marshall, depicting Washington as chosen by God also helped bolster the popularity of Federalist political ideology, which he perceived as potentially threatened by Washington's death and the subsequent election of Thomas Jefferson to the presidency. Marshall's vision of Washington as "the chosen instrument of Heaven" boosted patriotic nationalism and a particular political point of view simultaneously.

Even if history educators in the twenty-first century would like to set aside Washington as a providential force (as portrayed by Marshall and scores of other biographers and politicians over the last two hundred plus years), or at least to leave that for a class other than history, there is still a lot to be gained from Marshall's argument that learning about George Washington and the Revolutionary War offers a particularly good perspective on the history of the United States more broadly. A great many lessons about the Revolutionary War and the American Revolution can be creatively accomplished by teaching about George Washington as a Revolutionary War commander. Clear-eyed historical analysis, even without extreme hero worship, has a lot to offer today's students.

For one thing, Washington *was* extremely important as a military commander. He was neither the most effective tactician nor the best strategic commander of his age, but he proved adept at sustaining American forces under trying circumstances, collaborating with allies, and winning when it counted. As historian Jeffrey L. Pasley puts it, "While not always terribly effective as a field commander—he lost most of his battles—Washington's sheer gravitas, undergirded by genuine integrity and aided by iron control of his public demeanor and image, inspired enough confidence to carry the army and the country through the end of the war."[3] Overall, Washinton's decision-making contributed to military success, and though his battlefield losses were significant, his wins at Trenton and especially Yorktown proved his strategic competence.[4] John Marshall's reverent biographical tone, and the patriotic cult of George Washington erected around it, might be outdated and slightly beside the point for today's students, who need to understand historical lessons about the Revolutionary War. But this hero worship did arise, at least in part, from Washington's actual vital importance to the military and political foundations of the United States.

The Revolutionary War, which started more than a year before the Declaration of Independence, was essential to the political and social changes wrought by the broader American Revolution, but we must remember to teach it specifically as a war—one that had to be won in order for independence to be guaranteed. Teachers at all levels need to overcome concerns we might harbor about military history being *solely* a venue for mythmaking to explain how the Revolutionary War was an essential part of the American Revolution.[5] Students benefit from considering where the Revolutionary War and its consequences fit into the history of the founding era.

George Washington first led the United States in warfare. As commander in chief of the Continental Army, he defined the military character of the Revolutionary War and shaped how the military, as an institution, would subsequently relate to other aspects of American life and politics. He launched and sustained the US army and did much to establish its position in US society. Also, Washington's resignation from command in 1783 and his insistence on the subordination of military power to civilian power established a bedrock value of civilian control that became enshrined in the US Constitution. As the first president, Washington helped solidify this republican principle.[6] Understanding his importance to the Revolutionary era, then, really does necessitate talking with students about combat, service, and military decision-making—not always the most comfortable of topics for historians or social studies teachers trained in the post-Vietnam, post–Cold War, or Global War on Terror eras.[7]

Today, it is important for K–12 and college students to understand the Revolutionary War and George Washington's role in it, but that does not mean teaching a staid, outdated view of Washington or the war. Just as students need up-to-date historical interpretation of Washington himself (as a president, as an enslaver, as a leader), so too they need an up-to-date view of Washington at war. As the authors of a 2024 American Historical Association report on secondary US history education noted, "Historians of the revolution and early republic have periodically had difficulty squaring their view of a dynamic and diversifying subfield with the folk enthusiasms and civic rationales that have kept the Founding era alive in K–12 curriculum and popular culture."[8] But we need to take on that task. It is our responsibility as historians and educators to make "dynamic and diversifying" history accessible to students at every level and the larger American public. Thoughtful study of George Washington at war can show just how much the history of warfare has changed since the eighteenth century, allow new and important insights about the United States, and form the basis for changing notions of civic education. Providing the very best historical and civic education *does* mean including lessons about George Washington and the combat history of the Revolutionary War. But it also should mean far more.

Teaching about the Revolutionary War should go beyond the old-school "military chronicle" that has been used to shore up the mythologized view of George Washington in curricula for decades.[9] Many academic historians harbor suspicions of military history. Don Higginbotham, who largely founded the "new military history" of the Revolutionary War in the last days and aftermath of the Vietnam War, wrote in the 1980s that even he, one of the foremost American military historians, at times "shied away from combat studies because it seemed that one might be branded as an antiquarian or a super patriot" for writing battle-focused histories.[10] Since the 1980s, scores of new historians have followed Higginbotham's scholarship to create new perspectives that fuse interpretations of combat with social, political, and cultural history in ways that make it possible to use lessons about the Revolutionary War to teach about exactly the kind of conflicted, contingent past with which students most need to grapple.[11] The history of the Revolutionary War need not be a stale combat history written only in heroic terms.

Any lesson about George Washington in the Revolutionary War is also a chance to broaden students' views, allowing them to see many varied experiences of warfare. A huge range of people participated in and suffered from the effects of military power and military conflict, even as they also resisted or helped create the American nation.[12] Teaching about George Washington and the Revolutionary War offers a way to teach students about how war and society affect one another, a process that had particular consequences in the founding era. If students look at George Washington in the Revolutionary War, good teaching should allow them to see right alongside him enlisted men (White and Black), women (White and Black), and poor people (enslaved and free). As historian Judith Van Buskirk writes, "Washington's army was an integrated operation," even in the face of Washington's own early efforts to ban Black soldiers from the ranks.[13] Women accompanied Washington's troops throughout the war, ranging from Martha Washington, who visited George's headquarters during almost half of the war, to the relatives of enlisted men who traveled with the army, to the female laborers who sold supplies, cooked and washed, and supported military operations. It is impossible to understand Washington's wartime experiences without seeing all those others.

The person literally standing closest to General Washington throughout the Revolutionary War was William Lee, an enslaved man purchased by Washington in 1768. Lee, though never formally enlisted in the militia or Continental Army (as were an estimated ten thousand other Black men), provided essential labor as Washington's valet, organizing his papers, maintaining military equipment, and caring for Washington's horses and personal bodily needs.[14] Like almost every other Black man who served with the American military in the Revolutionary War, Lee received his freedom in return, though in his case it took until Washington's death in 1799—a time when Lee's own health was also exhausted after decades of forced labor.[15] Lee was famously, and exotically, depicted by artist John Trumbull in a 1780 military portrait. In the painting, Lee supports Washington (on horseback) as they overlook the Hudson River; Trumbull emphasized the closeness of the two men and showed Lee's importance to Washington as commander of the Continental Army.[16] Lee also played a role in advancing the memory of George Washington's military reputation. Until his own death, in 1810, early tourists and dignitaries visiting Mount Vernon sought Lee out as a valuable eyewitness to the Revolutionary War and General Washington, the creation of the new nation, and Washington's presidency.[17] Lessons about George Washington in the war that do not also touch on the life of William Lee would be incomplete.

Since the Vietnam War era, military history generally and Revolutionary War history specifically have been greatly enriched by connecting battlefield events to larger themes in social and political history. Histories that leave out the social dynamics of war fail to present a full picture of the military conflict. Most contemporary military historians—even most operational combat historians—make efforts to connect war and society and to write histories that are inclusive and adopt multiple perspectives.[18] Because, as historians John Resch and Walter Sargent put it, "the Revolution had no single home front," scholarship about the Revolutionary War provides material with which to teach about war and a huge variety of diverse social relationships.[19]

Considering Washington and the Revolutionary War in both local and global perspectives enriches the social history of war and helps students function in a modern, globalized world. Students can see in Revolutionary War events examples of Washington working with allies (European and Indigenous) and against enemies (European, American, and Indigenous).[20] Teaching about George Washington's personal and professional relationship with the Marquis de Lafayette, who is mentioned in many states' social studies standards, offers a great opportunity to put US history in a global context for students. It connects to many localities, too, since Lafayette traveled widely during the Revolutionary War and visited all twenty-four states on his nostalgic tour of the United States in 1824–1825.[21]

Lessons emphasizing the globalized social history of the Revolutionary War could also center on the story of Harry Washington, an enslaved man who was among seventeen who escaped from Mount Vernon in 1781 to board the British ship *Savage*, anchored in nearby Alexandria, much to George Washington's chagrin. Harry then fought in the Revolutionary War with the British Royal Artillery, was transported to Nova Scotia after the war, and later resettled in Sierra Leone, where he then fought against British colonial control.[22] Just as the Revolutionary War became a global contest over power in North America, so too was it a power contest between people and institutions on an everyday basis. This kind of military history necessitates looking at the consequences of conflicts for both civilian and military populations: looking at George Washington, Harry Washington, and the history of Mount Vernon can really bring those consequences home for students.

The broader political and social approach to military history does, however, present some challenges for teaching the Revolutionary War, especially to younger students. Teaching in a way that connects war and society means, increasingly, drawing on a historiography that emphasizes the brutal hardships of war. Even scholars who do not want to center themes of White supremacy or settler colonialism in their accounts of the Revolutionary War increasingly emphasize the bloody, bitter aspects of warfare.[23] While lesson plans about the Revolutionary War have for decades emphasized the trenchant partisan conflicts between Patriots and Loyalists in areas such as the Carolinas, New York, and New Jersey and the rather cinematically depicted starvation at Valley Forge, thinking about how to integrate scholarship about physical punishment, coerced labor, rape, illness, and disability into the primary and secondary curriculum necessitates even greater care. Luckily, Revolutionary War scholars and teachers can take pedagogical insights from our colleagues who have focused for decades on other "difficult" subjects, including the Holocaust, Native American boarding schools, and American slavery.[24] Lessons need not delve into the gruesome details of abuse but can still acknowledge the true threats to life and autonomy posed by military conflict.

Using George Washington as a reference point can provide ways to carefully infuse difficult themes in Revolutionary War historiography (in age-appropriate ways) into the classroom. It is true that Washington was hailed as a heroic commander, but he was also a government official trying on a daily basis to deal with sickness, misbehavior, food shortages, and near mutiny in the ranks.[25] Washington struggled, at times, to control civilian and political rage at prisoners of war, who were also poorly cared for by the Continental Congress.[26] Washington complained about camp followers and the deleterious effects of women who were pregnant or had children with them, even as his army relied on women's labor to keep fighting.[27] General Washington revealed the social dynamics of power when he ordered corporal punishments for soldiers and enslaved people and when he explicitly approved scorched-earth tactics against Indigenous soldiers and civilians.[28] John Marshall worried that he had to edit his biography of Washington "especially that part of it which details the distresses of the army during the war," so that his readers might be "relieved from tedious repetitions of the same sufferings." But now Revolutionary War pedagogy has probably removed too much of the suffering, and Washington's biography provides a way to judiciously add back in some of the "dark side" of the war.[29]

Using the Revolutionary War as a lesson on consent could provide one such opportunity. While the war was certainly being fought to guarantee the existence of a republican form of government founded on the "consent of the governed," the conditions of war fighting also sometimes emphasized the limits of individual consent and the degree to which marginalized people in eighteenth-century society (including children, women, and the enslaved) were understood not to possess the full personhood that would enable free consent.[30] The examples of George Washington and his relationship to enslaved men like William Lee and Harry Washington show the importance, and the limits, of consent in the time of the American Revolution and in the circumstances of the Revolutionary War. Historian Holly Mayer has written that while "there is no evidence that the army as an organization ever owned slaves itself . . . it readily accepted the labor of slaves on loan (whether willingly or unwillingly furnished)," and Washington assented to the treatment of enslaved people as property whose labor could be forced to support army operations (as it was during the winter at Valley Forge).[31] After the Battle of Yorktown, Washington issued specific orders designed to keep enslaved people who had escaped their enslavers from being harbored by American officers, explicitly limiting the rights of such people to seek freedom by consent, even if they were contributing to the American cause.[32] Observing the tensions in notions of consent, even and especially to those closely connected with George Washington, creates an accurate picture of the possibilities and limits of the broader American Revolutionary era.

Teaching about George Washington and the Revolutionary War in the twenty-first century is both essential and difficult. In the current context of political polarization and historical "culture wars," teaching in a manner informed by current scholarship becomes even more important, even if it involves some very real public challenges.[33] Political battles over how to teach George Washington are nothing new. John Marshall had an explicitly nationalist purpose in mind when writing the history of Washington, and his biography was tied up in the polarized political contests of the early nineteenth century. He published his biography, with its frankly Federalist interpretation of events, at a time when the Federalist party was trying to hold on to power after the ascendency of rival Democratic-Republican Thomas Jefferson.[34] Today's educators need to have a sense of how politicized this history has always been. This knowledge can help us put our own pedagogical struggles in context and should encourage us to engage with the real history of the Revolutionary War on an even deeper level.

Because the founding era retains a central place in civics and history education and because many state standards require instruction on the Revolutionary War for middle and high school students, educators have the opportunity to make the most of updated approaches. Students can study George Washington and the Revolutionary War to develop a full, nuanced picture of the American Revolution. Of course, state education departments approach the subject from a number of political and educational viewpoints. Some state standards are quite up to date in their approach, but almost all of them leave ample room for teachers to use the history of the Revolutionary War to teach creatively about Washington and the larger American Revolution. Across various geographical, ideological, and pedagogical spectra, educational standards about Revolutionary War instruction allow quite a bit of room to explore important topics with students.

Consider, for example, the state standards for eighth-grade history in Texas, which, because of partisan education battles, one might assume to be rather narrow.[35] The Texas Essential Knowledge and Skills (TEKS) standards for eighth-grade social studies specify "depth" of understanding for students as they "study the history of the United States from the early colonial period through Reconstruction." The TEKS standards prescribe that in order for eighth graders to understand "the foundations of representative government in the United States," they must study the accomplishments of George Washington and military events including "fighting the battles of Lexington and Concord, Saratoga, and Yorktown; enduring the winter at Valley Forge; and signing the Treaty of Paris of 1783."[36] The list of Revolutionary-era figures included in the Texas standards who could be used in lessons is diverse, including, alongside George Washington, "Abigail Adams, John Adams, Wentworth Cheswell, Samuel Adams, Mercy Otis Warren, James Armistead, Benjamin Franklin, Crispus Attucks, King George III, Patrick Henry, Thomas Jefferson, the Marquis de Lafayette, [and] Thomas Paine."[37] What better lesson about the connections between military, social, and political history than the life of James Armistead, an enslaved man who impersonated a runaway in order to serve as a spy for Washington's troops under General Lafayette and then successfully petitioned the Virginia legislature for his freedom in 1786, believing that he should be granted "that Freedom" that he "in some degree contributed to establish"?[38] It is possible to teach up-to-date lessons about Washington and the Revolutionary War adhering to these standards and to infuse social and cultural context into the lessons.

Massachusetts social studies standards provide clear guidance to make up-to-date instruction even easier, but they are not wholly different from instruction standards in Texas. In Massachusetts, Revolutionary War instruction (with an emphasis on Massachusetts history) is mandated in fifth grade, where students learn to describe "the impact of events" in the Revolutionary War and to explain "the factors leading to American victory and British defeat."[39] The fifth-grade standards include instruction about George Washington and Lafayette, but they also explicitly recommend teaching about the role of women in "raising funds for the war, and supporting the Continental Army" and encourage teachers to use the National Park Service "Patriots of Color" project to teach about Black and Indigenous New England men who fought against the British early in the war.[40] Revolutionary War coverage in the eighth-grade Massachusetts standards is a bit more traditional, specifying that students should be able to "[d]escribe the key battles of the Revolution (e.g., Lexington, Concord, Bunker Hill, Trenton, Saratoga, Yorktown); the winter encampment at Valley Forge; and key leaders and participants of the Continental Army."[41] Still, this leaves teachers quite a bit of room to build upon the social context of war introduced in the fifth grade and to link the Revolutionary War and George Washington to the politics of the larger Revolutionary era, which form the main focus of eighth-grade instruction. Lessons could focus on a figure like Prince Hall, the free Black veteran of the Battle of Bunker Hill. Starting in 1777, Hall repeatedly petitioned the Massachusetts legislature to end the institution of slavery, arguing that opposing slavery would allow the government of Massachusetts to be consistent in "their present glorious struggles for Liberty" once that concept could apply to all residents of the state.[42] Prince Hall and George Washington were both military men whose service influenced their (at times conflicting) ideas of liberty and freedom.

Scholars and teachers alike can count on the fact that no matter how controversial social studies curricula become in the United States, states will likely continue to include George Washington and the Revolutionary War at the heart of civics education standards. As John Marshall knew, George Washington is a symbol of national identity as well as a figure of historical significance. The outcome of the Revolutionary War secured the fate of the American Revolution and the early existence of the United States, and the collective memory of the war has helped define US national identity since the eighteenth century.[43] That is partly why political forces have often sought to shape and contest what can, and should, be taught about them—and why teaching about these topics will likely continue to be contested.[44] As commander in chief of the Continental Army, the actual and symbolic head of American military power, Washington occupies a central role in the history and memory of the Revolutionary War, and he is likely to remain a focus of state education requirements. Teaching about Washington can be a way to provide an entrée into instruction about people and topics that have traditionally been more marginalized and might be perceived as "controversial."

Students can handle an accurately complex vision of the past. Especially in a time of heightened political conflict, it is vital to teach students how to think about, and through, the events of the Revolutionary War and to understand the broad range of people who were involved in and affected by it. George Washington's own words in his 1796 Farewell Address are the best advice to historians and teachers: "Honesty is the best policy."[45]

Notes

Citations of Founders Online documents do not include individual links, as each source can be found by searching the site at https://founders.archives.gov/.

1. John Marshall, "Preface," in *The Life of George Washington*, vol. 1 (London, 1804), xx.
2. Marshall, "Preface," xii. On Marshall's biography, see Virginia Museum of History and Culture, "A Connected Legacy: John Marshall and George Washing-

ton," https://virginiahistory.org/learn/connected-legacy-john-marshall-and-george-washington; Eileen Ka May Cheng, *Historiography: An Introductory Guide* (New York: Continuum, 2012), 53.

3. Jeffrey L. Pasley, *The First Presidential Contest: 1796 and the Founding of American Democracy* (Lawrence: University Press of Kansas, 2013), 19.
4. Edward Lengel, *General George Washington: A Military Life* (New York: Random House, 2005), 365–71; John Ferling, *Almost a Miracle: The American Victory in the War of Independence* (New York: Oxford University Press, 2007), 136–37, 571–72; Ricardo A. Herrera, "'Our Army Will Hut This Winter at Valley Forge': George Washington, Decision Making, and the Councils of War," *Army History* 117 (Fall 2020): 6–27.
5. See Michael Howard, "The Use and Abuse of Military History," *Army Doctrine and Training Journal* 6, no. 2 (2003): 18.
6. Caroline Cox, "Integrity and Leadership: George Washington," in *The Art of Command: Military Leadership from George Washington to Colin Powell*, 2nd ed., ed. Harry S. Laver and Jeffrey J. Matthews (Lexington: University Press of Kentucky, 2017), 13–34. On the army as part of the early US state, see Gautham Rao, "The New Historiography of the Early Federal Government: Institutions, Contexts, and the Imperial State," *William and Mary Quarterly* 77, no. 1 (2020): 112–13.
7. Don Higginbotham, "American Historians and the Military History of the American Revolution," *American Historical Review* 70, no. 1 (1964): 18–34.
8. American Historical Association, *American Lesson Plan: Teaching US History in Secondary Schools* (Washington, DC: American Historical Association, 2024), 150; Jane Kamensky, "Two Cheers for the Nation: An American Revolution for the Revolting United States," *Reviews in American History* 47, no. 2 (2019): 308–18.
9. American Historical Association, *American Lesson Plan*, 152.
10. Don Higginbotham, "Preface," in *War and Society in Revolutionary America: The Wider Dimensions of Conflict* (Columbia: University of South Carolina Press, 1988), ix. On Higginbotham's contributions to the history of the Revolutionary War, see his obituary "Scholar of Colonial America; Pioneer of 'New Military History,'" *American Historical Association Perspectives on History* 47 (2009). Other notable contributors to this "new" military history in that era include John Shy, Charles Royster, Ira Gruber, and Richard Kohn; see Edward M. Coffman, "The New Military History," *Military Affairs* 48, no. 1 (1984): 1–5.
11. For a broader look at the "cultural" turn in American military history (which encompasses the Revolutionary War), see Wayne E. Lee, "Mind and Matter—

Cultural Analysis in American Military History: A Look at the State of the Field," *Journal of American History* 93, no. 4 (2007): 1116–42.

12. See Harry M. Ward, *The War for Independence and the Transformation of American Society* (London: UCL Press, 1999).
13. Judith L. Van Buskirk, *Standing in Their Own Light: African American Patriots in the American Revolution* (Norman: University of Oklahoma Press, 2017), 22.
14. Jessie MacLeod, "William (Billy) Lee," in *The Digital Encyclopedia of George Washington,* George Washington's Mount Vernon, https://www.mountvernon.org/library/digitalhistory/digital-encyclopedia/article/william-billy-lee; Mary V. Thompson, *"The Only Unavoidable Subject of Regret": George Washington, Slavery, and the Enslaved Community at Mount Vernon* (Charlottesville: University of Virginia Press, 2019), 53–54.
15. Philip D. Morgan, "'To Get Quit of Negroes': George Washington and Slavery," *Journal of American Studies* 39, no. 3 (2005): 404–5.
16. See John Trumbull, *George Washington and William Lee,* 1780, Metropolitan Museum of Art. For the museum's recent update to include Lee as part of the title and interpretation of the painting, see "George Washington and William Lee (George Washington)," Metropolitan Museum of Art, https://www.metmuseum.org/art/collection/search/12822. See also Alexandra Eaton, "His Name Was Bélizaire': Rare Portrait of Enslaved Child Arrives at Met," *New York Times,* August 14, 2023, https://www.nytimes.com/interactive/2023/08/14/video/belizaire-frey-children-portrait-met.html.
17. Matthew Costello, *The Property of the Nation: George Washington's Tomb, Mount Vernon, and the Memory of the First President* (Lawrence: University Press of Kansas, 2019), 87; Jessie MacLeod, "William (Billy) Lee," in *Lives Bound Together: Slavery at George Washington's Mount Vernon,* ed. Susan P. Schoelwer (Mount Vernon, VA: Mount Vernon Ladies' Association, 2016), 14–16.
18. See, for example, Tami Davis Biddle and Robert M. Citino, "The Role of Military History in the Contemporary Academy," *Army History* 96 (Summer 2015): 26.
19. John Resch and Walter Sargent, "Preface," in *War and Society in the American Revolution: Mobilization and Home Fronts,* ed. John Resch and Walter Sargent (DeKalb: Northern Illinois University Press, 2007), viii.
20. Maria O'Malley and Denys Van Renen, eds., *Beyond 1776: Globalizing the Cultures of the American Revolution* (Charlottesville: University of Virginia Press, 2018).
21. Harlow Giles Unger, *Lafayette* (New York: John Wiley & Sons, 2002); Sarah J. Purcell, *Sealed with Blood: War, Sacrifice, and Memory in Revolutionary America* (Philadelphia: University of Pennsylvania Press, 2002). See also Harrow

Strickland, "The Marquis de Lafayette and Celebrity Culture (Lesson Plan)," American Revolution Institute of the Society of Cincinnati, https://www.americanrevolutioninstitute.org/master-teacher-lesson-plans/the-legacy-of-the-revolution/the-marquis-de-lafayette-and-celebrity-culture.

22. Cassandra Pybus, *Epic Journeys of Freedom: Runaway Slaves of the American Revolution and Their Global Quest for Liberty* (Boston: Beacon Press, 2006); Thompson, *"Only Unavoidable Subject,"* 439; Douglas R. Egerton, *Death or Liberty: African Americans and Revolutionary America* (New York: Oxford University Press, 2009), 194–221.
23. Holger Hoock, *Scars of Independence: America's Violent Birth* (New York: Crown, 2017); Harry M. Ward, *Between the Lines: Banditti of the American Revolution* (Westport, CT: Praeger, 2002). A similar trend in Civil War historiography has caused some debate over how historians should best present "the dark side" of that conflict; see Gary W. Gallagher and Kathryn Shively Meier, "Coming to Terms with Civil War Military History," *Journal of the Civil War Era* 4, no. 4 (2014): 487–508.
24. See "Guidelines for Teaching About the Holocaust," United States Holocaust Memorial Museum, https://www.ushmm.org/teach/fundamentals/guidelines-for-teaching-the-holocaust; Harvard Graduate School of Education, "Justice in Schools," https://www.justiceinschools.org; Sarah Militz-Frielink, La Vonne I. Neal, and Alicia L. Moore, "Learning Series: African Americans in Times of War; Triumphs of Tragedy," *Black History Bulletin* 80, no. 2 (2017): 6–15.
25. Caroline Cox, *A Proper Sense of Honor: Service and Sacrifice in George Washington's Army* (Chapel Hill: University of North Carolina Press, 2004); Resch and Sargent, *War and Society;* Ann M. Becker, "Smallpox in Washington's Army: Strategic Implications of the Disease During the American Revolutionary War," *Journal of Military History* 68, no. 2 (2004): 381–430.
26. T. Cole Jones, *Captives of Liberty: Prisoners of War and the Politics of Vengeance in the American Revolution* (Philadelphia: University of Pennsylvania Press, 2020).
27. "General Orders," August 4, 1777, Founders Online; Holly A. Mayer, *Belonging to the Army: Camp Followers and Community During the American Revolution* (Columbia: University of South Carolina Press, 1999); Holly A. Mayer, ed., *Women Waging War in the American Revolution* (Charlottesville: University of Virginia Press, 2022).
28. Cox, *Proper Sense of Honor;* Andrea Lynn Smith and Nëhdöwes (Randy A. John), "Monuments, Legitimization Ceremonies, and Haudenosaunee Rejection of Sullivan-Clinton Markers," *New York History* 101, no. 2 (2020): 343–

65; Colin G. Calloway, *The American Revolution in Indian Country: Crisis and Diversity in Native American Communities* (New York: Cambridge University Press, 1995), 129–57.

29. Marshall, *Life of George Washington*, viii.
30. Gillian Brown, "Consent, Coquetry, and Consequences," *American Literary History* 9, no. 4 (1997): 625–52; Lauren Duval, "'A Shocking Thing to Tell Of': Female Civilians, Violence, and Rape Under British Military Rule," in Mayer, *Women Waging War*, 77.
31. Mayer, *Belonging to the Army*, 163; Ricardo A. Herrera, *Feeding Washington's Army: Surviving the Valley Forge Winter of 1778* (Chapel Hill: University of North Carolina Press, 2022), 110–12, 132–33.
32. Mayer, *Belonging to the Army*, 164.
33. See American Historical Association, *American Lesson Plan*.
34. Eileen Ka-May Cheng, "Plagiarism as Dialogue: George Chalmers, William Robertson, and John Marshall's 'Life of George Washington,'" *Transactions of the American Philosophical Society* 111, no. 4 (2022): 3–18.
35. Joshua Blank, "Seven Observations About Texas Public Opinion on Public Education," The Texas Politics Project at the University of Texas at Austin, April 3, 2023, https://texaspolitics.utexas.edu/blog/seven-observations-about-texas-public-opinion-public-education.
36. Texas Administrative Code, Title 19 (Education), Part 2, Chapter 113, Texas Essential Knowledge and Skills (TEKS) for Social Studies, Subchapter B (Middle School), Rule §113.20, Social Studies, Grade 8, Adopted 2022.
37. TEKS, Rule §113.20, Social Studies, Grade 8, Adopted 2022.
38. "James Lafayette Petition for Freedom, 1796," Library of Virginia, https://edu.lva.virginia.gov/dbva/items/show/277.
39. Massachusetts Department of Elementary and Secondary Education, Massachusetts Curriculum Framework—2018: History and Social Science Framework, Grades Pre-Kindergarten to 12, 2018, [5.T2], 74.
40. Massachusetts Curriculum Framework, [5.T2], 73, 74; "Patriots of Color—Minute Man National Historical Park (U.S. National Park Service)," https://www.nps.gov/mima/patriotsofcolor.htm.
41. Massachusetts Curriculum Framework, [USI.T1], 121.
42. "Petition for Freedom (Manuscript Copy) to the Massachusetts Council and the House of Representatives, [13] January 1777," Massachusetts Historical Society Collections Online, https://www.masshist.org/database/557; Abigail Swanson, "Prince Hall," Black Past, https://www.blackpast.org/african-american-history/hall-prince-c-1735-1807.
43. Purcell, *Sealed with Blood*.

44. See Nikole Hannah-Jones, Caitlin Roper, Ilena Siverman, and Jake Silverstein, eds., *The 1619 Project: A New Origin Story* (New York: One World, 2021); Sarah Schwartz, "Lawmakers Push to Ban '1619 Project' from Schools," *Education Week,* February 3, 2021, https://www.edweek.org/teaching-learning/lawmakers-push-to-ban-1619-project-from-schools/2021/02.
45. George Washington, Farewell Address, September 19, 1796, Founders Online. The text is also available at the Yale Law School Avalon Project site: https://avalon.law.yale.edu/18th_century/washing.asp. Of course, to be fully honest, we should acknowledge the irony that Washington may have collaborated, at least with Alexander Hamilton, in writing the Farewell Address, so the words might not be Washington's "own." See Jeffrey J. Malanson, "'If I Had It in His Hand-Writing I Would Burn It': Federalists and the Authorship Controversy over George Washington's Farewell Address, 1808–1859," *Journal of the Early Republic* 34, no. 2 (2014): 219–42; Pasley, *First Presidential Contest,* 218–22.

ENGAGING MIDDLE SCHOOLERS IN THE COUNTRY'S FOUNDING HISTORY

JOHN CLINTON WALSH

In my almost twenty years of teaching, I have picked up some wisdom on engaging middle schoolers in the country's founding history. Those lessons, however, still largely reflect my experience in my corner of central Florida. My work with the George Washington Teacher Institute at Mount Vernon (GWTI) has provided me with the opportunity to meet innovative teachers from across the country. I have also been blessed to collaborate with great educators within my school, district, and state. These interactions have improved my practices and made me a better teacher. In an attempt to capture some of the wisdom of these educators, I surveyed my friends and colleagues in the spring of 2024 about their experiences teaching history in middle school. Collaboration is essential among educators—especially at the middle school level. Therefore, I have taken that approach here. Teaching students in the thick of early adolescence has its challenges, but it also provides some opportunities unique to the middle school years. My survey of GWTI alumni and work colleagues revealed some trends. Teachers who want to engage middle schoolers in our nation's founding history should make history relevant, embrace controversy, be inclusive, emphasize humanity, utilize primary sources, and show their enthusiasm and passion.

Engaging middle schoolers in the country's founding history requires teachers to make it relevant to their students. Beth Doughty teaches in Battle Ground, Washington.[1] She refers to the founding era as "the backbone of middle school United States history." She finds that the process of creating the American republic links our understanding of all eras of American history. This includes its challenges, inspirations, conflicts, flaws, and successes. Since her state is named after George Washington, she makes a point of emphasizing the connection between his name and her state. Even though Washington state is on the opposite side of the North American continent from the original thirteen states, she stresses that connecting the East to the West has been a central concern throughout our nation's past.

Addressing one's blind spots as an educator can help make the nation's founding more relevant to students. Like Doughty, I teach outside of one of the thirteen original states. Unlike the state of Washington, however, the state of Florida was a British colony during the American Revolution. Technically, it was East Florida and West Florida, but both colonies chose not to rebel against the actions of Parliament and the king. I taught for years without making this connection in my classroom. Reading books such as Kathleen DuVal's *Independence Lost* (2015) helped me address blind spots in my own learning so that I can emphasize a relevant geographic connection in my lessons.[2]

Charles Gentry teaches with me at Discovery Middle School in Orlando, Florida.[3] He underscores the relevance of America's founding era and George Washington in particular. He recounts that it is difficult to establish a proper perspective on current events without an understanding of the nation's founding history. Without the proper historical context informing modern news events, it is too easy for students to take our nation's freedoms and ideals for granted. Gentry refers to George Washington as the central figure in our eighth-grade US History curriculum. Students' knowledge of the story of America would be incomplete if they did not engage with the influence and legacy of George Washington—from his work as a young surveyor to his roles as general, president, and everything in between. To Gentry, it is important to help students make connections between the past and the present. Students need to understand the purpose of learning this content. If students cannot make real-world connections, they become uninterested and disengaged.

I agree with my colleagues that students must understand the relevance of the nation's founding to understand our modern world. Samantha Worden, a teacher out of Rock Springs, Wyoming, stresses how founding-era principles still impact people today.[4] She does this through reenactments and hands-on activities. Carla Ljunggren of Billings, Montana, expresses a similar sentiment.[5] She states that many of today's events can only be fully understood through an examination of our history. This is where games such as Mount Vernon's *Be Washington* can be effective.[6] The online interactive game focuses on four pivotal decisions George Washington made as commander of the Continental

Army or president and challenges participants to role-play as if they were the decision-maker. Like Washington, players must weigh contradictory advice from multiple advisors before deciding on the best course of action. Leaders must be able to do this today; however, everybody else needs to be able to do it, too. I have led teachers and students in many rounds of *Be Washington.* It allows participants to practice critical thinking and decision-making, which are skills adolescents greatly benefit from improving.

Apathy can be a real obstacle to engagement in a middle school classroom. Leah Steehler of Las Vegas, Nevada, is challenged by students who decide they just cannot do history because it is too boring.[7] Even though most of her students tend to be engaged and responsive, there are some who are generally apathetic. The trick, for her, is figuring out what makes them tick in order to get them interested in the content. She insists that it is the teacher's job to bring history to life however he or she can in order to encourage student engagement. She does this through varying approaches: breakout rooms, simulations, project-based learning, and a mix of technology-based and paper assignments. Steehler considers it her responsibility to provide her students with a strong foundation on how the nation began. With this strong foundation, the rest of America's history makes more sense.

Students without an adequate understanding of the founding era become adults who lack proficiency in civics. In his Farewell Address, George Washington reminded us that in a republic, "it is essential that public opinion should be enlightened," since the structure of government provides proportional force to public opinion. Washington promoted institutions of learning as objects of "primary importance" for this reason.[8] This is why Amanda Goodwin, who teaches in Urbana, Ohio, finds it so disconcerting that her students lack background knowledge about our nation's founding history.[9] She has noticed that students too often have no knowledge about how the nation's government was formed. Unfortunately, this lack of civic knowledge can continue into adulthood. A 2024 study by the US Chamber of Commerce Foundation found that more than 70 percent of Americans lack basic civics literacy. This includes deficiencies in topics such as the three branches of government, the number of justices on the Supreme Court, and the basic functions of republican government. Only half of the survey respondents were able to correctly identify the branch of government specifically tasked with making laws.[10]

Disheartening trends such as these have prompted states to pass initiatives to bolster civics education in our nation's classrooms. One example is Florida's

Justice Sandra Day O'Connor Civic Education Act. Passed in 2010, it requires the creation and implementation of a course on civics at the middle school level.[11] More recently, Florida created the Civics Seal of Excellence Endorsement, which awarded teachers a three-thousand-dollar bonus for completing a course designed to increase their knowledge of America's founding and its constitutional government.[12] The Florida Department of Education has also hosted workshops such as the Summer Civics Education Professional Development Series for the same purpose.[13] I met Spencer LeBlanc, who teaches in Gainesville, at one of these events.[14] He emphasizes how vital it is for students to have meaningful engagement with historical topics related to civics and the American founding so that they grow into adults who can make informed decisions.

Middle school students are in a unique position to understand the history of America's founding in relation to their own experiences. Jeremy Stamm of Orlando, Florida, observes that our nation's founding seems to echo the experience of middle schoolers: "Just as our founders wrestled with creating a unified national identity, students struggle with who they are" and who they will become.[15] By studying the history of the founding of the United States, students get an opportunity to understand that struggling to achieve growth and positive change is acceptable. He focuses on making specific connections between his history lessons and his students' lives. This helps build a bridge between the events of the past and the lives of students today. Stamm contends that teachers must present history as "a living, breathing story that continues to impact the world today."

Lindsay McBride, who teaches in Fredonia, Wisconsin, similarly sees the nation's founding history to be emblematic of the tumultuous middle school years.[16] In their early teen years, students have a desire to learn about the world around them. They are beginning to apprehend where they came from and who they are. They are forming a personal history and identity for themselves. The middle school years—usually from ages ten through thirteen—are filled with both disruptive and formative relationships. Students are differentiating friend from foe while being tested with the difficulties that come with adolescence. They can shy away from these challenges or confront them head-on and grow. As McBride puts it, "When students learn about the period when our nation was teetering between success or failure, they can learn how to develop a growth mindset."

On a broader scale, middle school students are also becoming more engaged in current events. McBride observes that students are better positioned to evaluate the accomplishments and shortcomings of our nation's founders. Students will view some historical figures as heroes, but at the same time, they will also start to evaluate their imperfections.

Janine Brown, who taught civics at Discovery Middle School in Orlando, Florida, also notes that seventh and eighth graders are at a point in their lives where they can appreciate the impact of founders such as George Washington. They are endlessly curious. Confronting the struggles that went into forming our federal government really piques their curiosity. Brown finds this to be one of the most rewarding aspects of teaching this age group. She is thrilled when students make connections between current and previously taught topics.

Studying American history fosters a sense of identity and belonging. Jessica Watson of Bruceton, Tennessee, points out that civics and history naturally connect students to the larger story of America's past.[17] Students become empowered to develop into informed and active citizens. They hone skills needed to critically analyze current events within a historical context. Engaging students in the nation's founding history equips them with tools needed to contribute thoughtfully to the future of the American republic.

Thoughtful students can be critical, though. This is especially true of middle schoolers, as their parents well know. No longer are these parents unquestionably "cool" in the eyes of their children. Parents' flaws are visible and are sometimes pounced upon by their newly rebellious teenagers. Kelsey Ireland, a teacher from Coppell, Texas, notes that middle schoolers are at an age where they are beginning to question everything, from pop culture to politics.[18] Students turn these same critical eyes on the nation's founding history.

If middle schoolers are suddenly more inclined to notice their parents' flaws, it makes sense for them to be more attuned to the flaws of their nation's founders. My students are quick to notice the disconnect between what the founders said and what they did. Patrick Henry may have railed against metaphorical enslavement in his "Liberty or Death" speech, with its imagery of clanking chains, but he participated in the actual enslavement of fellow human beings.[19] Students see this as hypocrisy, and it is appropriate for teachers to allow space in the classroom for students to wrestle with this feeling. It indicates how they are critically thinking about the content. In this case, I ask students to explain their reasoning: What makes someone a hypocrite? In what ways are liberty and enslavement incompatible with each other? Do you believe that Henry saw them as incompatible? If he did, why do you think he continued to enslave people? Asking such questions provides an opportunity to foster critical thinking–based conversations among students. These conversations enhance their understanding of the founding and give them practice in dealing with complex topics.

Even though this age group can be critical, many of their teachers have been accused of encouraging hatred of the founding generation. Christina Lee of Corpus Christi, Texas, points out that our current political climate has made it more difficult to teach history, with each political party attempting to control the historical narrative.[20] The result is often false or misleading accounts of the past. Dodging controversy leaves a void that gets filled by the loudest voices, but not necessarily the most truthful ones. Lee believes that it is the task of educators to fill that void, even though it may come at the cost of threats and intimidation from government officials. She suggests a need to remove modern politics from history classrooms or risk raising a generation devoid of critical-thinking skills. Students predisposed to see flaws in their historical heroes will still see those flaws, but they will wonder why their teachers are ignoring them. Acknowledging controversy meets middle schoolers where they are, provides a more inclusive history, and increases engagement in the classroom.

Engaging middle school students in the nation's founding history enables them to confront complex aspects of America's story and provides them with an opportunity to learn about diverse individuals and groups, including the enslaved people of African descent who shaped our nation's founding. Ginnie Holloway of Rochester Hills, Michigan, wants her students to think about the many different sides of Washington: the husband, the grandfather, the general, the president, the farmer, and the enslaver.[21] As president, Washington's administration set crucial precedents that influenced the development of the US government. At the same time, he relentlessly pursued his family's escaped enslaved maid, Ona Judge, who ran away from the President's House in Philadelphia in 1796.

Holloway uses many of Mount Vernon's *Lives Bound Together* resources, discussed within this volume by curator Jessie MacLeod, to teach about enslavement and Washington's relationship to it. Holloway includes the story of Judge as well as biographies of William Lee, Washington's enslaved valet; Hercules Posey, his enslaved cook; and Tom, an enslaved man sold into the Caribbean by George Washington in 1766 after he attempted to run away. She believes that it is essential for students to consider Washington's character as someone who was willing to put his country's needs over his own, but they must also recognize that he was a human with flaws, just like everybody else.

It can be difficult for middle school students to see founding-era leaders, such as George Washington, as mere humans. It does not help that many pieces of art depict the American founders as larger-than-life demigods. Becky Rasmussen of Millstadt, Illinois, acknowledges this dilemma.[22] She finds that Washington seems completely inaccessible to her students. He is a towering, giant figure because he was the first president of the United States. Rasmussen says that it is hard to portray him as just a man doing the best that he can. Ashley Penney, a teacher from Wichita Falls, Texas, considers this to be one of the most important reasons to teach about Washington's contributions and legacies.[23] Penney wants her students to know that he was not superhuman; instead, he was a person who stepped up when his country needed him. If Washington was capable of these selfless feats, other Americans (including students) are capable of them, too.

Recognizing the humanity of the founders is essential to engaging middle school learners. Jaimee Martin of West Bridgewater, Massachusetts, worries that people too often think of history as the rote memorization of dates and events.[24] In fact, our nation's history is more than just a series of chronological events. It includes the stories of many individual trials and tribulations. Collectively, these stories make up our American history, but they can also be applied to the ups and downs of modern life. Without a focus on humanity—warts and all—history does not resonate with middle school students.

A human-centered approach is recommended by many of the educators I interviewed. Casey Burrows, who teaches in Camdenton, Missouri, uses the human-centered approach to differentiate between trivia and true knowledge.[25] Trivia is knowing what happened, where it happened, and when it happened. True knowledge comes with understanding *how* something happened—the complexities of why historical events unfolded the way they did, along with their consequences. This more nuanced understanding develops students into learners who engage in meaningful discussions instead of simply recalling facts. Teachers assist students in understanding *how* and *why* an event occurred by emphasizing the human actions and contingency that are at the center of historical events. Burrows practices this in the language that he uses with his students. He avoids statements such as "The United States declared independence in 1776." Even though countries and governments are credited with carrying out many actions, it is the individuals leading them who make the decisions that drive those actions. For this reason, Burrows prefers more personal language, such as "members of the Continental Congress sent a declaration to King George III, declaring the U.S. to be an independent nation." He points out that these small changes to daily pedagogical practices can assist students in picturing the human beings behind the actions that constitute our nation's history.

As noted above, middle schoolers are likely to make critical moral judgments about the actions carried out by historical figures. Burrows states, "The question of morality is a complex part of the human condition." He notes that the study of history will lead students to ask whether a particular person, event, or nation was "good" or "bad." He cautions that this duality is more complex than it seems. He calls it a trap to apply personal morals to the study of history. Even though it may seem useful, modern sentiments may be inapplicable and ahistorical when applied to the past, reducing history to a battle of heroes and villains where most individuals do not fit neatly into either category.

At the same time, there is no need to avoid moral judgment entirely. Christina Lee finds that many of her students tend toward sweeping generalizations about the founding generation, such as that they were all enslavers. She addresses this by pointing to founding-era movements supporting the abolition of slavery. For instance, a petition from the Pennsylvania Society for Promoting the Abolition of Slavery reached the US Congress in 1790, during George Washington's first term. According to the petition, the society felt that the "blessings of liberty" contained in the preamble to the new Constitution "ought rightfully to be administered, without distinction of Colour, to all descriptions of People" within the United States.[26] It was signed by Benjamin Franklin, one of Washington's fellow delegates to the 1787 Philadelphia Convention. In his will, Washington immediately freed William Lee and set up plans for the emancipation of all the individuals that he had enslaved upon the death of his wife, Martha; even Washington, then, can be said to have changed his mind on the morality of enslaving fellow human beings.[27] Therefore, students are not imposing a modern morality when they judge the actions of past individuals who enslaved and killed people. People living during the founding era judged the morality of those actions as well.

In our classrooms, Gentry and I approach the question of morality through debate. Students evaluate the actions of historical figures through primary and secondary sources. Even though a hero or villain duality is initially applied, students quickly realize that categorizing each individual is much more complex. The debate format allows students to weigh the positive and negative impacts of each person's legacies while providing plenty of room for disagreement and reevaluation. It also increases engagement, with debates often spilling out of our classrooms and into the hallways, courtyard, and cafeteria.

Primary sources are invaluable for highlighting the humanity of those who witnessed historical events. Rasmussen uses them daily to compare the past with modern situations. Holloway utilizes primary sources to compare context and claims and examine multiple points of view. She acknowledges that primary sources can be challenging for students to understand, but they become accessible to students with enough dedicated time from the teacher. McBride utilizes as many primary sources as possible to allow students to interpret a particular historical moment for themselves. They ask difficult questions, which can lead to effective discourse. In fact, the use of primary sources was the most consistent practice emphasized by educators in their responses. It provides a direct connection to a historical figure or event, shows the humanity of people in the past, and provides history free of perceived political bias. Teachers worried about being accused of pushing political agendas can rely on the words and images of people involved in the nation's founding to drive the historical lesson. I find that Founders Online, run by the National Archives, is an excellent repository for primary sources about the nation's founding.

Passion and enthusiasm are also integral to engaging middle schoolers in the nation's founding history. Hayley Venner, who teaches this history in Leander, Texas, works hard to bring her subject to life.[28] She dresses up and engages students with strategies designed to tie an emotion or experience to her content. She firmly believes that her enthusiasm directly affects student excitement about learning. Venner stresses, too, the need for teacher reengagement. Participation in professional development opportunities such as GWTI helps educators become the best teachers that they can be for their students. She notes that stagnant teachers are boring teachers. They are probably grumpy, too.

Engaging teachers are storytellers. Laurie Westerfield of Orlando, Florida, says that story time is her students' favorite part of class.[29] She uses her acting skills to engage her students in events as if they were really there. She incorporates the weird, unique details that make the stories more interesting and encourages her students to participate as if they were reporting a bit of gossip for the newspaper or even social media. Westerfield urges students to include all the nitty-gritty details of the past. She calls her enthusiasm the most vital aspect of her teaching. Even though she might be sharing these stories with students for the hundredth time, it is new to her current students, and she loves seeing their excitement. It is the reason that she loves being a teacher.

Teachers who can make their content relevant, deal with controversy, provide an inclusive history, take a human-centered approach to the past, use primary sources, and show their enthusiasm are well equipped to engage their middle school students in founding-era history. Middle schoolers are not voters yet, but they will be soon. They are mature enough to realize that the actions of the government affect them and that their actions can affect the government, too—even if it is not at the ballot box. They are beginning to understand that they are part of a larger society that relies on their participation. Engaging students in our nation's founding history helps them understand the challenges that accompanied the desire to embark on this experiment in representative government. The Constitution that came out of the convention presided over by George Washington was not perfect. The framers of the Constitution presented it as a "more perfect union" than had existed under the Articles of Confederation. Since 1787, it has continued to be made more perfect by generations of Americans working to effect change. The fact that many of these individuals were also not able to vote should be especially relevant for early adolescents struggling to find their voices and be heard.

Notes

Citations of Founders Online documents do not include individual links, as each source can be found by searching the site at https://founders.archives.gov/.

1. Beth Doughty teaches eighth-grade US history, seventh-grade Washington state history, and seventh- and eighth-grade English language arts.
2. Kathleen DuVal, *Independence Lost: Lives on the Edge of the American Revolution* (New York: Random House, 2015).
3. Like me, Charles Gentry teaches eighth-grade US history.
4. Samantha Worden teaches eighth-grade US history.
5. Carla Ljunggren teaches eighth-grade US history.
6. To learn more about this project and play the games, visit the Be Washington Interactive Experience, George Washington's Mount Vernon, https://www.bewashington.org/.
7. Leah Steehler teaches US history to seventh graders in a course titled History & Geography 7.
8. George Washington, Farewell Address, September 19, 1796, Founders Online.
9. Amanda Goodwin teaches eighth-grade US history and seventh-grade world history.
10. "New Study Finds Alarming Lack of Civic Literacy Among Americans," US Chamber of Commerce Foundation, https://www.uschamberfoundation.org/civics/new-study-finds-alarming-lack-of-civic-literacy-among-americans.

11. Justice Sandra Day O'Connor Civics Education Act., S. SB 1096, 2010 Leg. (Fla., as passed, April 16, 2010), https://www.flsenate.gov/Session/Bill/2010/1096/.
12. "Florida Civics Seal of Excellence Course," Florida Department of Education, https://www.civicsliteracy.org/civics/course.
13. "2023 Summer Civics Education Professional Learning Series," Florida Department of Education Memorandum, May 5, 2023, https://info.fldoe.org/docushare/dsweb/Get/Document-9834/dps-2023-74.pdf.
14. Spencer LeBlanc was preparing to teach sixth-grade US history when I met him. He currently teaches government in high school.
15. Jeremy Stamm teaches eighth-grade US history.
16. Lindsay McBride teaches sixth-grade ancient world history and civics, seventh-grade US history, and eighth-grade international relations.
17. Jessica Watson taught seventh-grade English language arts and world history before moving to high school, where she teaches ninth-grade world history, eleventh-grade US history, and twelfth-grade statewide dual credit.
18. Kelsey Ireland teaches eighth-grade US history.
19. The Patrick Henry speech ("Give Me Liberty or Give Me Death") from March 23, 1775, is available at the Yale Law School Avalon Project site: https://avalon.law.yale.edu/18th_century/patrick.asp.
20. Christina Lee teaches language, US history, and social studies.
21. Ginnie Holloway teaches eighth-grade US history.
22. Becky Rasmussen taught sixth- and seventh-grade US history before switching to her current role as an eighth-grade English/language arts teacher.
23. Ashley Penney taught eighth-grade US history before switching to her current role as an academic counseling and internship coordinator at the university level.
24. Jamiee Martin teaches eighth-grade civics and social studies and ninth-grade world history.
25. Casey Burrows teaches eighth-grade US history.
26. "Benjamin Franklin's Anti-Slavery Petitions to Congress," National Archives, https://www.archives.gov/legislative/features/franklin.
27. "Washington's Last Will and Testament," George Washington's Mount Vernon, https://www.mountvernon.org/george-washington/death/washingtons-last-will-testament.
28. Hayley Venner teaches eighth-grade US history and seventh- and eighth-grade dance.
29. Laurie Westerfield teaches eighth-grade US history.

TOWN DESTROYER

Teaching George Washington, Native America, and the Founding of the United States

DAVID J. SILVERMAN

If you visit the monuments, homes, and libraries dedicated to the presidents of the United States, you might notice that almost none of them address the Indian policies of those figures, even though Indian policy has been a major feature of the country throughout most of its history and occupied a great deal of the early presidents' time and attention. American culture has always worked to make Indians disappear—both in history and in the here and now. The ideology of Manifest Destiny, which existed well before the name for it was coined during the US war against Mexico and continues to resonate to this very day, posits that God blessed the United States to serve as the vehicle for capitalism, Christianity, and democracy. Any human suffering along the way—which is to say, Indian suffering—was and is dismissed as incidental collateral damage.[1]

Consider also the tale of the First Thanksgiving, which defines Native peoples' role in the American mythos. The story has Indians making friends with the Pilgrims, feasting with them, handing off their country, and finally disappearing, so that the colonists' descendants can create the United States. Generations of US history curricula have promoted the same view by reducing Native people to bit parts in the country's history (when not ignoring them entirely). For over a century, maps in many American history textbooks failed to represent Indians after initial contact, as if they had vanished, while making it appear that European empires dominated practically all of North America from the beginning of the colonial era. It is as if the United States expanded with no obstacles other than time and its own sense of limits.[2]

None of this is history. It is ideology.

White Americans ignore Indians to spare themselves the shame of confronting the country's devastation of Native people in what historians are increasingly convinced should be characterized as a genocide. Regardless of whether one believes the use of that term is appropriate in the American context, there is nearly universal agreement that historic White Americans' violent subjugation of Native people and degradation of the survivors stand alongside slavery as the country's foundational human-rights disasters. Given that much of the public believes that the point of a history education is to cultivate patriotism, it is no wonder that educators of all sorts avoid the topic. Yet for those who believe that a history education involves confronting hard truths about the past to understand the present and chart a better future—and that Americans of all descriptions, including Native Americans, have a right to see themselves depicted accurately in their own country's history—this subject is essential. Neglecting it is bad history and, I contend, bad civics.

This essay submits that we should not and, indeed, cannot understand George Washington, the world in which he lived, and the world he helped create without Indigenous people front and center. Washington was important to Indians, and Indians important to him, in ways that reflected the intertwined lives of White and Native Americans east of the Mississippi River. Engaging this history unflinchingly reveals that relations between the two populations were primarily about land and power negotiated through violence. It also confronts us with the salience of racial ideology in that contest and American national identity. George Washington was not solely or mostly responsible for the horror the colonies or the young United States inflicted on Indigenous people, but he was thoroughly part of it. Indeed, this period exposes a pattern in American history: Whites were determined to seize Indian lands by whatever means, and elected governments could either channel this will or lose popular support. Washington understood this dynamic. He also expected that we would judge him and the country for it.

History instructors, for understandable reasons, often feel ill-prepared to teach Native American history, never mind deal with its fraught modern politics. To help them tackle the first problem, if not the second, when it comes to addressing Indians and George Washington, this essay provides a detailed road map for considering the period between the Seven Years' War (1754–1763) and the War of 1812 (1811–1815) as a single Sixty Years' War. During this era, Indians between the Appalachian Mountains and the Mississippi River were engaged in almost constant hostilities with White Americans from the East.

MAP 1. Indian Country between the Appalachian Mountains and the Mississippi River. (Map by Nat Case, InCase, LLC)

Their sovereignty, lands, cultures, and very existence hung in the balance. The struggle was punctuated by various formal wars that historians normally treat individually, based on the perspectives of White historical actors, but Native people did not experience these events as separate at all. For them, this time was a constant state of war, characterized by relentless mutual low-level raiding and occasional bursts of large-scale genocidal violence. To teach Native American perspectives, and the life and career of George Washington, we have to teach the stakes, conduct, and outcomes of this Sixty Years' War.[3]

Washington came of age in Virginia during a transitional stage in Indian-colonial relations. By the time of his birth in 1732, each of the mainland North American colonies had finished what might be called the first stage of major Indian wars. These conflicts initially threatened the colonies' very existence but ultimately gave them possession of territory stretching a hundred miles westward from the Atlantic coast. Indian warfare dominated life in Virginia from the 1610s through the 1640s and then again in the 1670s, but by Washington's boyhood such events were distant history. Consequently, Washington grew up on the Rappahannock River experiencing little contact with Indians. There was a small reservation nearby, containing a few dozen members of the Rappahannock tribe. On the route between his boyhood home and the Virginia capital of Williamsburg there were a handful of other reservations for the Mattaponi, Chickahominy, and Pamunkey communities. Washington might have encountered them occasionally, but not regularly, as wage workers, basket peddlers, or hunting guides.

As for the hundreds and perhaps even thousands of Indians enslaved by Virginia colonists during the mid- to late seventeenth century, most of them had produced children with enslaved Africans and those children were considered by Whites to be Black, which colonial society had made synonymous with "slave." Washington also might have occasionally witnessed political delegations from faraway tribes traveling through his neighborhood, but these would have been rare occasions. In terms of Washington's daily life, Indians were either remote and foreign or conquered.

The era of peaceful, unchallenged colonial dominance was coming to an end as Washington came of age. The surge of colonial expansion toward the foothills of the Appalachian Mountains was contested by some of the greatest Indian powers in eastern North America: the Six Nations Iroquois or Haudenosaunee in what is now upstate New York (consisting of the Mohawks, Oneidas, Onondagas, Cayugas, Senecas, and Tuscaroras), the Cherokees of the Smoky Mountains, and the Creeks or Muskogees of what is now the Georgia/Alabama border region. There was also a growing confederation of smaller groups in the Ohio Country, including Shawnees, Delawares, Wyandots, Miamis, Ottawas, Ojibwas, and others. These Ohio Indians were galvanized by religious prophets, who argued that the Great Spirit had created Indians and Whites separately, for distinctive purposes, and that therefore Indians needed to make common cause with each other to hold back the White tide.

Another factor in the renewal of warfare between the tribes and British colonists was the resumption of imperial warfare between Britain, France, and Spain after a brief lull just before Washington's birth. From 1739 until the end of the Napoleonic Wars (ca. 1799–1815), those powers remained at war almost constantly. North American Indians were both allies and enemies of these empires amid their own hostilities with White Americans from the East. Washington grew up in this world.

Not coincidentally, Washington and most of his White contemporaries conceived of Indians as bloodthirsty savages. Even when they did not have regular contact with Indians, Whites in the East had access to a steady stream of newspaper articles and fireside tales, real and imagined, telling of Indian atrocities committed against frontier families—men, women, and children alike. Colonists living in the backcountry, as British colonists called the western reaches of their settlements, lived these stories. Though colonists were as likely to commit acts of terror against Indians as suffer them, they focused only on the Indians' exploits, not their own. As such, it was second nature for Washington to refer to Indians as "inhuman savages," "barbarous," and "beasts of prey."[4]

Such language supported a racial ideology used to justify Indian dispossession, from which Washington profited mightily. To the extent that White colonists justified their seizure of Indian territory, they argued that Indians failed to improve the land to its fullest extent and thus should make way for those who did, which was to say, the colonists. They characterized Indians as inveterate hunters, roving the wilds instead of turning the wilderness into a fruitful garden. In this, Whites focused on Indian men's wide-ranging hunting instead of the intensive corn/beans/squash horticulture carried out by Indian women. They ignored the many Indians who had begun to adopt Christianity, raise livestock, and even, in some cases, use plows and fences, partly to convince colonists to tolerate their presence. They also ignored the White elites who sometimes claimed hundreds of thousands of acres as private property that they left unused as capital investment.

Washington became one of those elites, and the process tells us a great deal about him as a person, the Indian policy pursed during his presidency, and Indian-White relations in the eighteenth century. Following in his father's footsteps, Washington cut his teeth as a surveyor, traveling far into Virginia's western reaches to chart the land claims of the colony's most powerful men, claims that invariably rested on Indian cessions (past or future). Eventually, Washington began speculating in Indian land himself. Over the course of his life, he surveyed or had surveyed more than two hundred tracts of territory, giving him title to more than sixty-five thousand acres in thirty-seven different locations spread across what is now Virginia, West Virginia, Pennsylvania, Maryland, Kentucky, New York, the Ohio Valley, and Washington, DC. Most of this acreage was Indian land. Acquiring, managing, and trying to capitalize on these claims consumed as much of Washington's time and attention as anything else in his life.

Washington also acquired land claims through inheritance. Washington's half brother, Lawrence, was one of the organizers of the Ohio Company, which, after its incorporation in 1747, prevailed on Virginia's lieutenant governor, Sir William Gooch, and then the Crown to give it a grant of up to half a million acres from territory the Haudenosaunees had ceded at the Treaty of Lancaster in 1744. None of this land ever actually belonged to the Haudenosaunees; it belonged instead to the Shawnees, Delawares, Cherokees, and others. The speculators hardly cared, so long as their claims had some legitimacy, and the Haudenosaunees hardly cared, so long as they got paid and other tribes had to deal with the problem of the settler invasion they had caused.

Land companies could not cash in on their investments unless would-be settlers believed that the land titles they bought from those speculators were recognized both by Indians and by colonial and imperial governments. Given the underhanded methods of many (and perhaps most) speculators, usually their tenuous claims could not be secured without an Indian war. In the case of Washington's Ohio Company interests, the primary conflict was the Seven Years' War, stretching between 1754 and 1763. Washington's every action while he served in the Virginia ranks—from his opening mission to warn the French away from the forks of the Ohio River, to the building and defense of Fort Necessity, to his later service alongside British general Edward Braddock in the march against Fort Duquesne—involved his personal fortunes.

When Braddock began charting a road to allow his soldiers to besiege Fort Duquesne, at the site of modern Pittsburgh, Washington and his partners made sure that it ran through northwestern Virginia right to the company storehouse on Redstone Creek. The point was to encourage the troops to purchase their supplies there. The outcome of the war would also decide whether Washington could profit from two hundred thousand western acres that Virginia had promised to soldiers who served under him. None of this land was supposed to go to officers, but Washington was certain he could finagle a large piece for himself. He was right.

Washington's later approach to Indian affairs was shaped equally by his firsthand experience in the war, when he witnessed Mingo, Delaware, and Shawnee Indians fighting in a manner that he deemed barbaric. The greatest impression came during Braddock's march against Fort Duquesne in 1755. Braddock repeatedly ignored advice from Indian allies and Washington himself to employ scouts and flankers against potential ambushers. When the attack finally came, a combined force of French, Canadian, and Indian troops from several tribes killed or wounded 977 of 1,400 redcoats and colonial militiamen while losing only 39 themselves. Fortunately for the survivors, when Braddock fell dead, Washington took command and led an orderly retreat, the beginning of a career-long pattern of understanding when and how to give up the fight. It was also a key moment in that Washington concluded, like so many of his predecessors, that Indians were undeserving of the rules of "civilized" warfare.

When Britain finally defeated France in the Seven Years' War and convinced it to sign the Treaty of Paris, surrendering France's claims in North America, it seemed that Washington and other land speculators were primed to reap a fortune. There were only two problems: neither Indians nor the British government agreed.

No sooner had France surrendered than an unprecedented alliance of over a dozen different tribes from the Ohio Country and Great Lakes rose up in unison to sack most of Britain's western forts, put the holdouts Detroit, Pitt, and Niagara under siege, and strike frontier settlements in Pennsylvania, Maryland, and Virginia. British land encroachment was only one of several Indian grievances (the main one was Britain's refusal to adhere to the same Indian protocols as the French), but it was significant, as evident in the Shawnees' and Delawares' systematically pushing the line of Pennsylvania settlement within fifty miles of Philadelphia. The war ended in 1764 after nine months, but both sides knew it represented a pause rather than a firm peace.

The Crown was another problem for land speculators like Washington. In late 1763, King George III issued a Proclamation Line barring White colonists from settling west of the Appalachians and declaring all land titles within the region to be null and void unless they had been negotiated and approved by royal officials. Washington's individual land claims, and those held by the companies in which he had invested, no longer had any legal standing. The king's goal was for the Proclamation Line to bring order to Indian relations and thus avoid costly military operations when Britain was already saddled with debt from the Seven Years' War. Washington had different priorities. As a man on the make, he viewed the Proclamation Line as "a temporary expedient to quiet the Minds of the Indians & must fall of course in a few years . . . Any Person therefore who neglects the present opportunity of hunting out good Lands . . . will never regain it."[5] He had no intention of abiding by the law.

Washington did not have to wait long to see his predictions come true. It took only until the 1763 Treaty of Augusta and the Treaties of Hard Labor and Fort Stanwix in 1768 for the Crown's agents to negotiate Indian land cessions extending far west of the Proclamation Line. A flood of settlers followed, some with land titles, most without. Between 1760 and 1775, some forty thousand Scots, or about 3 percent of the entire population of Scotland, and fifty-five thousand Irish, or 2.3 percent of the total number of Irish, migrated to the colonies "for no other reason," one British official remarked, "but because they hope to live better."[6] Many of them pushed their way into the lands of the Haudenosaunees, Delawares, Shawnees, Cherokees, and Creeks, creating an environment of unrestrained, often alcohol-soaked violence. This situation also represented potentially enormous profits to land speculators if they could get these newcomers to buy their questionable titles.

The combination of the influx of settlers, aggressive land speculation, and boundary disputes between colonies meant that the region centered in present-day West Virginia, home to the Mingos, Shawnees, and Delawares, descended into anarchy. Virginians and Pennsylvanians engaged in shoot-outs over jurisdiction, Indians and Whites often murdered one another on sight and desecrated the bodies of each other's dead, and authority figures were at a complete loss as to what to do.

This crisis emerged at an opportune time for Virginia's government. The royal governor, John Murray, fourth earl of Dunmore, wanted to send troops into the Ohio Valley to defend Virginia's western claims against Pennsylvania's and to distract Virginians from the brewing imperial crisis. Land speculators in the colony's House of Burgesses wanted returns on their western land claims. To these ends, in October 1774, Dunmore led 2,400 men against Shawnee towns blocking Virginia's expansion. Following the Battle of Point Pleasant, Shawnee leaders signed a treaty ceding their claims to present-day West Virginia and Kentucky in exchange for Dunmore's promise to keep Whites south of the Ohio River. Both parties began to violate the agreement immediately.

Americans today usually think of the American Revolution only in terms of Patriots opposing Britain, including taxation without representation. Yet it emerged seamlessly out of Dunmore's War and involved Indians from the start. As colonial protests against British policies began turning into an armed rebellion, Indians throughout the East argued that they should be left out of it. But neutrality was next to impossible. First and foremost, Indians wanted to maintain the flow of trade goods, and practically all those items, including munitions, cloth, clothing, metal tools, cooking utensils, and liquor, came from Britain. Neutrality—or, after 1776, an alliance with the United States, which had little manufacturing—would produce nothing. Indians also aimed to secure their lands, and though Britain had shown little support for this goal, at least it paid lip service to Indian title. American colonists, by comparison, wanted to return to the chaotic expansion that preceded the Proclamation Line. Thus, the vast majority of independent tribes sided with the British. These groups included most of the Haudenosaunees, Delawares, Shawnees, and Cherokees and Ohio Country nations such as the Miamis, Wyandots, and Ottawas. Practically the only Indians who sided with the United States had no choice because they lived surrounded by or in close proximity to Whites. They included the Catawbas, Oneidas, Mohegans, Pequots, Narragansetts, and Wampanoags.

Meanwhile, the unruly inhabitants of the British colonies were organizing a rebellion and nation around a White identity defined in great measure against Indians. In December 1773, the participants in Boston's "Tea Party" protest disguised themselves as Indians to signal that, like Native people, they had ancestral ties to America and a commitment to liberty. Yet once real Indians entered the picture, the White public's mood went from bold and boisterous to terrified. In August 1775, George III declared the colonies to be in "open rebellion . . . for the purpose of establishing an independent empire" and began hiring Hessian mercenaries for American operations, offering enslaved Virginians freedom in exchange for British military service, and negotiating with Indian nations to attack exposed White settlements.[7] The *Pennsylvania Evening Post* reported (truthfully or not) that the king's northern superintendent for Indian affairs, Guy Johnson, then invited the northern tribes to "FEAST ON A BOSTONIAN AND DRINK HIS BLOOD."[8]

Up to this point, Americans, especially in the mid-Atlantic colonies, had resisted calls for independence because their dispute was with Parliament alone, not George III or their inclusion in the British Empire. As long as they retained their allegiance to the throne, they remained loyal to Britain. The king's negotiations with soldiers of fortune, enslaved men, and "savages" to butcher his own people severed their fidelity once and for all. When the Second Continental Congress declared independence in July 1776, it listed twenty-seven measures by which the king had caused this grave decision. The final one read, "He has excited domestic insurrections [slave revolts] amongst us and has endeavoured to bring on the inhabitants of our frontiers the merciless savages, whose known rule of warfare is an undistinguished destruction of all ages and conditions." Generations of diverse colonists, who shared a White identity defined against Blacks and Indians, considered no act more characteristic of a tyrant than this one—and no better vindication of their independence.

Once Washington took command of the Continental Army, he insisted that his troops engage only enemy soldiers in arms and leave White Loyalist noncombatants out of it, but he showed no such restraint toward Indians. During the Revolutionary War, Indian hit-and-run attacks on farmsteads, supply trains, and isolated posts paralyzed the trans-Appalachian region and added to Washington's chronic difficulty of recruiting for the Continental Army, for men were unwilling to leave their families unprotected when an Indian strike could come at any time. At the same time, word-of-mouth reports and the press magnified the terror by fixating on Indian atrocities against civilians. In the 1760s and early 1770s, Whites in Pennsylvania and Virginia had already effectively declared open season on all Indians, including Christians allied with the colonies—men, women, and children. This was the era that saw the rise of the saying "The only good Indian is a dead one." During the Revolutionary War, this bloody principle became even more widespread among the people Washington was pledged to defend. The general himself sometimes shared the sentiment.

Washington brought total war to Indians, making Indian Country as active a theater in the Revolutionary War as any in the East. The most notable example is US major general John Sullivan's 1779 raid against the Haudenosaunee. With a force of nearly 4,500 men, Sullivan invaded and destroyed an estimated forty villages and 160,000 bushels of corn and killed an unspecified number of people, with the express purpose of starving the population into submission. Washington's orders were "to extirpate them from the Country."[9] For the most part it worked, but at the cost of inspiring Haudenosaunee warriors to return the favor in the pattern of tit-for-tat terror. The Haudenosaunees never forgot Sullivan's march or who was ultimately responsible. As the Seneca chief Cornplanter told George Washington in 1790, "When your army entered the Country of the Six Nations, we called you the Town-destroyer [or Conotocarious] and to this day, when that name is heard, our women look behind them and turn pale, and our children cling close to the neck of their mothers."[10]

The Haudenosaunees were not alone. Attacks by White Americans during the Revolutionary era cost the Cherokees half their population, the destruction of most of their towns, and the torching of untold amounts of food and personal property. The Shawnees and Delawares suffered likewise, some of them at the hands of Virginia's George Rodgers Clark, who declared that "to excel [Indians] in barbarity was and is the only way to make war upon . . . and gain a name among them."[11] He added that "for his part he would never spare Man woman or child of them on whom he could lay his hands."[12] His orders from Virginia governor Thomas Jefferson was to effect the Indians' "extermination, or their removal beyond the lakes or Illinois river."[13] In exchange, Clark's soldiers would receive three hundred acres each from the land they conquered.

Under such circumstances, the end of the Revolutionary War should have come as a relief to the Indians, but it was a peace that brought no peace. The 1783 treaty between the United States and Britain made no mention of Britain's Indian allies and ceded to the United States all the land between the Appalachians and the Mississippi. Americans took this to mean that by defeating Great Britain they had also conquered its allies, an idea that, according to one observer, "made the Indians stare."[14] They were not struck dumb for long. The Haudenosaunees declared themselves "a free people subject to no Power on earth" and charged that the Peace of Paris was "an act of Cruelty and injustice that Christians only were capable of doing."[15] Clearly, like many enslaved African Americans and women denied the right to own property, own themselves, and vote, it did not take the Native Americans long to use revolutionary slogans to point out American hypocrisy when it came to respecting others' natural rights to liberty.

Indians refused to bend to the American demand that they vacate their homelands, even though the United States had grown to three million people; fewer than two hundred thousand Indians lived east of the Mississippi. With the Confederation Congress continuing to insist that Indians had been conquered, with states like New York, North Carolina, and Georgia constantly pressing them to cede more land, and with White squatters swarming into the Ohio Country, the Smokies, and the Georgia upcountry, Indians throughout the East decided to raid frontier settlements once again.

If Indians were faced with limited options, so was the US government. It not only wanted Indian land for obvious reasons; it needed it. During the Revolutionary War, the Continental Congress had recruited soldiers for the Continental Army by promising them land bounties that would be paid out of conquered or ceded Indian land. Now the war was over, and those land bounties were due. Furthermore, the country had borrowed massive amounts of foreign money to keep the war effort afloat—and after the war, it continued to borrow massive amounts of foreign money to keep the government afloat. These loans, on the part of creditor and borrower alike, were based partly on the assumption that the country would eventually possess and sell millions of acres of Indian land. This principle was crystallized in the Northwest Ordinance, enacted in 1787 under the Confederation Congress. The ordinance envisioned three to five new states between the Ohio and Mississippi Rivers without regard to the tens of thousands of Indians who lived there. The country also needed to sell Indian land to pay its operating expenses. Stifled by the requirement for state unanimity for taxes under the Articles of Confederation, the country collected precious little in revenue from its citizens, relying almost exclusively on port duties instead of property taxes. In so many ways, then, the nation was premised on forcing Indians from their homes.

Government officials in both the Confederation era and during Washington's presidency realized that they were partially responsible for this mess. Foremost among them was Henry Knox of Massachusetts, who, after the adoption of the Constitution, became Washington's secretary of war and his point man on Indian affairs. Knox's vision, which Washington eventually adopted, was to try to acquire Indian territory without excessive cost or warfare and without sacrificing the reputation of the young country. The key, he believed, was for the nation to return to the colonies' practice of *negotiating* with Indians for their land. After 1789, he also wanted the new federal government to assert its exclusive jurisdiction over Indian land cessions. The purpose was still to acquire Indian territory, but peacefully and cheaply.

Knox also advocated government action to promote Indian Christianity and civility. He thought that if the Indians adopted intensive agriculture and gave up hunting, they could make do with less land and cede the excess to Whites. Furthermore, if they coupled this change with the adoption of Christianity, theoretically, they could assimilate into White society. Knox and Washington commiserated that the only alternative was for the country to accept the responsibility—and the condemnation—for what they foresaw as the Indians' inevitable extinction, whether through extermination at White hands or through the effects of disease and alcohol abuse. That would mean, Knox predicted, "future historians" painting a picture of the early republic with "sable colors" on the basis that "our modes of population have been more destructive to the Indian natives than the conduct of the conquerors of Mexico and Peru."[16]

Washington's support for the Constitution in 1787–1789, and that of many other Federalists in the 1790s, had partially to do with the desire for a strong federal government that could negotiate with Indian nations and gain their peaceful concession to land sales or else punish them militarily when they refused. Washington also looked forward to the federal government's superseding the hopelessly parochial and bickering states when it came to conducting Indian diplomacy. With his support, the new federal Congress passed the Trade and Intercourse Acts of 1790, 1793, and 1796, which forbade trespass on Indian territory, provided for the punishment of crimes committed in Indian Country, and required licenses to trade with Indians. The 1793 act also provided for the distribution of "civilized" goods to Indian leaders, including livestock, plows, and spinning wheels, and made provision for White teachers to show the Indians how to use these things.

Meanwhile, Washington's administration forcefully asserted its jurisdiction over Indian diplomacy not only in the territories but even in New York, North Carolina, and Georgia. Collectively, these initiatives were part of President Washington's goal to make the federal government strong, competent, and respected in all its duties, including securing the land on which his and the nation's fortunes depended. There was a desperate need for such a plan, because Indians throughout the eastern interior were fighting to push Whites back within their treaty bounds.

Government policy, both under the Articles of Confederation and during Washington's presidency, risked rural rebellion and even secession by focusing on securing the Ohio Country and leaving the southern states to war against the Cherokees and Creeks on their own. The people of Mero County, Tennessee, spoke for frustrated settlers throughout the South when they declared in 1789 that "to treat with the Creek Nation will never avail us anything [until] an army is Sent into the heart of their Country Sufficient to extirpate their whole Savage race."[17] Between 1784 and 1788, Whites in the Watauga region of eastern Tennessee plotted to secede from North Carolina and form a new state called Franklin, partly because they wanted complete freedom to attack Indians and seize their land. When their effort failed, Franklin's leadership considered aligning with Spain, only for Cherokee attacks to drive them back into the

American fold. Just a few years later, a band of Georgians, in defiance of the 1790 Treaty of New York, invaded Creek territory west of the Oconee River and declared themselves an independent "Trans-Oconee Republic" before state and federal troops dispersed them. Everyone knew that if Indian attacks continued, however provoked, and the federal government failed to answer, it was only a matter of time before the next secessionist movement.

As leader of a country whose financial well-being and political stability rested on the appropriation of Indian land, by negotiation or force, President Washington made defeating the Ohio Indian confederacy his administration's primary order of business. In 1790, the United States sent an army under Josiah Harmar against the allied tribes, but Indian forces led by Blue Jacket (Shawnee) and Little Turtle (Miami) turned them back, killing or capturing 108 soldiers and 500 horses. The following year, the unlucky general was Arthur St. Clair. Of his 1,400 troops, the Indians killed 630 and the rest were captured, missing, or wounded. Only 20 or so Indians lost their lives. During the early 1790s, Indian warfare was consuming five-sixths of the federal government's operating budget, which, ironically, the government needed the sale of conquered Indian land to meet.

Yet Indian resistance was short-lived. In the Southeast, the Cherokees surrendered in 1794 after losing another 2,000 people (a sixth of their already reduced population), three-quarters of their remaining land, and more than half of their towns, following repeated attacks by White forces from the surrounding states. The war-weary Creeks followed two years later, after Spanish Florida stopped supplying them with munitions, rather than hazard war with the United States. It spoke volumes about how the Creeks' options had narrowed that when their leaders sat down to the negotiating table, they asked the federal government to station White troops along their border with Georgia to protect them from other White people. They knew they would need it. Federal officer Benjamin Hawkins was told by one of the Creeks' White neighbors, a woman named Ann Van Zandt, that "the doctrine in her neighborhood was, let us kill the Indians, bring on a war, and we shall get land."[18]

The 1790s also saw the end of Indian resistance in the Ohio Country. In 1794, General Anthony Wayne ("the Indian killer") led 3,000 US soldiers up the Maumee River against between 400 and 1,400 Indian warriors in what has become known as the Battle of Fallen Timbers. Wayne's troops rolled over the Indian forces and devastated the countryside, and by spring the Indians were starving. Seeing the writing on the wall, at the 1795 Treaty of Greenville, the Ohio Valley Indians had to concede defeat and cede to the United States southern and eastern Ohio. Washington and his country finally secured their coveted western lands, and the next round of the country's land speculation was on, continuing for many generations to come.

George Washington was at once a creator and a manifestation of this world. Throughout his life, he and his society so lusted after Indian land that they were willing to go practically to any length to obtain it. They developed elaborate racial ideologies to convince themselves that they were right in doing so. Washington did not want to have to slaughter Indians to secure this land. He and many other members of the ruling class hoped Native people would hand over their birthright voluntarily, ideally after adopting the White way of life. Yet when the Indians proved unwilling, he and the rest of his society repeatedly resorted to violence on a genocidal scale to force them to yield. When the government proved too deliberate in this process, many White settlers on the front lines of this invasion of Indian Country took matters into their own hands, even to the point of committing insurrection. Washington, and many presidents after him, had little choice but to bend to this electorate. He and his successors ultimately did so because they shared the frontiersmen's goals and their devaluation of Native people. It was basic to who they and the country were. An unflinching view of it should be basic to the history we teach.

Notes

Citations of Founders Online documents do not include individual links, as each source can be found by searching the site at https://founders.archives.gov/.

1. A note on terminology: I use the terms "Indian," "Native," and "Indigenous" interchangeably throughout this essay when referring to Native Americans in the aggregate, though I employ "Indian" the most, for two main reasons. The first is that most of the Native American people in the United States whom I know personally or have encountered through professional events and media continue to favor this expression. Over the course of centuries, their people have appropriated the "Indian" misnomer and made it a source of pride. Not all Indigenous people in the United States follow this practice, but my sense is that "Indian" remains the label of choice in most Native circles, as illustrated by its continued use in Native-run institutions like the National Congress of American Indians and *Indian Country Today*. My second reason is that "Indian" remains an official designation in United States law and government, as illustrated by the agency name of the Bureau of Indian Affairs and the area

known as Indian Country. When referring to particular Native peoples, I use tribal names.

2. For the history of Thanksgiving, see David J. Silverman, *This Land Is Their Land: The Wampanoag Indians, Plymouth Colony, and the Troubled History of Thanksgiving* (New York: Bloomsbury, 2019). Important books that counter these misleading myths include Colin G. Calloway, *The Indian World of George Washington: The First President, the First Americans, and the Birth of the Nation* (New York: Oxford University Press, 2018); Calloway, *The American Revolution in Indian Country: Crisis and Diversity in Native American Communities* (New York: Cambridge University Press, 1995); Gregory Evans Dowd, *A Spirited Resistance: The North American Indian Struggle for Unity, 1745–1815* (Baltimore: Johns Hopkins University Press, 1992); Patrick Griffin, *American Leviathan: Empire, Nation, and the Revolutionary Frontier* (New York: Hill and Wang, 2007); Woody Holton, *Forced Founders: Indians, Debtors, Slaves, and the Making of the American Revolution in Virgina* (Chapel Hill: University of North Carolina Press, 1999); Jeffrey Ostler, *Surviving Genocide: Native Nations and the United States from the American Revolution to Bleeding Kansas* (New Haven, CT: Yale University Press, 2019); Robert G. Parkinson, *Heart of American Darkness: Bewilderment and Horror on the Early Frontier* (New York: W. W. Norton, 2024); Alan Taylor, *American Revolutions: A Continental History, 1750–1804* (New York: W. W. Norton, 2016).
3. On the notion of a Sixty Years' War, see David Curtis Skaggs and Larry L. Nelson, eds., *The Sixty Years' War for the Great Lakes, 1754–1814* (East Lansing: Michigan State University Press, 2001); François Furstenberg, "The Significance of the Trans-Appalachian Frontier in Atlantic History," *American Historical Review* 113, no. 3 (2008): 647–77.
4. George Washington to Christopher Gist, October 10, 1755 ("inhuman foes"); George Washington to John Robinson, October 8, 1755 ("barbarous"); George Washington to the Massachusetts General Court, July 11, 1776 ("savages"); George Washington to James Duane, September 7, 1783 ("beasts"), all on Founders Online.
5. George Washington to William Crawford, September 17, 1767, Founders Online.
6. Bernard Bailyn, *Voyagers to the West: A Passage in the Peopling of America on the Eve of the Revolution* (New York: Vintage, 1988), 30.
7. "By the King, a Proclamation, for Suppressing Rebellion and Sedition," Massachusetts Historical Society, https://www.masshist.org/database/818.
8. Robert G. Parkinson, *The Common Cause: Creating Race and Nation in the American Revolution* (Chapel Hill: University of North Carolina Press, 2016), 181.
9. Calloway, *Indian World*, 248–50 (quotation on 250).

10. Seneca Chiefs to George Washington, December 1, 1790, Founders Online.
11. James Alton James, ed., *George Rogers Clark Papers, 1771–1781* (Springfield: Illinois State Historical Library, 1912), 298.
12. Richard White, *The Middle Ground: Indians, Empires, and Republics in the Great Lakes Region, 1650–1815* (New York: Cambridge University Press, 1991), 368.
13. Ostler, *Surviving Genocide,* 64.
14. Anthony F. C. Wallace, *The Death and Rebirth of the Seneca* (New York: Random House, 1969), 198.
15. Gary B. Nash, *The Unknown American Revolution: The Unruly Birth of Democracy and the Struggle to Create America* (New York: Penguin, 2005), 382.
16. Henry Knox, Report on Indian Affairs, December 29, 1794, Founders Online.
17. Citizens of Mero (Miro) District, North Carolina, to President and Congress, November 30, 1789, Founders Online.
18. *American State Papers: Indian Affairs* (Washington, DC: Gales and Seaton, 1832–61), 1:538.

PART III

ENSLAVED AMERICANS AND SLAVERY IN THE REVOLUTIONARY ERA

"YOU DON'T HAVE TO BE IN THE LIMELIGHT TO BE IMPORTANT"

Teaching Slavery at Mount Vernon Through the *Lives Bound Together* Exhibition

JESSIE MACLEOD

In October 2016, Mount Vernon opened its first large-scale exhibition on the topic of slavery. *Lives Bound Together: Slavery at George Washington's Mount Vernon* encompassed seven galleries—4,400 square feet—in the Donald W. Reynolds Museum and Education Center. Before closing in July 2021, the exhibition welcomed almost a million visitors, including nearly all attendees of the George Washington Teacher Institute.

Public conversations around George Washington and slavery retain an almost obsessive focus on what being an enslaver means for Washington's legacy. People are often uncomfortable sitting with the contradiction that Washington could have been indispensable to this nation's founding *and* someone who benefited from chattel slavery. Washington was well aware of the contradictions, eventually opposing slavery but keeping his concerns private and failing to extricate himself from the institution during his lifetime.

Almost by definition, Mount Vernon centers George Washington in nearly everything it does. But one way to teach about Washington and slavery is to shift focus away from the man and instead highlight the experiences of those who had no choice but to labor for his benefit, whose lives were affected by the decisions he made, and whose work contributed to his success. *Lives Bound Together* presented Washington's changing views on slavery, but its most powerful impact was bringing forward the stories of the hundreds of people caught in the crosshairs of the first president's ambivalence over enslavement.

In *Lives Bound Together,* curators used numerous interpretive strategies to highlight and humanize the enslaved people who lived and labored at Mount Vernon. This essay provides an overview of the exhibition and explores three of those strategies: reframing decorative arts collections as artifacts of slavery, using conjectural silhouettes to represent enslaved individuals, and collaborating with descendant communities to produce oral histories.

The opening of *Lives Bound Together* marked the culmination of decades of research into slavery at Mount Vernon. The most significant effort was undertaken by Mary V. Thompson, the estate's longtime research historian, beginning in the 1980s. Thanks to George Washington's meticulous recordkeeping, Mount Vernon is arguably the nation's best-documented eighteenth-century plantation. Yet Thompson was warned that there was very little information on enslaved people. Undeterred, she unearthed thousands of references—not only to their labor but also to their living conditions, personal lives, resistance, and resilience. While few primary sources survive from enslaved people themselves (a universal problem for scholars), George Washington and his family and hired employees left mountains of evidence on slavery, allowing Thompson to reconstruct the contours of an entire community.[1]

In addition to documentary research, archaeology at Mount Vernon began to reveal the material life of those enslaved on the plantation. In the mid-1980s, an excavation in the cellar of the "House for Families" quarter near the Washingtons' mansion revealed more than sixty thousand artifacts, including ceramic dishes, glass bottles, buttons and buckles, animal bones, and botanical remains. These fragments, which were linked directly to the enslaved residents of the quarter, provided a rich view of the private lives of those living in bondage.[2] Excavations at other sites across the estate, such as a midden (trash pit) south of the mansion and Washington's distillery, unearthed more artifacts that shed light on the experiences of the enslaved people laboring in the plantation's main house, kitchen, and workshops.

By the 1990s and 2000s, Mount Vernon staff began to incorporate this research into the site's public interpretation through updated signage and furnishings in outbuildings, a "Slave Life" walking tour (1994), and small displays in the new Museum and Education Center (2006). In 2010, the bunkrooms of the "Greenhouse Slave Quarter" near the mansion were refurnished for the first time in half a century. Still, slavery remained one of the most common questions raised by visitors, and staff recognized the benefit of an exhibition that would consolidate disparate strands of research in one place.[3]

In 2013, Mount Vernon's staff determined that the next special exhibition in the museum would focus on slavery and the enslaved community. The show was initially slated for a 1,100-square-foot gallery that held a series of rotating exhibits on special topics. But as planning commenced, it became clear that this small space could not do justice to such a complex subject. Instead, the decision was made to take over the entire fine and decorative arts museum, which had previously held a permanent installation of highlights from Mount Vernon's collection. While quadrupling the square footage presented many opportunities, this shift also came with challenges, as budgetary constraints and the temporary nature of the exhibit precluded making changes to the architecture or the floor plan beyond a few cosmetic updates. Curators found themselves fitting an exhibition on slavery onto the footprint of a traditional gallery space (crown molding, marble floors) designed for another purpose. Yet this seeming contradiction led to beneficial conversations, upending visitors' expectations about how the story of slavery fit into Mount Vernon's history.[4]

Working with exhibit designer Charles Mack (who designed the original museum space) and graphic designer Sally Wern Comport (Art at Large, Inc.), curators developed an exhibit framework centered on the idea that the lives of George Washington and those he enslaved were deeply interconnected ("bound together," in more ways than one). Historian James Oliver Horton has declared that "slavery was not a sideshow [in American history]. It was the main event."[5] So, too, was slavery central to the history of Mount Vernon. Stemming from that "big idea," curators identified three main messages they wanted visitors to take away:

1. enslaved labor was critical to the operation of the Mount Vernon plantation,
2. George Washington's views on slavery changed over time, and
3. the enslaved met the conditions of bondage with resistance, resilience, and creativity.

In addition to these content-oriented goals, curators developed affective and process-oriented outcomes, namely, humanizing the stories of the enslaved and showcasing "how we know what we know" by making visible the archival record, in both its richness and its silences.

The finished exhibition featured seven galleries, though interpretation began outside the space itself. As they entered the museum lobby, visitors saw a large glass wall holding the doors to the museum. Through the glass, visitors could see a rotunda with a bust of George Washington, a feature of the previous installation that was retained. Overlaid on the doors were the names of individuals enslaved at Mount Vernon, so that visitors had to look through the names to see Washington's image, emphasizing the theme of interconnectedness (see fig. 1).

The first gallery, the rotunda, included introductory panels outlining the exhibit's major themes and background on slavery at Mount Vernon and in eighteenth-century America. One panel offered a primer on why the exhibition favored the term "enslaved people" rather than "slaves." This important language choice emphasized enslaved peoples' humanity rather than a condition imposed by others. This gallery also featured an infographic with differently colored icons representing the population breakdown of Mount Vernon in 1799: 5 Washington family members, 17 hired White servants and their family members, and 317 enslaved people (see fig. 2). A small theater off the rotunda

FIGURE 1. Entrance to the exhibition, featuring the names of enslaved people. (Photograph by Gavin Ashworth, courtesy of The Mount Vernon Ladies' Association)

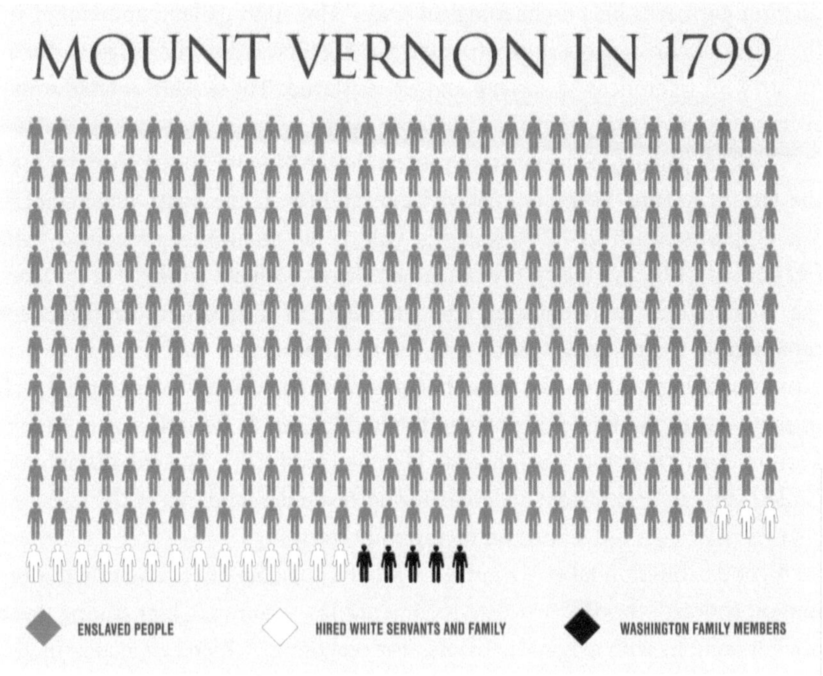

FIGURE 2. Infographic showing the population of Mount Vernon in 1799. (Courtesy of The Mount Vernon Ladies' Association)

played a short video introducing visitors to the topic and some of the enslaved individuals they would encounter in the exhibit.

The second gallery, "Slavery in Washington's World," displayed decorative arts while highlighting the Washingtons' connections to the transatlantic slave trade and the centrality of slavery to their domestic world at Mount Vernon. From here, visitors entered a small gallery, "Soldier, Statesman, Slaveholder," which presented George Washington's evolving views on slavery, culminating in his decision to free those he enslaved directly—123 of 317 people—in his will. (Washington directed that they be freed at his wife's death; she ultimately freed them earlier, on January 1, 1801.)

The fourth gallery, "Daily Life on Mount Vernon's Five Farms," was the largest, showcasing many archaeological artifacts and exploring enslaved people's families, living conditions, health, and resistance. An adjacent alcove, the fifth gallery, presented enslaved people's clothing and personal style through reproduction garments and archaeological finds. The sixth gallery, sponsored by the Gilder Lehrman Institute of American History, displayed original documents with references to slavery and the enslaved. These were rotated every six months, owing to paper's sensitivity to light.

The final gallery, "Slavery and Freedom in the Nineteenth Century," traced the fate of Mount Vernon's enslaved community in the years after George Washington's death in 1799. Roughly half of the community received their freedom in 1801, and the rest remained enslaved, with most inherited by Martha Washington's grandchildren after her death in 1802. Many families were separated in the process. Continuing the motif of names, this last gallery featured a snaking, ribbon-like panel hanging from the ceiling—a memorial wall of sorts—with the name of every individual known to be enslaved at Mount Vernon during George Washington's lifetime (see fig. 3). The exhibition concluded with an oral history video featuring seven descendants of the enslaved sharing their own reflections on their family stories.

A good exhibition takes advantage of what a museum offers that other information sources—books, articles, documentaries—cannot. Chief among these are interactions with original artifacts, "the real thing," which can inspire in visitors a sense of wonder and personal connection to the past. Cultural anthropologists Catherine M. Cameron and John B. Gatewood designated this sacred

FIGURE 3. A view of the final gallery with the memorial "ribbon" above. (Photograph by Gavin Ashworth, courtesy of The Mount Vernon Ladies' Association)

quality of original objects as "numen," from the Latin for "divine presence." They identified "numen-seeking" as a top reason that tourists visit historic sites.[6] In developing an exhibition, curators place these objects in conversation with one another and with accompanying text, imagery, and multimedia (videos, interactives, soundscapes) to convey a narrative in physical space. Museum visitors thus undergo a particular kinetic and sensory experience—and often a social one as well, as most people visit museums with others. An exhibit should never be a "book on the wall" but instead should capitalize on the nonlinear, multidimensional, and interactive possibilities that the medium offers. Below are three examples of the strategies that the curators and designers of *Lives Bound Together* used to take advantage of the exhibit's unique capabilities in teaching about slavery at Mount Vernon, especially foregrounding the stories of enslaved people themselves.

Reframing decorative arts as artifacts of slavery. *Lives Bound Together* featured hundreds of original artifacts, including many archaeological fragments that could be linked directly to the enslaved community, a powerful connection. But one of the unexpected ways in which the exhibit interpreted Mount Vernon's collections was in presenting decorative arts objects as artifacts of slavery as well. A porcelain sugar bowl, a mahogany dressing table, a silver coffee urn—all of these "elegant" objects can be linked directly to the transatlantic slave trade as well as to the enslaved people whose labor made the Washingtons' lifestyle possible.

The first case that most visitors encountered in the exhibition, titled "Sugar and Slavery," explored how this staple of the Washingtons' table was in fact harvested by enslaved Africans on Caribbean plantations, where brutal conditions meant frequent injuries and high mortality rates. On the label, visitors encountered a quote from a seventeenth-century pamphlet vividly describing the dangers enslaved laborers faced in the mills where sugarcane was processed: "If a Mill-feeder be catch'd by the finger, his whole body is drawn in, and is squees'd to pieces, If a Boyler gets any part into the scalding Sugar, it sticks like Glew, or Birdlime, and 'tis hard to save either Limb or Life." In the case above these words, visitors viewed original Washington objects associated with sugar and sweetened beverages—a punch bowl, tea service, coffee and chocolate pots, tongs, and other accessories (see fig. 4). Traditionally celebrated for their elegant forms, beautiful designs, and expensive materials, these objects were instead being linked to the violence inherent in the products they held.

FIGURE 4. A view of the "Slavery and the Washingtons' World" gallery, with the "Sugar and Slavery" case at center. (Photograph by Gavin Ashworth, courtesy of The Mount Vernon Ladies' Association)

Of course, the violence of slavery could be found right at Mount Vernon. As visitors progressed through the gallery, they encountered vignettes that presented the Washingtons' tableware and furnishings through the lens of the enslaved household staff who interacted with the objects. Indeed, if you consider who was washing, polishing, dusting, moving, and otherwise managing these things, enslaved people probably interacted with them as much as—if not more than—the Washingtons themselves. The Sèvres porcelain service on the Washingtons' dining table tells the story of their entertainments, but it can also illuminate the lives of cooks Hercules Posey and Doll, who skillfully prepared the sumptuous food, and waiters Christopher Sheels and Marcus, who brought the dishes laden with delicacies from the detached kitchen to the dining room.

This reinterpretation offers a material version of the "reading between the lines" that scholars of slavery must undertake in the archival record. Even when enslaved people are not explicitly mentioned in documents, carefully analyzing the silences can provide a window into their experiences and perspectives. To help visitors understand this process, one section of the exhibition paired a vignette of objects with a close reading of a primary source—Benjamin

Latrobe's July 1796 diary account of his visit to Mount Vernon—to illuminate the hidden role of enslaved people in making the Washingtons' hospitality possible.[7] The label unpacked lines in Latrobe's text to reveal which individuals likely performed the labor his statements passively imply. For example:

> Having alighted, I sent in my letter of introduction and walked into the portico next to the river.

Though not an invited guest, Latrobe brought a letter of introduction from George Washington's nephew Bushrod. He probably handed it to the butler, Frank Lee.

> . . . the horses came to the door.

Cyrus or Wilson, Mount Vernon's grooms, likely cared for Latrobe's horses, boarding them in the stable overnight and bringing them back to the house for his departure.

Behind the label, visitors viewed a vignette showing a small tea table laden with silver and porcelain accoutrements for coffee, which Latrobe enjoyed on Mount Vernon's piazza during his visit. After seeing a close reading of Latrobe's account, visitors were primed to "read" the objects on display for multiple meanings.

This strategy of reframing decorative arts reveals a limited part of enslaved people's experience: their labor for the Washingtons. But broadening the stories that objects "owned" by the Washingtons can tell democratizes Mount Vernon's collection. No longer could anyone claim that the institution lacked material with which to interpret slavery. The stories were just hidden in plain sight.

Giving enslaved people physical presence. The lack of images of enslaved people poses a particular challenge for exhibitions on eighteenth-century slavery.[8] In the period before photography, most depictions of people were portraits, a medium available primarily to the White and wealthy. The abundance of portraits of George Washington makes this contrast especially stark. Most Americans are quite familiar with the first president's face, literally carrying it in their pockets in the form of quarters and dollar bills. In an exhibit on those enslaved at Mount Vernon, it was paramount to provide enslaved people with a presence that could counter the ubiquity of Washington's image.

The exhibition team was faced, then, with the challenge of evoking the presence of enslaved people without any historical images of them.[9] After much

FIGURE 5. Conjectural silhouette of Kate, an enslaved midwife. (Designed by Sally Wern Comport, by permission of The Mount Vernon Ladies' Association)

discussion, the solution was to commission nineteen life-sized silhouettes from exhibit graphic designer Sally Wern Comport, who is also a talented illustrator (see fig. 5). The medium of silhouettes, a popular eighteenth-century art form, proved apt for several reasons. Silhouettes show only the figure's outline. While evocative, they leave many details unknown, just as many aspects of enslaved people's lives remain elusive. To avoid confusion for visitors about whether these were actual historical silhouettes, the forms did not appear in the traditional black-on-white. Rather, they were printed on frosted plexiglass in a pattern of lines and swirls reminiscent of a fingerprint.

Each silhouette represented a specific named individual who had been enslaved at Mount Vernon. Those depicted were selected based on the amount of documentation of their life and how well their story showcased the exhibit's themes, along with an eye toward showing diversity within the enslaved community. The featured individuals included a mix of men and women; house servants, craftspeople, and field hands; and those owned by George Washington directly (who were freed by his will) and by the Custis estate (who remained enslaved).

The details of the silhouettes were based on both documentation and conjecture. For a handful of individuals—such as William Lee and Ona Judge—details of their physical appearance survive through contemporary descriptions or runaway advertisements. For most, however, the designer imagined what the person might have looked like based on period-appropriate clothing styles, elements of personality that shine through in their story, and the emotions the exhibit team hoped to convey. Tom, whom Washington sold to the West Indies, appeared defiant. Caesar, a preacher, held his hands aloft as if mid-oration. Kitty, who was separated from her husband and seven of their nine daughters after Washington died, looked downcast.

The silhouettes were also placed in conversation with objects or visuals that related to their experience (see fig. 6). Doll, a cook, appeared beside a case of kitchen equipment; Priscilla and her young daughter Penny stood next to archaeological artifacts from the "House for Families"; Sambo Anderson, a carpenter, was featured by a case of tools. In the gallery focused on George Washington's changing views on slavery, silhouettes were in direct conversation with portraits of Washington. William Lee, the valet who served the

FIGURE 6. The silhouette of William Lee near a graphic including a portrait of George Washington. (Photograph by Gavin Ashworth, courtesy of The Mount Vernon Ladies' Association)

general throughout the Revolutionary War, peered through a spyglass at a mural reproduction of John Trumbull's 1780 military portrait of Washington. Hercules Posey, the chef for the presidential residence, stood proudly facing one of Gilbert Stuart's many versions of his famous "Athenaeum" portrait.

The silhouettes were also enhanced by touch screen interactives that allowed visitors to explore additional details about the person's life through moments when they appeared in the documentary record, whether in the "weekly reports" detailing labor on the plantation, Washington's correspondence and ledgers, or visitor accounts. The interactives also included family trees along with an explanation of how the silhouettes were developed. For those unable or uninterested in engaging with the digital interactive, a panel surrounding the touch screen featured a basic biography of the person that foregrounded their personal relationships. For example, Priscilla was identified this way:

> —Priscilla
> —Wife of Joe
> —Mother of Sophia, Savary, Penny, Israel, Isrias, and Christopher
> —Field Worker
> —Dogue Run Farm
> —Owned by George Washington[10]
>
> Shown here with her ten-year-old daughter Penny, Priscilla had six children. She lived with them in a small cabin on Dogue Run Farm. Her husband, Joe, lived and worked at Mansion House Farm, so she was separated from him six days a week. Priscilla tried to run away from Mount Vernon at least twice but was recaptured both times.

Ultimately, the silhouettes proved to be one of the most striking and effective aspects of the exhibition. Even if visitors read almost no labels (and, despite curators' best efforts, they often do not), the power of these human figures was unmistakable. Reading about the experiences of Kate, who served as midwife to her fellow enslaved women, is one thing. It is quite another thing to encounter a life-sized representation of her, holding a baby aloft, engaged in a universal and inescapably human moment of connection.

"Shared authority" through descendant engagement and oral histories. From the beginning of planning, it was evident to the exhibition team that outreach to the descendants of those enslaved at Mount Vernon—and incorporating their perspectives—would be a crucial part of the process. Such outreach forms part of the practice of "shared authority," popularized by historian Michael Frisch, in which professionals collaborate with community members and stakeholders rather than engaging in a top-down approach that privileges the institution's "expertise."[11] Such collaboration is especially important in contexts where the community has historically been excluded from the institution, as has often been the case with descendants of the enslaved.

In an exhibit on slavery, "shared authority" recognizes that the knowledge and perspectives of descendants are necessary partners to the academic research and framing performed by historians and curators. Mount Vernon had worked with descendants before; Mary V. Thompson had cultivated relationships with some individuals over the course of her research, and several were interviewed for a video in the "slavery" gallery of the 2006 Education Center. But community engagement had never been built into the exhibition planning process, and outreach to descendants was often *ad hoc* rather than part of a sustained project of relationship-building.

To bring Mount Vernon in line with the field's best practices, significant outreach was part of the development process for *Lives Bound Together*. Exhibition team members held one-on-one and group meetings with descendants and other stakeholder groups, such as Black Women United for Action, a local organization that conducts a memorial ceremony at Mount Vernon's African American cemetery every year. At key benchmarks, more formal focus groups were conducted, in which descendants and other audiences (such as staff and supporters of the Alexandria Black History Museum) reviewed label text and design elements, including the silhouettes. These sessions led curators to make several key changes that significantly improved the final exhibition.

For visitors, the most visible result of this outreach was a twenty-minute oral history video that featured excerpts from interviews with seven descendants.[12] This video played in the last area of the exhibition, which also had several benches available for visitors who wanted to spend time resting and reflecting before exiting back onto the estate. The lack of written sources documenting the perspectives of enslaved people makes oral history a critical tool in researching and interpreting slavery. Often, oral traditions were the only way that family stories were passed down.[13] The moments featured in the exhibition were highlights from longer interviews with descendants, usually over an hour, that were conducted by a trained oral historian hired by Mount Vernon. The full videos and transcripts are housed in Mount Vernon's archive for future researchers to access. The goal is to expand the number of interviews as more descendants are identified.

In the interviews, descendants reflected on their ancestors' fortitude and resistance, the grueling labor they were forced to perform, and the comfort family and community provided amid this hardship. A recurring theme was their ancestors' humanity. As ZSun-nee Matema, the great-great-great-great-granddaughter of Caroline Branham, expressed, "My Caroline was real. She was a real person. . . . She could suffer disappointments. She could have hurts. She could feel slighted. She could feel joy and happiness." Some interviewees also expressed ambivalent feelings about George Washington and how their ancestors contributed to his legacy. Shawn Costley pointed out, "We helped make the president who he was. . . . That was important. And you don't have to be in the limelight to be important." For many descendants, Mount Vernon continued to be an important place for their families. Judge Rohulamin Quander recalled that when he was a child, his family visited Mount Vernon "all the time," but he did not understand until he was older that they were "paying respects to the Quander ancestors." Still, descendants' relationships to the site remain complex. "On the one hand, it's exhilarating, because you're connected to the earliest parts of this country," remarked Steve Hammond. "On the other hand, it's frustrating to know how people were treated."

Hearing these reflections from descendants provided a powerful closing moment in the exhibition. Just as the silhouettes humanized the historical figures enslaved at Mount Vernon, the first-person narratives in the oral history video added a much-needed layer of emotion to the research presented earlier in the galleries. Furthermore, these interviews emphasized to visitors how the events and systems of the eighteenth century still have ramifications today.

When planning for *Lives Bound Together* began in early 2013, the exhibition team had little idea that the United States was on the brink of a national reckoning over racism and the history of enslavement. From the founding of the Black Lives Matter movement in 2013 to neo-Nazis marching on Charlottesville in 2017 to the murder of George Floyd in 2020, the legacy of slavery was suddenly at the forefront of Americans' consciousness and a source of deep polarization. The early 2020s saw efforts to restrict how race and slavery are taught in schools, with fearmongering over "critical race theory" and "wokeness" leading certain states to restrict what teachers can discuss with students. Such efforts intensified during Donald Trump's second administration, as the federal government undertook anti-DEI initiatives, cut funding to humanities organizations, and expanded scrutiny of the history presented at the Smithsonian and at National Park Service sites.

Within this polarized landscape, the role of exhibitions like *Lives Bound Together* becomes more important than ever. In surveys, Americans across the demographic and political spectrum have consistently ranked museums as very trustworthy sources of information, typically second only to friends and family.[14] This trust provides institutions like Mount Vernon with a critical opportunity to educate a large audience (over one million visitors a year) on topics like slavery. Significantly, Mount Vernon has never accepted any government funding, insulating the institution from both federal budget cuts and content censorship. This independence allows Mount Vernon to play a unique role in preserving and relaying an honest telling of American history.

While the original *Lives Bound Together* exhibition closed in 2021 (after being extended for three years beyond its planned two-year run), its legacy lives on in several ways. A virtual 360-degree tour allows visitors to explore the galleries and watch the introductory and oral history films.[15] Much of the exhibit's content has also been placed on Mount Vernon's website.[16] These resources offer classroom teachers ways to engage their students in the stories of enslaved people, and Mount Vernon's Education Department has developed lesson plans that aid educators in using biography and material culture to teach slavery. In June 2025, Mount Vernon installed a smaller version of *Lives Bound Together* in a historic quarter that housed enslaved people in the eighteenth century. Focused on uncovering the lives and voices of the enslaved through artifacts and ancestral histories, this version of the exhibit is permanent.

Beyond the exhibit itself, *Lives Bound Together* also influenced the overall visitor experience at Mount Vernon, as the research and themes of the exhibition have been incorporated into the site's general interpretation. Tour guides now mention enslaved people by name in every room of the mansion. A revamped "Enslaved People of Mount Vernon" walking tour tells the story of enslavement through the lens of biography, just as *Lives Bound Together* did. In 2022, a new exhibition opened in the museum space. *Mount Vernon: The Story of an American Icon* incorporates the contributions of enslaved people and uses several of the interpretive techniques mentioned in this essay. In addition, new staff positions focused on African American interpretation and outreach have codified the engagement efforts begun during *Lives Bound Together.* These initiatives are now improved, thanks to the 2021 establishment of the League of Descendants of the Enslaved at Mount Vernon, an independent 501(c)(3) that can bring forward descendants' ideas and concerns as well as collaborate with Mount Vernon on projects such as a slavery-focused audio tour. Descendants have also become important participants in sessions of the George Washington Teacher Institute each year.

George Washington's participation in slavery continues to be a divisive topic in public discourse. From those who condemn him entirely to others who rationalize his activity, the appetite for nuance, contradiction, and complexity remains low. But the positive response to the exhibition has shown that there can be entry points that encourage people to move beyond reflexive outrage or defensiveness and consider the human side of the topic. Learning about slavery at Mount Vernon through the lens of the enslaved community can remind everyone that Washington's story is not the only one that matters.

Notes

1. Thompson compiled her years of research in the comprehensive volume *"The Only Unavoidable Subject of Regret": George Washington, Slavery, and the Enslaved Community at Mount Vernon* (Charlottesville: University of Virginia Press, 2019).
2. Artifacts from the House for Families have been digitized on Mount Vernon's website: see "House for Families," George Washington's Mount Vernon, https://www.mountvernon.org/preservation/archaeology/archaeology-online?project=3.
3. A timeline of Mount Vernon's slavery interpretation from the founding of the Mount Vernon Ladies' Association to 2016, featured in *Lives Bound Together,* can be found online: see "Interpretation of Slavery at Mount Vernon," George Washington's Mount Vernon, https://www.mountvernon.org/george-washington/slavery/timeline-of-interpretation-of-slavery-at-mount-vernon.
4. *Lives Bound Together* drew inspiration from other groundbreaking exhibitions on slavery, especially *Slavery at Jefferson's Monticello: Paradox of Liberty* (2012), organized by the National Museum of African American History and Culture in partnership with Thomas Jefferson's Monticello.
5. Glenn Collins, "A 'Main Event' in Old New York," *New York Times,* September 27, 2005.

6. Catherine M. Cameron and John B. Gatewood, "Excursions into the Unremembered Past: What People Want from Visits to Historical Sites," *Public Historian* 22, no. 3 (2000): 107–27.
7. Latrobe's diary is owned by the Maryland Center for History and Culture, and excerpts have been published in Jean B. Lee, ed., *Experiencing Mount Vernon: Eyewitness Accounts, 1784–1865* (Charlottesville: University of Virginia Press, 2006), 56–67. The diary is an especially rich text because Latrobe also made several sketches during his time at Mount Vernon. One shows a group on the piazza with an enslaved man, likely Frank Lee, in the background. (The sketch is owned by the Maryland Center for History and Culture: see "Sketch of a groupe for a drawing of Mount Vernon," https://www.mdhistory.org/resources/sketch-of-a-groupe-for-a-drawing-of-mount-vernon/.) In Latrobe's finished drawing of the scene, the figure is missing, a symbolic moment of erasure. (This drawing is in Mount Vernon's collection: Benjamin Henry Latrobe, *View of Mount Vernon with the Washington Family on the Piazza*, 1796, George Washington's Mount Vernon, W-5307, https://emuseum.mountvernon.org/objects/17513.) In the exhibition, graphics of both images supplemented the interpretation described above.
8. Different exhibitions have taken varying approaches to solving this dilemma. Steven Lubar details some of them in his article "Representing the Pain of Others: Telling Stories of Violence, Suffering and Death in Museum Exhibits," *Human Remains and Violence* 8, no. 2 (2022): 40–57.
9. Some eighteenth-century paintings of George Washington feature an enslaved person in the background, including John Trumbull's 1780 portrait (Metropolitan Museum of Art) and Edward Savage's *The Washington Family* (National Gallery of Art), but linking definitively to specific individuals is difficult. Moreover, the depictions are either not sufficiently detailed (Savage) or clearly utilize racial stereotypes of the era (Trumbull), making them unsuitable as reliable references for physical appearance.
10. Norms and best practices around language when interpreting slavery have shifted considerably in the last decade and continue to evolve. Today, the phrase "owned by" would likely be replaced with "enslaved by."
11. Michael Frisch, *A Shared Authority: Essays on the Craft and Meaning of Oral and Public History* (Albany: State University of New York Press, 1990).
12. This video is available online: "Oral Histories with Descendants of the Enslaved Community," George Washington's Mount Vernon, https://www.mountvernon.org/video/view/J5pf3-zRykU.
13. Thomas Jefferson's Monticello initiated one of the first large-scale oral history projects with descendants of the enslaved with the Getting Word African

American Oral History Project, which has conducted more than one hundred interviews since its founding in 1993. See the Getting Word website at https://gettingword.monticello.org/.

14. American Alliance of Museums and Wilkening Consulting, "Museums and Trust, Spring 2021," https://www.aam-us.org/2021/09/30/museums-and-trust-2021/.
15. *Lives Bound Together: Slavery at George Washington's Mount Vernon* (virtual tour), Hull Film, https://hullfilm360.com/projects/livesbound/360tour.
16. "Lives Bound Together Online," George Washington's Mount Vernon, https://www.mountvernon.org/george-washington/slavery/lives-bound-together-online.

STRATEGIES FOR TEACHING ABOUT GEORGE WASHINGTON AS AN ENSLAVER

MORGAN SMITH

Teaching about George Washington and his role in forming the new nation is a common standard in the K–12 world. His leadership skills and his legacy make it easy for students to make connections and understand why he gained the nickname "Father of His Country." Christopher Jackson's portrayal of President Washington in *Hamilton* highlighted his humanity, bringing him to life in a way that students could grasp. What often does not get explored as much is the depth of Washington's role as an enslaver. There are tales of his using enslaved people's teeth for his dentures, and enslaved manservant Billy (William) Lee is acknowledged as Washington's ever-present valet. The fact of Washington's freeing the enslaved people he "owned" upon his death is shared far and wide, too. But accounts of this manumission frequently leave out key parts of the story. Not all of the enslaved people at Mount Vernon were set free. And those who were set free under the terms of his will were not immediately released from the chains of slavery after Washington died.

In my experience, once students learn that the Father of His Country was also an enslaver, there is surprise, confusion, sometimes even anger, and questions. How does a teacher responsibly support the inquiry and emotions that come with learning about revered individuals who enslaved other human beings, especially when one of them was George Washington? Creating a culture that involves thinking routines, historical skills, space to process new and challenging information, posing questions, and researching answers is a supportive approach.

I like to use Harvard University's Graduate School of Education Project

Zero Thinking Routines to help me create this supportive classroom environment. The Thinking Routines Toolbox provides teachers with a scaffolded opportunity to have students think critically and collaboratively and then communicate their responses orally or in writing. Educators Ron Ritchart, Mark Church, and Karin Morrison describe how "the steps of the routine act as natural scaffolds that can lead students' thinking to higher and more sophisticated levels."[1] When these routines are executed well, they also provide space for processing hard history like enslavement.

The beginning of a unit on George Washington and his participation in the institution of slavery could start with one of these thinking routines: step in—step out—step back.[2] While students process and participate in the routine, they could independently or in partnerships fill out a graphic organizer to help them move through the thinking routine. Teachers can ask students to step in and think about what they think George Washington knew, felt, or wondered about the institution of slavery. It is an important element to have students simply consider Washington's thoughts and use evidence from a text or schema to support their claims (as opposed to students' taking on the mindset or role of Washington). Next, students would be asked to step out and consider what they would want to or need to learn in this unit to understand his perspective better. Lastly, for the step-back portion of the routine, students would be asked what they noticed about their own perspective and what it takes to consider someone else's perspective. Once students have answered these three questions, independently or with partners, the teacher would seek volunteers to share their thoughts.

This routine not only warms students up to think about George Washington as an enslaver but also provides the teacher with a chance to see what students already know or want to learn about Washington and his role in enslavement. Sometimes students ask questions that not only surprise a teacher but can create the driving question to explore throughout a unit: Did Washington command the Continental Army the same way he ran Mount Vernon? What impact did enslavement have on George Washington as the first president of the United States? Structuring simple thinking routines around the hard truth of George Washington's being a willing participant in the institution of enslavement can take learning "a step further and push students to go below the surface of things and consider the complexity of issues and ideas."[3]

Once teachers introduce George Washington and enslavement with a thinking routine that supports inquiry, it is important to be intentional in providing multiple sources that students can explore independently, in partnerships, in small groups, or even with the whole class. Factors to consider include accessibility of the sources, language, reading skills, and different modalities in learning. For example, using a short video clip with captions like BrainPOP to provide background knowledge can support students whose first language is not English or who may have a reading disability. Diving into another thinking routine, like "see—think—wonder" around an image of George Washington in the foreground and William Lee in the background, can also help students.[4] While examining a painting like the one painted by John Trumbull in 1780 (see fig. 1), students can answer these questions: What do you see? What is it making you think about? What do you wonder or what questions do you have now?

Taking the "wonder" portion a step further, teachers can ask students to analyze what types of questions they come up with: Do the questions you ask have easy answers? Would the answers change people's perspective on George Washington? This type of thinking could be sparked by a simple visual or from a source like the "George Washington and Slavery: Key Events" timeline on Mount Vernon's website, which combines information in a visual way.[5] It

FIGURE 1. *George Washington and William Lee*, John Trumbull, 1780. (Metropolitan Museum of Art, New York)

provides a timeline that includes historic events, enslaved people, Washington in public, Washington in private, and the Mount Vernon Ladies' Association. The timeline provides not only specifics around enslavement and Washington's connections to it but also broad historical information, including the 1705 Virginia slave code.

It is also important to use primary sources that present Washington's own words in order to analyze his views on slavery. The focal point of discussions around Washington and enslavement is often that he freed the enslaved people at Mount Vernon on his deathbed. Not only is the story a bit more complicated than that, but it is also important to note how he lived as an enslaver as well as how his public views on the institution changed over time. Using letters available on the Founders Online archive, coupled with historical thinking skills like comparing and contrasting, determining cause and effect, or critical analysis of sources, provides ways to explore Washington's views on slavery through classroom instruction.[6]

For example, in 1766 Washington wrote to Joseph Thompson, a contact in the West Indies, to initiate the sale of a man he had enslaved, Tom, in return for items such as limes, molasses, and rum.[7] In 1772, Washington wrote to Daniel Jenifer Adams describing the physical specifications he required for the enslaved people he would accept in return from the sale of flour.[8] After having students read through both letters, have them compare and contrast the letters. What is similar about their content or requests, and what is different? Then move on to letters Washington wrote that document how he struggled with his role as an enslaver. In 1786 he wrote to John Francis Mercer: "I never mean (unless some particular circumstances should compel me to it) to possess another slave by purchase." He also explained he wished to "see some plan adopted by the legislature by which slavery in this Country may be abolished by slow, sure, & imperceptible degrees."[9]

After reading these primary sources together, teachers could have students make a claim about Washington's stance on slavery at the time of the most recent letter(s) and identify evidence from the letter(s) to support the claim, ending with students asking a question related to their claim. Finally, a lesson could incorporate a letter from April 1791, when Washington wrote to Tobias Lear, his personal secretary. In this letter Washington outlines a plan to send enslaved workers out of Philadelphia, where the US capital and president's residence were located at the time, to prevent them from gaining their freedom. Pennsylvania had passed emancipation laws and begun the process to abolish slavery in 1780. Washington told Lear that he wanted to move people he enslaved out of the state "under pretext that may deceive both them and the Public."[10] After reading Washington's directions, use the "what makes you say that?" thinking routine to ask students to explain what is going on in this letter. Then they can use evidence from the primary source to answer the question, What makes you say that?[11]

Analyzing the letters in chronological order can help lead students to appreciate the complexity and duality of George Washington, because one goal of a history teacher is to help students think critically about the past in a way that develops a more complete picture. Examining Washington not just as a commander of the Continental Army or the first president but also as an enslaver helps develop a more complete picture of his history and allows for other perspectives to be considered, too.

Another way to teach about George Washington through a lens of enslavement is with biographies and stories of the enslaved at Mount Vernon. In 1799, the year that George Washington passed away, more than three hundred enslaved people lived and worked at Mount Vernon. It would make sense to consider Washington as an enslaver through the eyes of someone whom he had enslaved. One well-known enslaved person at Mount Vernon is Ona Judge, who ended up successfully running away.

Ona Judge was Martha Washington's personal maid. In 1796, at the end of Washington's presidency and as the Washingtons were transitioning from Philadelphia back to Mount Vernon, Ona escaped further north; two days later, George posted a runaway advertisement for Ona. Engaging in the thinking routine "connect—extend—challenge" around the advertisement would be a great use of the primary resource.[12] Have students independently or in a partnership peruse the source as they answer these questions: How is the information connected to what you already knew? What new ideas did you get that broadened your thinking or extended it in different directions? What challenges or puzzles emerge for you as you read this ad? The teacher can either have students share their thoughts in a small group or bring the questions to the whole group.

Another teaching strategy to consider is to have students analyze the advertisement and answer the questions independently in writing. Next, using the Mount Vernon biography database, teachers can have students read the story of Ona Judge. There they will come across the great efforts George made to recover Judge from New Hampshire and bring her back to Martha in Virginia. In fact, when Judge was found the first time and was asked to return to the Washingtons, she replied that "she would rather suffer death than return to Slavery & liable to be sold or given to another person."[13] Letters document George's frustration with her refusing to return when she was located two different times.

While Judge was happy to risk her life to gain her freedom, enslaved men and women took their freedom however they could. Teachers can opt to provide students with words from other former enslaved workers at Mount Vernon, such as Sambo Anderson, who gained his freedom in 1801 by the terms of Washington's will. Anderson expressed that he "had a good kind master to look after all of [his] wants, but now [he'd] have no one to care for [him]."[14] Students can then revisit the connect—extend—challenge thinking routine to analyze Anderson's words.

I recommend ending the unit or short series of lessons on Washington and his role in the institution of slavery by revisiting the driving question—hopefully a question students asked on the first day. This is when students can use any notes, graphic organizers, conversations, and anchor charts created during the unit to answer that driving question. They can provide answers in an essay format, a video, a podcast, or whatever other creative way the teacher and/or students devise. This is important, because it asks students to think about both independent and collective learning and to synthesize. This concluding activity allows students to show what they know rather than simply locating a correct answer in a multiple-choice assessment.

The intentionality of such thinking routines applied to these kinds of sources allows students to participate in driving the instruction with their teacher. This supportive classroom culture makes everyone responsible for the cognitive load via thinking, talking, posing questions, and researching the answers to those questions. The hope is that students will discover George Washington's legacy as a great leader and the first president of the United States while they develop a more complete picture that includes his role in the institution of slavery.

Notes

Citations of Founders Online documents do not include individual links, as each source can be found by searching the site at https://founders.archives.gov/.

1. PZ's Thinking Routines Toolbox, Project Zero, https://pz.harvard.edu/thinking-routines; Ron Ritchhart, Mark Church, and Karin Morrison, *Making Thinking Visible: How to Promote Engagement, Understanding and Independence for All Learners* (San Francisco: Jossey-Bass, 2011), 47.

2. "Step In—Step Out—Step Back," Project Zero, 2022, https://pz.harvard.edu/resources/step-in-step-out-step-back.
3. Ritchhart, Church, and Morrison, *Making Thinking Visible*, 50.
4. BrainPOP, https://www.brainpop.com/discover/; "See—Think—Wonder," Project Zero, 2022, https://pz.harvard.edu/resources/see-think-wonder.
5. "George Washington and Slavery: Key Events," George Washington's Mount Vernon, https://www.mountvernon.org/george-washington/slavery/timeline-of-george-washington-and-slavery.
6. Founders Online contains over fifty thousand word-searchable letters to or from George Washington.
7. George Washington to Joseph Thompson, July 2, 1766, Founders Online.
8. George Washington to Daniel Jenifer Adams, July 20, 1772, Founders Online. Washington directed: "If the Return's are Slaves let there be two thirds of them Males, the other third Females—The former not exceeding (at any rate) 20 yrs of age—the latter 16—All of them to be strait Limb'd, & in every respect strong & likely, with good Teeth & good Countenances—to be sufficiently provided with Cloaths."
9. George Washington to John Francis Mercer, September 9, 1786, Founders Online.
10. George Washington to Tobias Lear, April 12, 1791, Founders Online.
11. "What Makes You Say That?," Project Zero, 2022, https://pz.harvard.edu/resources/what-makes-you-say-that.
12. "Connect—Extend—Challenge," Project Zero, 2015, https://pz.harvard.edu/resources/connect-extend-challenge. A transcription of the advertisement is presented in the essay in this collection by Laura J. Ping.
13. Joseph Whipple to Oliver Wolcott, October 4, 1796, quoted in Fritz Hirschfeld, *George Washington and Slavery: A Documentary Portrayal* (Columbia: University of Missouri Press, 1997), 114–15.
14. "Mount Vernon Reminiscences Continued," *Alexandria Gazette*, January 1, 1876, transcript, Mount Vernon Ladies' Association, in research notebook, "Early Descriptions After 1800."

THE MYTHS WE CARRY

Recovering Enslaved People's Experiences, Perspectives, and Legacies

KATHRYN M. SILVA

The glow of the sunrise over the Potomac River is a gorgeous sight from Mount Vernon's piazza. During the George Washington Teacher Institute (GWTI) each summer, teachers and facilitators board an early morning bus to catch a glimpse of the orange sky as bald eagles, affectionately nicknamed George and Martha, fly overhead. Most think of the Washingtons dining in this spot while catching a glimpse of the watershed view—a view later preserved by the Mount Vernon Ladies' Association, whose members have sought to keep this historical site as the Washingtons would have experienced it in 1799.

The land across from Mount Vernon, the majestic landscape surrounding the Potomac, is the ancestral home of the Piscataway and a reminder that George Washington's Mount Vernon did not belong just to the Washingtons; the land belonged to others first. I have had the privilege to sit on the chairs that adorn the piazza, and when I am in this space, I think of the Piscataway people who lived on these grounds before English colonizers (and, eventually, the Washington family) claimed it, as well as those who lived on this property during George Washington's lifetime, not by choice but by force, for their entirety of their lives. While some think of this space from the perspective of the presidential family, or maybe that of the Mount Vernon Ladies' Association, which restored the property to its eighteenth-century appearance, one educational purpose of the GWTI is to acknowledge Mount Vernon as a place of bondage and hard labor.

The labor of Mount Vernon's enslaved community created wealth for the mansion's White inhabitants. When thinking of their labor, the view off the piazza shifts; it reminds me of the lives of people walking to complete their daily tasks, leaving their homes and their children, to serve the Washingtons. Their long days could sometimes be rewarded with the companionship of their families in the evenings, but not always. These men and women lived and loved in ways we will never know, had thoughts that we will never read, and upheld values we can never capture fully in the little bit that we know of their lives from the extant records left by those who held them in bondage.

Mount Vernon provides a revealing opportunity to study the lives of enslaved people and teach about early American slavery. Teachers who participate in GWTI connect on a human level through the experiences of the more than three hundred enslaved men, women, and children on the estate. In my classes and as a lead scholar for the GWTI, I use a multipronged approach to teaching this history, beginning with conversations on truth, facts, and honest perspectives gleaned from primary documents to explore the violence and coercive nature of slavery. I recommend that teachers include local narratives, deriving from the wider Atlantic slave trade, as well as the Washingtons' views on slavery. Critical to connecting teachers to the eighteenth century is Mount Vernon's ongoing conversations with the descendants of the enslaved community. The descendants are integral sources, linking teachers to the ancestors who lived and labored at Mount Vernon. During the GWTI, the history of the enslaved community includes these conversations—bridges from the past to the present—before concluding with a modern history of Jim Crow and racism. It is an emotional week. It often shatters long-held beliefs as teachers confront personal and community sentiments. However, the week is also a transformative example of how we can continue to combat racist tropes and ideologies through education.

As historians debate George Washington's changing views on slavery, the best strategy for teaching the history of the enslaved at Mount Vernon is through their agency. Presenting this history challenges teachers who have varying degrees of familiarity with African American history in general and slavery in particular. Furthermore, for many teachers, local and state politics and the racism that persists today increasingly constrict their ability to teach an inclusive and diverse history. The anti-diversity, equity, and inclusion (anti-DEI) and anti-"woke" sentiments of recent years have increased tensions in K–12 classrooms. Our nation's changing political landscape often creates anxiety for teachers who participate in Mount Vernon's GWTI week focused on enslavement. The current controversies over interpretation and whose stories are told may shape what teachers can teach—but not what they can learn at the GWTI, which aims to present the most inclusive, current, and historically accurate discussion possible of the lives of the enslaved.

In the time I have led the "Lives Bound Together" sessions at the GWTI, our conversations regarding the history of enslavement have evolved from focusing exclusively on the historical figures directly impacted to a broader understanding of slavery across the Atlantic world. To foster an environment in which to discuss this history, the first "Lives Bound Together" session begins with thought exercises and approaches to foster openness and mutual respect and situate our weeklong conversations in a forum that allows for brave comments. Conversations led by Braden Paynter, director for methodology and practice of the International Coalition of Sites of Conscience, and Richard M. Josey, founder and principal consultant of Collective Journeys, allow teachers to discuss the idea of truth and reconciliation, to consider approaches to fostering inclusive history, and to discuss who can tell this history, and how.[1]

Setting rules of engagement provides a strong, open foundation for our week of study. Additionally, one of the most important things to me is grounding the history of enslavement in Africa itself—precolonial Africa. Discussion of the lives of Africans and African Americans begins on the African continent, with its various traditions, religions, and cultures. Africans, of course, are not a monolith. Time and place are essential to the interpretation of that history as well as the history of slavery and how it changed over time. I am careful to discuss the different experiences of men and women, particularly regarding their experiences in the Middle Passage and the vulnerability of women and children on slave ships.

The GWTI week benefits from the terrific work of scholars who have added to our knowledge on enslaved communities in the Americas. With greater access to this scholarship, our understanding of the African diaspora is wider. The approach to the week is through a narrative history of slavery in the Atlantic world. In four days, we discuss perspective, agency, and family, placing emphasis on individual stories to discuss a collective history. Just as I began my work with GWTI, scholars such as Erica Armstrong Dunbar and Mary V. Thompson published their work on Ona Judge and the enslaved community at Mount Vernon, respectively.[2] The brilliant work of Mount Vernon curator Jessie MacLeod (a contributor to this volume), the archaeology team, led by Jason Boroughs, and the numerous scholars who pulled together the stories of the enslaved community in the *Lives Bound Together* museum exhibition shaped teaching and learning on the estate. Academic historians' presentations of the history of the enslaved allow for a dialogue that too seldom exists between the ivory tower and K–12 educators. The critical issue is to ensure a truly inclusive history of slavery. The challenges we encounter stem from presenting history to teachers with varying degrees of familiarity with the history of slavery.

What stories do we tell—and how? Teaching the history of slavery, whether it is the history of Mount Vernon or the Atlantic world more broadly, centers on the labor of generations of enslaved people. The emotional, intellectual, and physical labor of our enslaved and freed ancestors built the world we live in today. Honoring our Indigenous and African ancestors from the moment we begin our week grounds the scholars, teachers, and facilitators in the work of uncovering stories, discovering new interpretations, and challenging long-held beliefs. This emotional and rewarding work starts with a land acknowledgment at the beginning of the week to honor the Piscataway. At the end of this profound week of academic labor, we honor the ancestors in a Homegoing Ceremony at the resting ground, the cemetery of the enslaved situated just a few hundred yards from George Washington's tomb. This is the place where many who spent much, if not all, of their lives as enslaved people tied to the first president of the United States, his wife, Martha, and their families found their eternal rest.

In terms of historiography, the work of Black feminist scholars is the foundation for the week and for the stories we discuss. As the authors of *The Black Women's History of the United States* explain, "To write a history about the United States from the perspective of Black women is to chart a course where the incredible, the fantastic, and the triumphant meet, mix, and mingle, often simultaneously, with hardship, and terror."[3] So much of the interpretation of slavery, especially of the late colonial, Revolutionary, and early republic eras, relies on reading primary sources that were produced by White men and women for the benefit of their power and posterity. Black feminist historians rely on these writings of oppressors and enslavers; I, too, rely on these sources when I teach, including teaching teachers, about enslaved women.

One way I interpret and teach the story of enslaved women (and men and children) is by reading "runaway advertisements" through the lens of freedom seekers.[4] The people who paid for the advertisements wanted to recover their "property," but the people they targeted knew that their legal status did not define their humanity. I ask teachers to interpret these freedom-seeking advertisements. The activity allows teachers and, once they return to their classrooms, their students to see the depth and complexity of Black Americans at a glance, in an interpretation of a moment of decision in their lives. In each of these advertisements, we can learn something about the human being obscured by the law as property, even though the advertisements are skewed toward the White enslaver's or bounty hunter's view. We can sometimes learn individuals' names, their families, and the reasons why they took the dangerous path toward freedom. Ona Judge and Hercules Posey, who both ran away from the Washingtons, are examples I use regularly. Their stories undermine some myths taught to us through years of purposeful misinformation and the lack of inclusive history—as, for example, the idea that people with fairer complexions, sometimes called "house slaves," fared better in slavery than field workers.

The advertisements placed in eighteenth-century newspapers by both male and female enslavers, including the Washingtons, point to a lie that we often tell ourselves: that slavery was better for some than others, especially as it was tied to the wealth, power, and prominence of the enslaver. Some teachers have attachments to the myth and memory of George Washington. Washington is worthy of our admiration in many ways; that he was also an enslaver can be difficult to reconcile with this appropriate veneration. A question often arises about whether Washington and/or his contemporaries were "good slave owners." Teachers ask for themselves and for their students. The stories we can recover from advertisements to recapture enslaved people can help us answer such questions, not from the perspective of George and Martha Washington but from that of people they enslaved.

Ona Judge, who was fair-skinned, and Hercules Posey, Washington's celebrated chef, both sought their freedom in Philadelphia during Washington's presidential years. Clearly, both decided that an unpredictable, perhaps dangerous flight was far preferable to life with the Washingtons. Judge's story is especially helpful in dispelling the idea of a "good master," because the surviving records include her voice and perspective—a rarity for the eighteenth century. After she escaped, and later, when she lived in New Hampshire, Judge explained that she would rather be poor and free than ever be returned to slavery in the Washington household.[5]

Writing and speaking through the lens of the enslaved community at Mount Vernon requires being attuned to the human story. The empathy needed is deep. It can be soul-crushing to read these stories and to tell them with integrity and without nostalgia. On the other hand, we can recover the experiences and perspectives and skills of enslaved individuals, which can be empowering. Such an opportunity arose in 2024, when a cache of bottles filled with cherries and other fruits was discovered during an archaeological dig from the ongoing renovation of the Mansion House. The discovery brought to the forefront an enslaved cook called Doll, who had likely filled or supervised the filling of the bottles centuries before. Doll's story allows us to reconsider a common and misogynist view that only men were skilled laborers (whether enslaved or free). While there is no doubt of the immense skill and craft of Hercules Posey, Doll also fed the Washington family and their thousands of visitors. While gender shaped her experience with enslavement, she, no less than Posey, was highly skilled. These are the kinds of stories that can be discovered if we are expansive in our use of sources and inclusive in our analysis.

Many teachers arrive at the GWTI assuming that they will primarily learn about George Washington's views on slavery. They and their students want to know: Where did he stand on the matter? Did he change his mind? Throughout his life, Washington was always an enslaver. His choices, rhetorical and in action, reflected his belief system. Washington traded enslaved people; he bought and sold human beings. Tom, who is often discussed during the week on slavery, is representative of Washington's knowing complicity in the violent institution of slavery. Washington sold Tom, who sought freedom one too many times for Washington's liking, to the Caribbean in exchange for limes and other small items. Because Caribbean slavery was so brutal, violent, and disease-plagued, selling Tom was an almost certain death sentence for him. And Washington knew this. Washington ordered overseers to punish the enslaved men and women on his estate. He rented enslaved people. He fully participated in the institution and determined, to a great extent, his enslaved laborers' destinies.

I always make a point of connecting Washington's writings with the advertisements we investigate to help teachers critically engage with what it meant to be an enslaver, helping them understand why it is inaccurate to label enslavers operating in an inherently evil institution as "good" or "bad."

We link, too, Washington's leadership of the Continental Army and the new nation to the power he exerted at the Mount Vernon estate. Many teachers point to Washington's exacting nature and selfless repudiation of power as part of the myths that surround him. But it is important to remember that this is how he behaved on the battlefield and in government. The difference is that the people whom he dealt with in those situations were free men. This is not the case with his vast plantations. The White men and women who labored under the Washington family were free and could leave at any time. His Black laborers could not. Washington also chose to marry Martha, a wealthy widow whose riches came from her late husband's ownership of enslaved people. The enslaved men, women, and children inherited by Martha and her children were referred to then, and sometimes now, as "dower slaves" and, because of the complexities of the Custis estate, they could not be freed by George or Martha. George knew this upon marrying Martha, and he also inherited and bought enslaved people to bring human property into the marriage. Thus, although Washington's views evolved over time and he eventually questioned his relationship to slavery, he did not end that relationship with the institution, either personally or politically. Mount Vernon, as it stands today, reflects the wealth he acquired from being an enslaver.

Mount Vernon was owned by the Washingtons, but it was a Black-majority space, and the estate provides visitors, students, and teachers the opportunity to learn about the working lives of the enslaved community in the places where they labored. Teaching slavery in a place-based learning setting helps teachers connect to the stories we can tell from advertisements, the writings of enslavers, and archaeology. Mount Vernon is also directly connected to the descendant community, and oral histories are another rich source for uncovering the experiences and perspectives of enslaved people. We regularly invite members of the League of Descendants, including members of the Branham and Quander families, to speak about their ancestors' stories, which helps teachers connect the often abstract idea of slavery to the families themselves. It is humbling to meet those descendants whose families labored and lived on the estate.[6]

Descendants describe the lives and experiences of people enslaved at Mount Vernon through generations of oral histories. They share how their ancestors walked under the bright full moon, the time when husbands could do what Washington referred to as "night walking." The enslaved men on Washington's vast eight-thousand-acre properties walked for miles at night to visit their wives and children. Worship, family, and friendship, not to mention romance, took place under the moon. A moonlit night also held the promise of emancipation: the moon gave enough light, and direction, for freedom seekers making their way out of slavery and into a new life as autonomous individuals able to make choices for themselves, even within the complicated legality of their enslaved status. For those who remained behind, choices took place in the mundane spaces of life.

One additional resource for recovering these stories at Mount Vernon is the group of wonderful professional character interpreters, who take on difficult roles in portraying enslaved people to an often hostile and racist public. For several years, the GWTI included the portrayal of Priscilla in the teachers' learning experience. From a historical character interpreter, we meet Priscilla, who lived on River Farm, and her husband, Joe, who lived on the Mansion House Farm. It was quite a walk from the mansion to Priscilla's cabin, but Joe would make that trek every week to see his wife and children. We know of Joe through Washington's complaints—memorialized in his correspondence to his overseers—regarding enslaved men walking at night because he felt their desire to see their families overrode his desire for their work productivity. Washington believed that "night walking" made Joe and men like him too tired to work. For Joe, and countless other men, their agency and their families mattered more to them than Washington's feelings and his demands of control over their bodies. And for this—for being human under such oppression—Joe and Priscilla and others faced punishment, including, but not limited to, being prevented from seeing their loved ones.

All these kinds of evidence and approaches advance the difficult, but essential, responsibility of teaching about slavery and the lives of enslaved people. Teaching those topics to our nation's educators is an honor and a privilege, and it is some of the most profound work I have undertaken in my career. Sharing enslaved people's stories always evokes strong emotions: stories about Priscilla, Joe, Ona, and Hercules; about George and Martha; about ourselves, in the twenty-first century; about our nation's history; about what many love about history in the first place, nostalgia. The powerful energy of Mount Vernon can also overwhelm those who stand on the hallowed ground where the ancestors labored and lived.

One of the most significant consequences of this work is dispelling gender and racial stereotypes associated with African Americans and the history of slavery. In place of myths and stereotypes, half-truths and nostalgia, we can begin to answer new questions: What was it like to be an enslaved woman in the home of her enslaver? When did an enslaved woman wake? Did she get rest? When did she see her children? The constant watchful eyes of the enslaver, the family, and those who supported slavery are a profound part of her story. Being a woman who could not escape the desires of her enslaver was dangerous for

Black women. Black women, and enslaved women in particular, had no legal rights in eighteenth-century America—and for Black women, none that were upheld by social norms or law. Enslaved women did not even have a right to combat abuse, whether physical, mental, or sexual. George Washington's Mount Vernon was a site of such abuse, perpetrated by the members of the family and their visitors.

By dispelling myths, we can broaden understanding. The surviving sources reveal that enslaved people worked toward self-emancipation, and their freedom-seeking took many forms. As historian Deborah Gray White has illustrated in her groundbreaking work on enslaved women, their resistance included not only flight but also slowdowns, feigning sickness (or resisting by vocalizing illness), and short-term freedom-seeking.[7]

Our expanded understanding, in turn, raises yet other questions, including about what is missing in the classrooms of our nation's schools because so many of us were taught old stories of slavery that were rooted in racist tropes. Many of our educators and the public they serve, particularly parents, may never have encountered histories that were truly inclusive in their educational journey. What strikes me the most, year after year, is the sincerity of teachers who constantly seek to "get it right." I admire them and hope to help them do so.

Resistance to studying slavery arises from the comfort of ignorance. Once you wake up and learn this brutal history, you cannot go back to sleep. Plantations no longer remain simply places of elegance and wealth; they become sites of bondage and inhumanity, too. Yet plantations cannot only be seen as places of violence to the descendants of the enslaved. They are also homes: places of joyful births, mourned deaths, and the mundane occurrences of everyday lives. The work of the GWTI is to prepare teachers with the sources, tools, and perspectives to lead those kinds of hard conversations about enslaved people and the country's founding era. And, always, we want to embrace the humanity of the enslaved and remember that George Washington's Mount Vernon is their Mount Vernon, too.

Notes

1. See Sites of Conscience, https://archive.sitesofconscience.org/en/leaders/braden-paynter/, and Collective Journeys, https://www.collectivejourneys.org/about.
2. Erica Armstrong Dunbar, *Never Caught: The Washingtons' Relentless Pursuit of*

Their Runaway Slave, Ona Judge (New York: Atria, 2017); Mary V. Thompson, *"The Only Unavoidable Subject of Regret": George Washington, Slavery, and the Enslaved Community at Mount Vernon* (Charlottesville: University of Virginia Press, 2019).

3. Daina Ramey Berry and Kali Nicole Gross, *A Black Women's History of the United States* (Boston: Beacon Press, 2020), 1.
4. Freedom on the Move is a large and growing database of advertisements teachers and students can access to investigate self-liberating peoples' experiences: see https://freedomonthemove.org/.
5. For a brief essay about her experiences, see Jessie MacLeod, "Ona Judge," in *The Digital Encyclopedia of George Washington*, George Washington's Mount Vernon, https://www.mountvernon.org/library/digitalhistory/digital-encyclopedia/article/ona-judge.
6. To learn more about the League of Descendants of the Enslaved at Mount Vernon, visit their website, https://www.leagueatmountvernon.org/. To learn more about how Mount Vernon interprets slavery and enslaved peoples' experiences, start here: "Interpretation of Slavery at Mount Vernon," George Washington's Mount Vernon, https://www.mountvernon.org/george-washington/slavery/timeline-of-interpretation-of-slavery-at-mount-vernon.
7. Deborah Gray White, *Ar'n't I a Woman? Female Slaves in the Plantation South* (New York: W. W. Norton, 1985).

PART IV

MARTHA WASHINGTON'S WORLD

THE FAMILY LIFE OF GEORGE AND MARTHA WASHINGTON

LYNN PRICE ROBBINS

A month after the siege of Yorktown in 1781, General Nathanael Greene wrote to General George Washington. Despite the Continental Army's success in the Virginia port town, the man in charge of the southern theater foresaw continued struggles ahead. Greene perceived that "we have still much to fear. Clouds of discontent hang over our heads, and a feild of difficulties lies before us." However, military concerns were not the only thing occupying Washington's mind. Greene also wrote, "I sinserely condole with Mrs Washington on the loss of her amiable Son—a loss which will be more sensibly felt from your continual absence."[1] John Parke Custis, Martha Washington's last biological child, died on November 5, 1781, three weeks shy of his twenty-seventh birthday. And while George Washington may have wished to be a comforting presence in his wife's time of grief, the nascent nation continued to struggle through the sixth year of war with Great Britain, and he was responsible for the military. In a circumstance that would repeat itself throughout his married life, his family and work life clashed.

The George Washington highlighted in history textbooks—a stalwart leader of the Continental Army and first president of the United States—certainly did exist. But he did not exist in a vacuum. From the age of twenty-seven until his death, George was also a husband, a father, a guardian, and a grandfather. By examining the lives of George and Martha Washington as well as those of their children and grandchildren, we discover new and relatable themes, including struggles with health and medicine, family tensions and tragedies, growing pains and awkward phases, and work/life balance. The man seen everywhere today, from our wallets to our national capital, experienced the same joys and traumas as all of humanity. George was a human being who accomplished great things, a possibility available to every student of history.

George Washington and Martha Dandridge Custis married on January 6, 1759. Washington had just resigned as colonel of the Virginia Regiment and commander of all Virginia forces and had no plans to make military service his career. The son of a second-tier Virginia planter from a second marriage, Washington leased Mount Vernon from his brother Lawrence's widow rather than owning it outright. As he stepped away from the military, Washington turned his attention to being a successful Virginia planter.[2]

Martha Custis, a widow, brought two children and considerable wealth to the union. She had married Daniel Parke Custis, a man twenty years her senior, in May 1750. Their seven-year marriage produced four children: Daniel Jr., Frances, John, and Martha. At the time of Daniel Sr.'s death, Martha had already lost Daniel Jr. and Frances. Her late husband's estate consisted of 17,779 acres of land, a furnished house in James City County, approximately 289 enslaved workers, liquid assets at £8,500 sterling, and £1,650 in the Bank of England. As one of the wealthiest widows in Virginia at the time, Martha did not need to choose a partner based on his money. She did, however, want a father figure for her surviving children, John "Jacky" Parke Custis and Martha "Patsy" Parke Custis.[3]

Upon the death of Daniel Parke Custis, Martha became the common-law guardian of the children—Jacky, age two, and Patsy, still a baby—but she wished to have assistance in managing the Custis estate. When John Robinson, speaker of the House of Burgesses, was approached, he refused to take on the responsibility. Nevertheless, Robinson readily agreed to act as guardian to manage lawsuits, offering their mother some respite, if not all that she had sought.[4] When George Washington married Martha Custis, he undertook the management of the large estate. However, he did not become the children's legal guardian until October 1761.[5]

In addition to managing an estate and the inheritance of his new wife's children, George took on the role of father when he married Martha. One aspect of this new role meant caring for the children's material needs. Washington purchased necessary items such as stockings, fabric, shoes, and schoolbooks for Patsy in 1760. Likewise, records show he bought Jacky a horse, children's books, and a Greek grammar book. He also purchased gifts for the children.

For example, in June 1761, Washington paid cash for a "Wax Baby" for Patsy. He acquired fiddle strings for Jacky, as well as a crystal for his watch, in 1767.[6]

In the upper echelons of Virginia society in the eighteenth century, money and material items loomed large in fatherhood. But perhaps the most challenging aspects of becoming a parent in any class level were emotional and psychological rather than financial. Patsy experienced serious health issues that would eventually take her life at the tender age of seventeen. Jacky was a rambunctious little boy who prized fun above all else—in many ways the opposite of his organized, detail-oriented stepfather. Martha understandably grew increasingly anxious for her children's safety with each passing year. And as George sought to care for his family as best he could, the North American colonies inched toward revolution.

Patsy Custis likely suffered from epilepsy. The first known written record of her having a seizure came via a letter Martha Washington wrote on September 29, 1760. Martha said that "my dear little girl is much better she has lost her fitts & fevours bout and seems to be getting well very fast." Medicine had been administered, including bitters, which were often used for stomach pain. It marked the beginning of an intense thirteen-year struggle to find relief for young Patsy.[7]

The Washingtons sought out and took the advice of many doctors. On March 12, 1768, Dr. William Rumney treated Patsy with valerian, a root used to treat nervous disorders. He also administered powders and some type of plaster. Later that month, Dr. Rumney created a medicinal brew for young Patsy that included twelve "Nervous Powders."[8] In July 1768, a Dr. Lee visited Mount Vernon for Patsy. The next year, in January 1769, Dr. Rumney consulted with Dr. Hugh Mercer about Patsy's treatment. This resulted in a new way of treating her "fitts," as the seizures were most often labeled, that included mercury and purging pills. Other doctors found in primary sources include Dr. William Pasteur, Dr. George Steptoe, and Dr. John Johnson.[9]

Medicine was not the only method employed to treat Patsy's illness. She underwent bloodletting in November 1768. On February 16, 1769, George recorded in his diary that "Joshua Evans who came here last Night put an Iron Ring upon Patcy (for Fits)."[10] In the latter half of the eighteenth century, physicians thought that rings called cramp rings could cure seizures. During the summer of 1769, George and Martha took Patsy to Warm Springs, Virginia, in the hopes that the mineral waters could offer a cure. George declared the test a failure and the method to be of little benefit.[11] While medicine in the eighteenth century differed greatly from today's medical knowledge, Martha and George acted like parents would today under similar circumstances. They stopped at nothing to heal Patsy, and yet they could not provide the relief that she urgently needed.

It is easy to imagine George's and Martha's distress as they helplessly watched their young daughter fall into fits again and again. To quantify the events, George kept marginal notes in his almanac during the summer of 1770. Between June 29 and August 31—sixty-four days—Patsy had twenty-seven seizures, which took a terrible toll on her body. As she became weaker, her parents grew more worried and desperate.[12]

Saturday, June 19, 1773, was a typically hot summer day in Virginia. The Washingtons spent the day at home and gathered for dinner in the afternoon. According to George, Patsy appeared in better health and spirits than she had for some time, and she arose from dinner at about 4 p.m. But then "she was siezd with one of her usual Fits, & expird in it, in less than two Minutes without uttering a Word, a groan, or scarce a Sigh." George continued: "this Sudden, and unexpected blow, I scarce need add has almost reduced my poor Wife to the lowest ebb of Misery; which is encreas'd by the absence of her Son (whom I have just fixed at the College in New York, from whence I returnd the 8th Instt)." Martha, devastated by the loss of her third child, could only wish for the presence of Jacky, who had gone away to school.[13]

Martha harbored intense anxiety about Jacky long before Patsy's death. The simple fact of his not being at home sent her imagination into overdrive. She wrote to her sister Anna Maria "Nancy" Dandridge on August 28, 1762, describing a test she had given herself to be without Jacky, who was seven years old at the time. That July, Martha had taken Patsy and ventured to Westmoreland County, Virginia, for two weeks to visit George's younger brother John Augustine Washington and his wife, Hanna Bushrod Washington. Her impatience grew as each day passed, and she expressed her fears for Jacky to her sister: "if I at aney time heard the doggs barke or a noise out I thought thair was a person sent for me I often fansied he was sick or some accident had happend to him so that I think it is impossable for me to leave him as long as mr washington must stay when he comes down."[14]

As was common among eighteenth-century elites, George and Martha sent Jacky to boarding school in 1768. This longer-term separation no doubt heightened his mother's apprehension about her children. However, Jacky was going to inherit great wealth, and George understood that education was necessary for his success as a Virginia gentleman—and to ensure that Jacky's love of fun did not result in his gambling away his inheritance. George reached out to Jacky's new tutor, the Reverend Jonathan Boucher, describing the young man as his son-in-law. "He is a boy of good genius," George explained, "about 14 yrs of age, untainted in his Morals, & of innocent Manners." He added that Jacky was "a promising boy—the last of his Family—& will possess a very large Fortune—add to this my anxiety to make him fit for more useful purposes, than a horse Racer &ca."[15]

At first, Boucher wrote in glowing terms about the young man. But by the summer of 1769, he discussed with George Jacky's laziness, which the tutor hoped was not incurable. In May 1770, Boucher wrote a bleaker appraisal of Jacky: "The chief failings of his Character are that He is constitutionally, somewhat too warm—indolent, & voluptuous." By the end of that year, he confessed to George: "I never did in my Life know a Youth so exceedingly indolent, or so surprizingly voluptuous: one wd suppose Nature had intended Him for some Asiatic Prince."[16] George struggled to strike a balance. Martha wanted Jacky with her, particularly with Patsy's illness. Yet each letter from his tutors only reinforced George's belief that Jacky required a proper education—as well as an attitude adjustment.

When Jacky's tutor offered to have him inoculated for smallpox, George agreed, but he kept it a secret from his wife. George implored Boucher to proceed immediately, knowing that the recovery period could be several weeks. His plan was to tell Martha that Jacky had successfully been inoculated (and was back to normal) before they left for a planned trip to Williamsburg. He explained, "Mrs. Washington I am convinced, would never agree to leave home till she had received the most Authentick advices of his being well over it; and this might be extreamely prejudicial to my Business."[17] George went so far as to ask Boucher to send his letters through Lund Washington in a handwriting not his own for fear that Martha might come across one of the letters and figure out the plan. George justified his strategy by sharing what Martha had previously admitted to him: "she having often wishd, that Jack woud take & go through the disorder without her knowing of it; that she might escape those Tortures which Suspence wd throw her into little as the cause might be for it." Jacky's inoculation proved successful, and Boucher kept the secret, understanding Martha's concerns. "I know," Boucher told George, "She will be anxious & impatient till it be over."[18]

Jacky surprised his parents in February 1773, when he was nineteen years old, by announcing that he was engaged to a young woman named Eleanor

"Nelly" Calvert. While it is easy to imagine Martha excited about this turn of events, George only grew more exasperated. He believed that as Jacky's guardian, it was his duty to see that the boy completed a proper education before getting married. He also did not believe that Jacky could be a proper husband without that schooling. George therefore wrote to Nelly's father, Benedict Calvert, hoping to find an ally in postponing the wedding. He assured Benedict that he approved of the match but strongly encouraged a delay in marriage until a later date. Thrilled that George approved of his daughter, Benedict agreed that a delay of matrimony was best.[19] Jacky moved to New York in May 1773 to attend King's College (present-day Columbia University), and his fiancée visited Mount Vernon a month later to spend time with her soon-to-be in-laws. The timing could not have been worse. Less than a month later, Patsy took her last breath.

Patsy Custis's death erased George's triumph in his quest for Jacky to delay his marriage and to finish his education. As George confessed to the president of King's College, Myles Cooper, Martha wanted her last living child at home. And the rest of the family, save George, agreed with her. He expressed his disappointment to Cooper but was not willing to push Martha too far: "at length, I have yielded, contrary to my judgment, & much against my wishes, to his quitting College."[20] Had the young man been a biological son, George might have felt it more appropriate to insist that Jacky remain in school. For his part, Jacky, who had never been fond of school, also seemed to understand that his mother needed him. Less than a month after Patsy's death, Jacky informed his stepfather that though he himself was overcome with sadness by the loss of his sister, he now concerned himself with how his mother was bearing the grief. Jacky wrote to Martha that day as well, trying to comfort her. He urged his "dear Mother" to "comfort yourself with ref[l]ecting that she now enjoys in substanc[e] what we in this world enjoy in imagination, & that there is no real Happiness on this side of the Grave." Jacky left college and married Nelly on February 3, 1774.[21]

During the first fifteen years of their marriage, George and Martha's life centered on their family and their family's home, Mount Vernon. Appearance was everything in colonial Virginia, and so the couple decorated their home in the latest styles. George's improvement in social status from his marriage to Martha also led him to expand and improve upon the Mount Vernon mansion, including building an additional story and refurbishing the entire house.[22] The Washingtons owned people, whose labor kept the estate maintained and profitable. In addition to the eighty-four enslaved people whom Martha inherited from her first marriage, George purchased more than sixty additional individuals prior to the American Revolution. These would have included domestic and field workers as well as artisans.[23]

Although George Washington would have likely described his career in the years between his wedding to Martha and the outbreak of the Revolutionary War as that of a gentleman farmer, he also held a seat in the Virginia House of Burgesses and experienced a public life away from his family. Between 1758 and 1765, he represented Frederick County, and from 1766 to 1775, he represented Fairfax County.[24] This meant traveling often to Williamsburg and time away from Mount Vernon and his family. It also meant a front-row seat to the growing tensions in the colonies toward Great Britain, leading up to the outbreak of war. In August 1774, George attended the first Continental Congress, departing from Mount Vernon for Philadelphia with Patrick Henry and Edmund Pendleton. Pendleton described Martha as cheerful—though she was likely just playing the role of a proper host. He wrote, "I was most pleased with Mrs. Washington and her spirit. She seemed ready to make any sacrifice and was cheerful though I knew she felt anxious."[25]

The military and political history of the years preceding the Revolutionary War are well covered in countless monographs and history books. But for George Washington, the events that all schoolchildren learn about came in addition to his private responsibilities, including his role as a nurturing and dependable husband and father. For example, in US history courses, the year 1773 is often remembered for the passing of the Tea Act by Great Britain, followed by the colonial response in the form of the Boston Tea Party. This "party" is seen as the spark that lit the fire of revolution in New England. And yet most do not know that during this time, George Washington was mourning the loss of his stepdaughter Patsy after spending years trying to find a cure for her illness. It was almost exactly two years after her death that he accepted a commission as commander in chief of the Continental Army. Would he have hesitated to assume that role if Patsy had still been alive and he was still searching for a cure?

George Washington accepted the role of commander in chief on June 16, 1775. With the benefit of hindsight, it is easy for students to perceive this assignment and the eventual American victory as inevitable. Yet at the time, a British defeat was almost unimaginable in a war against the North American colonies, and General Washington faced a plethora of hidden dangers that seldom appear in the history books. He could not have foreseen that he would be away from his beloved Mount Vernon for eight years. He could, however, understand that in the war against Great Britain, he would be labeled by the Crown as a traitor. With the danger of his situation clear, George confronted the fact that he had to leave his wife and her one remaining child while he proceeded into the unknown. And he was worried about them.

How would Martha Washington deal with her husband's being away at war? George was unsure. Upon his assignment as commander of the army, he wrote to Martha that he had not sought the position, nor did he think himself up to it. He did not want to leave her and the family, he insisted. And he needed her to face the challenge with strength and resolve: "My unhappiness will flow, from the uneasiness I know you will feel at being left alone—I therefore beg of you to summon your whole fortitude & Resolution, and pass your time as agreeably as possible." The next day, George wrote to Martha's brother-in-law, asking him to check in on her. "I have no expectations of returning till Winter & feel great uneasiness at her lonesome Situation," he pleaded. He then sent a letter to Jacky, explaining his expectations of the young man: "I therefore hope, expect, & indeed have no doubt, of your using every means in your power to keep up her Spirits, by doing every thing in your power, to promote her quiet—I have I must confess very uneasy feelings on her acct." He added that he hoped Jacky and Nelly would spend time with Martha at Mount Vernon to ensure her peace of mind.[26]

Another concern for George, and anxiety for Martha, stemmed from the possibility that the enemy might attempt to kidnap Martha for revenge. George reached out to Mount Vernon's caretaker, Lund Washington, hoping for reassurance that Virginia's royal governor, Lord Dunmore, would never stoop so low. Lund responded a month and a half later, explaining that a rumor of Martha's possible kidnapping had likely started in Alexandria and spread all the way to London, but it was just that: a rumor. Lund assured George that "she does not believe herself in danger, nor do I." However, George's apprehension escalated Martha's anxiety, and Lund wrote again to share with George: "Mrs Washington I believe was under no apprehension of Lord Dunmores doing her an injury until your mentiong it in several of your last Letters."[27]

Less than six months into his new role, George asked Martha to join him in winter quarters in Cambridge, Massachusetts. In the eighteenth century, war rarely continued uninterrupted in the winter months. This meant time for other activities, and family was on George's mind. He wrote to his brother in

October 1775, "seeing no great prospect of returning to my Family & Friends this Winter I have sent an Invitation to Mrs Washington to come to me, altho' I fear the Season is too far advanced . . . to admit this with any tolerable degree of convenience."[28] Martha agreed to the trip, which would mark her first time leaving Virginia. She arrived in Cambridge on December 11, 1775, with Jacky, Nelly, and George's nephew George Lewis.

With this visit to winter quarters in Massachusetts, Martha Washington bid farewell to her dream of a quiet domestic life and stepped into the spotlight as a new celebrity. Along the way, she was greeted with parades in her honor, and her arrival was announced in the newspaper.[29] She attended all eight winter encampments of the war: Cambridge, Massachusetts (December 1775–April 1776); Morristown, New Jersey (March–June 1777 and December 1779–June 1780); Valley Forge, Pennsylvania (January–June 1778); Middlebrook, New Jersey (February–June 1779); New Windsor, New York (December 1780–June 1781); Yorktown, Virginia (Williamsburg and Eltham, October–November 1781); and Newburgh, New York (March–July 1782 and November 1782–October 1783). Because of the prevalence of smallpox in the camps, Martha underwent inoculation in May 1776.[30] The years of travel took a toll on her health, as she suffered from exhaustion and a variety of illnesses throughout the war.

While the nascent United States struggled to become an independent nation, George and Martha happily watched their family unit expand. Jacky excitedly wrote Martha in August 1776 announcing the birth of her first grandchild, Elizabeth "Eliza" Parke Custis (Law). He noted, "I wish You were present, You would be much more pleased."[31] Jacky and Nelly went on to have three more surviving children: Martha "Patty" Parke Custis (Peter) (born 1777), Eleanor "Nelly" Parke Custis (Lewis) (born 1779), and George Washington "Washy" Parke Custis (born 1781). Because of her travels to visit her husband, Martha was only present for the birth of Patty at Mount Vernon.

Martha may have been Jacky's only biological parent, but a letter he wrote to George in June 1776 reveals that Jacky saw George as his father. Jacky almost gushed: "I am extremely desireous (but I am at Loss for Words sufficiently expressive) to return you Thanks for your parental Care which on all Occasions you have shewn for Me. It pleased the Almighty to deprive me at a very early Period of Life of my Father, but I can not sufficiently adore His Goodness in sending Me so good a Guardian as you Sir." Perhaps, as a young man in his early twenties, Jacky had become more aware of the difficulties he had caused

George as a boy, with his short attention span, lackadaisical attitude toward schoolwork, and penchant for pleasures. Poignantly, Jacky added, "He best deserves the Name of Father who acts the Part of one."[32]

John Parke Custis stayed clear of the battlefield during the Revolutionary War, a decision no doubt insisted upon by his mother. However, as the 1781 siege of Yorktown was winding down, Martha believed it safe enough for him to visit George in the well-protected officers' quarters. Jacky had been unwell before his departure, but when writing to Martha from Yorktown on October 12, 1781, he assured her that he was feeling much better. He also implored her to visit as well, informing her that her relatives in New Kent, Virginia, were desirous to see her. She agreed to the trip.[33]

What began as a visit to see her husband and son turned into Martha's worst nightmare. Along with Nelly and her daughter little Eliza, Martha set out from Mount Vernon for Williamsburg at the end of October. They arrived at Eltham to learn that Jacky had become gravely ill. George abruptly left his headquarters at Yorktown and rushed to his stepson's bedside.[34] On November 5, the family watched Jacky take his last breath. The twenty-six-year-old left behind a wife and four children. General Henry Knox described the grievous loss: "His Excellency the General & Mrs Washington amidst flattering public prospects have Received the most fatal blow to their domestic felicity—the amiable Mr Custis, Mrs Washingtons only child has just been obliged by the rigid hand of fate to pay his last Debt to nature." Martha's last child was gone—and George could only comfort her for a short time before he once again had to focus on war.[35]

Jacky's death left Martha and George's four grandchildren fatherless. Just as Martha had sought a guardian for young Jacky and Patsy in 1757, a guardian was sought for the four grandchildren now. Four days after Jacky's death, Martha's brother Bartholomew Dandridge contacted George with an offer to help with the estate or in any matter necessary. George took the opportunity to ask Dandridge to serve as a temporary guardian of the children until their mother remarried. Dandridge tried to push the responsibility back onto George but was met with resistance. George made it clear that even if the war were to end shortly, he would have neither the time nor the energy to embrace the role of his grandchildren's guardian. After yet another round of letters pushing off the responsibility to the other, Dandridge eventually relented exactly one year after Jacky's death—but not wholeheartedly. He insisted, "I am still conscious of my unfitness for the Office, and depend upon resigning it to you whenever you return in Peace, or to some more proper Person than myself as soon as one can be had."[36]

The Revolutionary War ended with the signing of the Treaty of Paris in September 1783, and that same year Jacky's widow married Dr. David Stuart. The oldest grandchildren, Eliza and Patty, stayed with their mother and their new stepfather. The care of Nelly and Washy was taken over by their grandparents, George and Martha, at Mount Vernon. They would grow up there as the Washingtons essentially started the parenting process over, with a young girl and boy to raise. Mount Vernon grew by three more young relatives as well. George took responsibility for the education of his orphaned nephews, George Steptoe Washington and Lawrence Augustine Washington, eleven and nine years old. Martha's niece, Frances "Fanny" Bassett, also moved into Mount Vernon. Martha's dream of raising a family at Mount Vernon appeared to be coming true. But that hope did not last long.

Eight years of war and travel caught up with Martha, and her health suffered. After an illness in the fall of 1784, George told a friend in January 1785 that Martha remained in poor health. In March he wrote another friend sharing that Martha still had not improved much. "Mrs Washington," he explained, "is too often troubled with bilious and cholicky complaints, to enjoy perfect health." The next month, Martha lost her mother, Frances Jones Dandridge, and her brother Bartholomew in the span of two weeks. In September 1785, George wrote that Martha was almost never well. Her health concerns did not allow the positive new beginning for which she had so long hoped.[37]

More service and long absences from Mount Vernon followed. George Washington attended the 1787 Philadelphia Convention, which ultimately resulted in his election as the first president of the United States. Just as she had during the Revolutionary War, Martha traveled to New York, the site of the nation's first capital under the Constitution, to be with him. She took along their grandchildren. Her domestic life at Mount Vernon was once again on hold, and she was unhappy about it. Then, just a few months into her new, unwelcome lifestyle, in the summer of 1789, George became seriously ill and as a result underwent surgery on his thigh. The nation fretted over the future of their leader until he recovered. And Martha complained, "I live a very dull life hear and know nothing that passes in the town—I never goe to any publick place—indeed I think I am more like a state prisoner than any thing else."[38]

The Washingtons initially settled into the presidential mansion on Cherry Street in New York, but, finding that house too small, they moved to a house on Broadway in February 1790.[39] Upon arriving in New York, Martha immediately set out to ensure that the grandchildren's needs were met, including acceptance into a good school. Nelly, whom Martha described in 1789 as a little wild creature, attended a prominent school run by Isabella Graham, where she was instructed in music, dancing, drawing, and foreign languages. She was also tutored alongside Washy.[40]

By November 1790, the Washingtons, including Nelly and Washy, were moving again, this time to the new capital, Philadelphia. The President's House was rented from Revolutionary War financier Robert Morris. The family lived there for the remainder of George's presidency. However, although Philadelphia offered many benefits of a metropolitan area in the eighteenth century, there were also downsides.

The yellow fever epidemic hit Philadelphia hard in 1793. At least five thousand people lost their lives from the disease. Martha, deeply concerned for the health and safety of her family, insisted that they remove themselves to Mount Vernon until the danger passed. Upon leaving, George explained to Tobias Lear, "It was my wish to have stayed there longer; but as Mrs Washington was unwilling to leave me amidst the malignant fever which prevailed, I could not think of hazarding her & the Children any longer by my remaining in the City."[41]

George's eight years as president, like his eight years as commander in chief, took their toll on the Washingtons as they tried to balance competing demands on their time: public and private, political and familial. With illness, an epidemic, travels, and ensuring that Nelly and Washy were cared for and happy, there was always some pressing family-centered matter to take George and Martha's focus away from their public roles. Near the end of their time in Philadelphia, John Adams described the Washingtons: "The P[resident] looks to me worried and growing old faster than I could wish and his Lady complains of Infirmities of Age and lowness of Spirits for the first time."[42] At the end of George's presidency, the family moved back to Mount Vernon in 1797. Martha would enjoy fewer than three years of domestic life before George Washington died, on December 14, 1799, at age sixty-seven. She lived a bit longer, dying on May 22, 1802, at age seventy.

George Washington was a surveyor, a general, and a president. He led the United States to independence and steered it through its formative years. But what most history books and classes forget is that he was also a father and grandfather. While a group of colonies fomented a revolution, war raged on, and a new nation struggled to stay together, Washington was also caring for his tough but anxious wife, raising children, losing family members, and attempting to set up a bright future for his young charges. By removing his personal life from the narrative, only half of the story is told. With the whole story, we can reach a greater comprehension of Washington's world, the American Revolution, and the founding of the United States.

Notes

Citations of Founders Online documents do not include individual links, as each source can be found by searching the site at https://founders.archives.gov/.

1. This and all other primary source letters are transcribed exactly as written and therefore include misspelled words and abbreviations from the originals. Nathanael Greene to George Washington, November 22, 1781, George Washington Papers, Digital Collections, Library of Congress, https://www.loc.gov/collections/george-washington-papers/about-this-collection/ (hereafter DCLC).
2. Address from the Officers of the Virginia Regiment, December 31, 1758, and George Washington to John Stanwix, March 4, 1758, both in George Washington Papers, DCLC; Lease of Mount Vernon, December 17, 1754, Fairfax County Court House, Fairfax County Deed Book C, 1750–54, 822–25; Bruce A. Ragsdale, *Washington at the Plow: The Founding Farmer and the Question of Slavery* (Cambridge, MA: Harvard University Press, 2021), 22. Washington wrote Stanwix, "I now see no prospect of preferment in a Military Life." Ragsdale notes that it was not until Washington resigned from the military that he pursued diversification of crops rather than relying on managers and overseers to simply keep the farm running.
3. Patricia Brady, *Martha Washington: An American Life* (New York: Viking, 2005), 32; Custis family tree in *The Papers of Martha Washington* (Charlottesville: University of Virginia Press, 2022), lxii; editorial note, Report of the Commissioners to Settle the Estate [ca. October 1759], and Combined County Inventory of Slaves and Personal Property in the Estate, [1757–58], in *The Papers of George Washington, Colonial Series*, ed. W. W. Abbot et al. (Charlottesville: University of Virginia Press, 1969–), 6:201–9, 215–17, 220–32.
4. Queries to John Mercer, April 20, 1759, Founders Online. See note 4 in this source for John Mercer's correspondence with Martha Custis regarding guardianship of Jacky and Patsy. The lawsuit requiring the assistance of a guardian, dubbed the Dunbar Case, is described in note 5 in this source.

5. Washington's Appointment as Guardian, October 21, 1761, Founders Online.
6. George Washington Papers, DCLC, Series 5, Financial Papers: General Ledger A, 1750–1772, 59, 146, 188, 237, 255, 262.
7. Martha Washington to Martha Bolan Green, September 29, 1760, in *Papers of Martha Washington*, 75; "Bitters," in *The Oxford English Dictionary*, ed. James A. H. Murray et al. (Oxford: Oxford University Press, 1961), 886.
8. Receipt from William Rumney, February 18, 1769, Custis Family Papers, Virginia Historical Society; John Hill, M.D., *The Virtues of Wild Valerian in Nervous Disorders* (London: R. Baldwin, 1758), 3–5. A medicinal plaster consisted of a thick salve, alone or spread on a bandage, that was impregnated with items such as herbs that contained healing properties. William Ellis, *The Country Housewife's Family Companion* (London: Looking-glass, 1750), 267.
9. George Washington, diary entries for July 6, 1768, and January 31, 1769, note 1, Founders Online; George Washington Papers, DCLC, Series 5, Financial Papers: General Ledger A, 1750–1772, 299, 333, 345.
10. George Washington, diary entries for November 9, 1768, note 1, and February 16, 1769, Founders Online.
11. William Jones, *Finger-Ring Lore: Historical, Legendary, and Anecdotal* (London: Chatto & Windus, 1890), 154; George Washington to John Armstrong, August 18, 1769, Founders Online.
12. George Washington Papers, DCLC, Series 1, Exercise Books, Diaries, and Surveys 1745–99, Subseries 1B, Diaries 1748 to 1799: Diary, January 1–December 31, 1770, Library of Congress, Manuscript/Mixed Material, https://www.loc.gov/item/mgw1b.701/.
13. George Washington to Burwell Bassett, June 20, 1773, Founders Online.
14. Martha Washington to Anna Maria Dandridge Bassett, August 28, 1762, in *Papers of Martha Washington*, 78–79.
15. George Washington to Jonathan Boucher, May 30, 1768, Founders Online.
16. Jonathan Boucher to George Washington, August 2, 1768; Jonathan Boucher to George Washington, July 20, 1769; Jonathan Boucher to George Washington, May 21, 1770 (first quotation); Jonathan Boucher to George Washington, December 18, 1770 (second quotation), all on Founders Online.
17. George Washington to Jonathan Boucher, April 4, 1771, Founders Online.
18. George Washington to Jonathan Boucher, April 20, 1771, Founders Online; Jonathan Boucher to George Washington, April 11, 1771, Founders Online.
19. George Washington to Benedict Calvert, April 3, 1773, Founders Online; Benedict Calvert to George Washington, April 8, 1773, Founders Online.
20. George Washington to Myles Cooper, December 15, 1773, Founders Online.
21. John Parke Custis to George Washington, July 5, 1773, Founders Online; John

Parke Custis to Martha Washington, July 5, 1773, in *Papers of Martha Washington*, 85–87; George Washington, diary entry for February 3, 1774, Founders Online.

22. Fielding Lewis to George Washington, February 7, 1757, Founders Online.
23. Mary V. Thompson, *"The Only Avoidable Subject of Regret": George Washington, Slavery, and the Enslaved Community at Mount Vernon* (Charlottesville: University of Virginia Press, 2019), 13–14.
24. Lucille Griffith, *The Virginia House of Burgesses, 1750–1774* (Tuscaloosa: University of Alabama Press, 1970), 94–98.
25. Ellen McCallister Clark, *Martha Washington: A Brief Biography* (Charlottesville: University of Virginia Press, 2002), 28.
26. George Washington to Martha Washington, June 18, 1775; George Washington to Burwell Bassett, June 19, 1775; George Washington to John Parke Custis, June 19, 1775, all on Founders Online.
27. George Washington to Lund Washington, August 20, 1775; Lund Washington to George Washington, October 5, 1775; Lund Washington to George Washington, October 15, 1775, all on Founders Online.
28. George Washington to John Augustine Washington, October 13, 1775, Founders Online.
29. *Pennsylvania Gazette* (Philadelphia), November 22, 1775.
30. George Washington to John Augustine Washington, May 31–June 4, 1776, Founders Online.
31. John Parke Custis to Martha Washington, August 21, 1776, in *Papers of Martha Washington*, 115–17.
32. John Parke Custis to George Washington, June 10, 1776, Founders Online.
33. John Parke Custis to Martha Washington, October 12, 1781, in *Papers of Martha Washington*, 138. Eltham, the home of Burwell Bassett and Martha's late sister Anna Maria Dandridge Bassett, was not far from York, Virginia.
34. George Washington, diary entry for November 5, 1781, note 1, Founders Online.
35. Henry Knox to Clement Biddle, November 11, 1781, Gilder Lehrman Institute of American History, https://www.gilderlehrman.org/collection/glc0243701287.
36. Bartholomew Dandridge to George Washington, November 9, 1781; George Washington to Bartholomew Dandridge, November 19, 1781; Bartholomew Dandridge to George Washington, March 20, 1782; George Washington to Bartholomew Dandridge, April 20, 1782; Bartholomew Dandridge to George Washington, May 13, 1782; George Washington to Bartholomew Dandridge, June 25, 1782; Bartholomew Dandridge to George Washington, November 5, 1782 (quotation), all in George Washington Papers, DCLC.

37. George Washington to Elias Boudinot, January 31, 1785; George Washington to William Gordon, March 8, 1785; George Washington to Richard Varick, September 26, 1785, all on Founders Online.
38. James McHenry to George Washington, June 28, 1789, note 1, Founders Online; Martha Washington to Frances Bassett Washington, October 22, 1789, in *Papers of Martha Washington*, 193.
39. George Washington, diary entries for February 1 and February 23, 1790, Founders Online.
40. Martha Washington to Frances Bassett Washington Lear, June 8, 1789, in *Papers of Martha Washington*, 187–88.
41. George Washington to Tobias Lear, September 25, 1793, Founders Online; Kenneth R. Foster, Mary F. Jenkins, and Anna Coxe Toogood, "The Philadelphia Yellow Fever Epidemic of 1793," *Scientific American* 279, no. 2 (1998): 89, 92.
42. John Adams to Abigail Adams, February 10, 1796, Founders Online.

MARTHA WASHINGTON

A Case Study for Teaching Gender-Inclusive History for High School Students

BONNIE A. BELSHE

In 2004, I started my teaching career in Cupertino, California. I have been at the same school for over twenty years now. I teach both the US history survey and Advanced Placement US history, but I specialize in women's history, and I include a focus on it in all my courses. Women's history was not always my focus, nor would I have considered myself a specialist in it when I first began teaching. Almost every new teacher is told somewhere along the way that there will be a moment in your first couple of years teaching where you realize just how little you know. I was no exception.

My second year of teaching US history at Monta Vista High School made it clear to me that I needed to know more: I needed more content to include in my lessons, and I needed to know more about the professionalization of history to better teach my students. In order to teach my students as historians-in-training, I needed the training of a historian as well as that of an educator. Fortunately, there was a wonderful master's in history program at San José State University with night classes that encouraged teachers to become immersed in teaching history. I remember sitting in Dr. Patricia Hill's class one evening in 2007 when she dropped a truth so simple, so plain, so clear, that it would permanently shape the next two decades of my teaching career. "Male," she said, "is not neutral and it is not default." Of course! The lightbulb went off over my head, and I knew then that my teaching philosophy needed to be centered around adding women and gender issues into all aspects of my classroom.

It is imperative for all students to understand the importance of including women and gender issues in our collective study of the past. When I was asked to contribute to this volume on learning from and teaching about George Washington in the twenty-first century, I interpreted that invitation as one to write about teaching Martha Washington in the twenty-first century. My goal for my students is to have them understand the complexities of American women's history, and Martha Washington provides a lens through which to see the perspective of elite eighteenth-century women. Because I teach AP US history chronologically, colonial history and the founding of the new nation are some of the earliest lessons of the year. This allows me to use Martha Washington and her personal history as a case study for understanding gender, race, politics, and economics in early America. Yet there is a critical question that I must contend with: How do I teach with Martha Washington as a case study for eighteenth-century history without her becoming representative of *all* eighteenth-century history?

I answer this question with the four core components of my teaching philosophy: include women as examples, teach diverse narratives, include women-specific topics, and read against the grain. At first glance, using Martha Washington as a case study may not appear to fit all four of these criteria. But, in fact, she was deeply immersed within her eighteenth-century world as a wife, mother, grandmother, friend, wife to the nation's first president, enslaver, and more. By engaging with the nuances of her interactions with enslaved women, with paid White domestic servants, and with other wealthy White women, students find Martha's world an expansive one. This approach also includes examining her relationship with George and the changes brought into her daily life with his military service, presidency, and ultimate retirement. A case study focused on Martha allows me to teach more complexity and subtlety within the confines of my high school US history survey.

The first three of my components are self-evident, I hope. But what does it mean to "read against the grain"? This method offers a tool for looking at primary source documents and material culture that assists students in moving beyond reading the obvious, or superficial, meaning of the source. Reading against the grain encourages students to draw deeper insights, interpretations, connections, and inferences from the text. For example, reading against the grain might inspire a student to ask, How can power dynamics be understood through this source? How can students perceive efforts at resistance to slavery from the sources left behind by enslavers, for instance? Nuanced questions arise from reading against the grain. This method helps students develop historical empathy and scrutinize historical beliefs, and it asks students to examine the gaps left in the historical records—a technique especially helpful when studying marginalized groups.

I believe that the reading against the grain technique is applicable to all students and can be applied to all topics in the classroom. This critical analysis of Martha Washington offers one model that I have found particularly successful within my classroom. In the following primary source, Martha Washington is writing to her niece Frances (Fanny) Bassett Washington. While the Washingtons were in Philadelphia for the presidency, Fanny was helping watch over Mount Vernon. Through this letter, students can learn about the system in which the Washingtons moved enslaved people back and forth, from Virginia and Philadelphia, to avoid Pennsylvania's 1780 act for gradual emancipation. This letter also helps students understand why and how enslaved people, such as Hercules Posey, self-emancipated (that is, ran away). Students learn about Martha Washington's taking advantage of living in a seaport city and the many purchases that she made during this time. But they can consider other questions as well: Who handles the cloth, runs the errands, and tends to the sick child? Who performs the labor related to these purchases and activities? By reading against the grain, students rightfully place enslaved people at the center of this letter and their learning.

> Philadelphia June the 5th 1791
>
> My dear Fanny,
>
> Your letter of the 29th of May, did not reach my hands till yesterday—I was then very sick having got cold by the change of weather;—or I would have got and sent by Hercules the silk and &—I will as soon as I am well enough to go out make the best collection I can and send it by a safe hand. I believe they are to be had in this city. As to fine muslin I have never been able to find a yard of fine Jaconet muslin in this place. nor is the Book fine—I will lay the money out in the best way I can.—I sent by Hercules some rufles for my little Boys bosom which I beg you will make Chariot hem—and ship them ready to sew on and send me six at a time as his old ruffles are worne to raggs—Hercules comes home to be ready for his master—I have got several things for kitchen use but—the vessel will not sail in time to be there as soon as he will—I also send some East India sugar—it seems to be clean and while I was in hopes it would have arrived in time to preserve and dry

> cherreys—I have had letters from the President from savanna—and expect he will be with you by this day week. I should be very happy to come on to see you and meet him but that is out of my power, I am not well enough to bear the journey—and if I was—I could not come so long a way without a gentleman—and Mr. Lear could not leave this to come with me—if you can get timothy for half a crown in town it is much cheaper than it can be had hear—the last India vessels has brought nothing but tea and nankeens and the very coarse set kind of callacos—and such muslin that sells for four and five shillings a yard—I was thinking to get some of the coarse cotton to make her under coats she must have them of some kind or other—it would be well for the major to mention it to the General—I sent to Betty Custis a pr. of stays which Mrs. Stuart says will fit her and she sent them to Mr. Snow to return to me if they will suite Miss Harriet she may as well keep them—as to have a pair made for her—I have seen no timothy hear sold for less than four & six pence and that but one piece—I got what was left and sent it to the girls.
>
> Batt Dandridge arrived hear yesterday he is as yellow as a mulato,—he is inoculated this day for the small pox—Mr. Lear's child has got quite well, and grows finely—the children are both well—and so is all our family except myself—and god only knows wheather—I shall ever be in tolerable health again—I am sorry to hear that your little Boy is not in good health—worms is the cause of all complaints in children—I have sent three Butter printers send one of the larger ones to Mrs. Stuart and—keep the others until I come.—my love to the major—kiss the children.—and believe me my dear Fanny.
>
> Your most affectionate
> M Washington[1]

Perhaps you are wondering how I am able to incorporate these case studies of Martha Washington into my classroom. What K–12 educators need most to support their teaching is time and access to primary and secondary sources. George Washington's Mount Vernon privileged me with both. I was honored to have been selected as one of the Life Guard Teacher Fellows for Mount Vernon in 2017–2018. This program allowed six teachers to live on the grounds of Mount Vernon in researcher housing, with access to dedicated research space at the Washington Library, Mount Vernon's expert staff, and the primary source documents and material culture of the estate.

Over the course of two summers, I immersed myself in study at Mount Vernon. My research focused on Martha Washington, and I built my case study around her for my own use as well as for other high school history teachers. I particularly wanted to highlight how to teach historical-thinking skills in the classroom. Using Mount Vernon's resources, I developed five lesson plans using Martha Washington and resources related to her life. These lessons were designed to give students the chance to look critically at historical content for colonial women's history in three key areas: private versus public spheres for women, coverture and the colonial family ethic, and slavery. I also developed two lesson plans for historical-thinking skills: perspective analysis and historiography. Using Martha Washington for these historical-thinking skills lessons sets the foundation for students to question the assumption of men's history as the default, neutral perspective.

Perspective analysis. I use perspective analysis in my lessons as a teacher facilitator during the George Washington Teacher Institute (GWTI) in what we affectionately call "Women's Week." Its official title is "The Worlds of Martha Washington and the Women of the Eighteenth Century." This professional development week brings together about twenty-five teachers from around the United States for an in-depth study of place-based learning, material culture, and primary source analysis. Along the way, the teachers work with leading scholars and build a teacher learning community. My role as teacher facilitator is to connect the learning from academic scholars, such as those who contributed to this volume, with the work of K–12 history educators. I lead sessions on incorporating eighteenth-century women's history into K–12 classrooms and facilitate a debrief every day. The debrief allows teachers to process our collaborative learning and share what they will add or change in their teaching when they arrive back home. Teachers call this type of summer professional development "teacher camp," so being a teacher facilitator means that I am, in effect, the camp counselor. These weeks are always the highlight of my summer, and they give me energy to start each new school year.

GWTI is an experience that enriches more than just the teachers who attend. Attendees go back and share what they learned with their colleagues and, of course, with their students in the classroom. For the teachers participating in

Women's Week, that means learning about Martha Washington as a case study for examining the eighteenth century. I begin the week by displaying different portraits of Martha; some of the portraits are of her as an older woman, with graying or white hair and a grandmotherly look about her. This is a familiar image and one that both students and teachers expect. What surprises the teachers is when I ask them to compare elderly, matronly Martha Washington to young Martha Dandridge—and then to compare Martha Dandridge Custis to the older, but still youthful, Lady Washington. Through portraiture—a readily accessible primary source—I broaden the ways in which teachers think about Martha Washington. This is only our introduction to the week. We then can spend the rest of the week complicating the narrative of women's roles in early America and thinking critically about the legacy of Martha Washington as well as the ways her life intersected with enslaved women, laboring women, and other elite women.

Historiography. "Historiography" is a term that strikes many people as a little "inside baseball," especially for those who love history but are not historians or history teachers. What is historiography? As I explain to my students, historiography is the study of how historians have written about the past and the ways in which schools of thought developed around patterns that we can study. I have found that high school students are particularly interested in historiography because they like understanding the ways that current events shape how we write about, interpret, and understand the past. With their exposure to the modern twenty-four-hour news cycle, constant social media presence, and barrage of videos and pictures at a speed that we can barely comprehend, history students today seem to appreciate historiography, as it encourages them to pay attention to their communities, both large and small, and bring that connection with them into the classroom and our study of the past.

This is where Martha Washington's case study also comes into play. My students come into my classroom with the bare minimum of familiarity with Martha Washington—they know her as President Washington's wife, and that is about it. Sharing with them excerpts from works authored by Marie Jenkins Schwartz, with her focus on Martha Washington as an enslaver; Helen Bryan, who emphasizes Martha as a businesswoman after the death of her first husband; and Patricia Brady, who depicts Martha as a shrewd and independent leader within her community, encourages students to see the complexity in Martha Washington's life.[2] By focusing these initial conversations on the historians writing about Martha Washington, I can encourage students to step into the historical debate themselves.

Coverture and family ethic. When incorporating women-specific topics into the classroom, I believe there is no more important topic for understanding the lives of eighteenth-century free women than coverture and the colonial family ethic. Coverture was the system of laws governing women's place in society and ensuring that women were legally subordinate to men, especially their husbands. The colonial family ethic offered a stable system in colonial life, with four basic principles: marriage, complementary roles for spouses, bearing and rearing children, and literacy. Colonial Americans expected remarriage after the death of a spouse because too many unmarried women of childbearing age were viewed as destabilizing to the community.

Students are always fascinated by coverture and the colonial family ethic. They draw direct connections to the gender wage gap today and the women's rights movement. Widow Martha Dandridge Custis understood the expectation and pressure to remarry when she married George Washington. My students read letters from the young widow acting as the business manager for her deceased husband's estate and a letter in which she provided her niece Fanny advice about whether she should marry.[3] This comparison allows students to create a nuanced picture of Martha Washington experiencing the colonial family ethic as well as coverture, but they also see her as a business leader, pushing the boundaries of gender expectations.

The various identities of Martha Washington. Examining Martha Washington as an enslaver allows students to critically examine the ways in which White women participated in and perpetuated the brutality of slavery. After the death of her first husband, Daniel Parke Custis, in 1757, Martha Dandridge Custis was entitled to the use of one-third of her husband's estate, including enslaved people, their labor, and the wealth produced from their work, for the duration of her life. After marrying George Washington in 1759, control of the "dower slaves"—that is, the enslaved people "owned" through the Custis estate—was brought to George Washington's Mount Vernon estate.

By having students compare Martha Washington's will to George Washington's will, we can encourage them to think critically about the ways that Martha embodied the role of southern plantation enslaver. While George's will stipulated that the enslaved laborers he "owned" would be freed, Martha never left any evidence that she questioned slavery.[4] George's will, and his decision to free the people he enslaved upon Martha's death, deserves much attention and study. While neither George nor Martha had the legal right to free the enslaved people owned by the Custis estate, Martha did not leave any indication that she ever intended to free them. Rather, her letters demonstrate how she benefited from and worked to perpetuate the system of slavery. When students learn to read against the grain, they can also see resistance to slavery within letters such as these.

Viewing the material culture and physical objects related to Martha Washington presents another opportunity to read against the grain. During the GWTI, we view, up close, Martha Washington's brown silk gown (see fig. 1).[5] I encourage teachers to ask themselves questions about who would have physically interacted with this dress. Who handled this dress in the mornings at Mount Vernon? Who sewed on its buttons? Who cleaned it when it was soiled? This is a form of reading against the grain, which, through the Mount Vernon

FIGURE 1. Brown silk gown, ca. 1790–1800. (Photograph by Gavin Ashworth, courtesy of The Mount Vernon Ladies' Association)

Museum digital collection, can be brought into my classroom in California—and those of teachers across the country.

Working with the teachers who participate in GWTI Women's Week inspired me recently to take up an adjunct teaching position at San José State University, where I offer an upper-level undergraduate course on US history for teachers. You will not be surprised to learn that I use Martha Washington as a case study for eighteenth-century history and as a model for reading against the grain in my university course, too. In discussion with these future teachers, I ask them to name the women they learned about in the elementary, middle school, and high school US history classes they took. The list is generally depressingly short. But one name is on that list every time: Martha Washington (except for the semester that a class could only remember her as "George Washington's wife").

Soon, these future teachers will be in charge in their own classrooms. I want to prepare them as best I can to teach the complexities of the past. For me, that means sharing the lessons of Martha Washington. Together, we examine the complexity of her private versus public life in Philadelphia during George's presidency. Comparing Martha's letters to Mercy Otis Warren and Abigail Adams to those she wrote to her niece Fanny Bassett highlights the tensions between George's political life and Martha's private life. On December 26, 1789, Martha wrote to Mercy Otis Warren her thoughts on George's decision to return to public life after the war was over:

> I little thought when the war was finished, that any circumstances could possible have happened which would call the General into public life again. I had anticipated, that from this moment we should have been left to grow old in solitude and tranquility togather: that was, my Dear madam, the first and dearest wish of my heart;—but in that I have been disapointed; I will not, however, contemplate with too much regret disapointments that were enevitable, though the generals feelings and my own were perfectly in unison with respect to our predilictions for privet life, yet I cannot blame him for having acted according to his ideas of duty in obaying the voice of his country.[6]

She writes of her personal disappointment but overall understanding of George's decision to heed the call of the nation. Yet just two months earlier, she had written to her niece Fanny of much deeper frustration and unhappiness with her life as the president's wife: "I live a very dull life hear and know nothing that passes in the town—I never goe to any publick place—indeed I think I am more like a state prisoner than anything else."[7] Future teachers examine such letters to develop an understanding of Martha Washington and how she both conformed to and resisted the limitations placed upon her from coverture, the colonial family ethic, and eighteenth-century gender, class, and race expectations.

While traditional textbooks have often relegated women's history to a side story—or, worse, ignored their stories entirely—in my high school classroom, college classroom, and involvement in Mount Vernon summer programs, Martha Washington and the women in and around her world take center stage. By engaging with Mount Vernon's resources in the classroom, students have a chance to look critically at early American history and the ways in which women, including Martha Washington, reflected and shaped that history.

Notes

1. This primary source is included in a series of lessons I wrote for Mount Vernon as part of the Life Guard Teacher Fellowship Program: "Integrating Women's History in the Founding Era," George Washington's Mount Vernon, https://www.mountvernon.org/education/for-teachers/lessonplans/lesson/integrating-women-s-history-in-the-founding-era. To learn more about the program, visit "Teacher Fellowship Program," George Washington's Mount Vernon, https://www.mountvernon.org/education/for-teachers/professional-development/teacher-fellowship-program.
2. Marie Jenkins Schwartz, *Ties That Bound: Founding First Ladies and Slaves* (Chicago: University of Chicago Press, 2017), 17; Helen Bryan, *Martha Washington: First Lady of Liberty* (New York: John Wiley and Sons, 2002), 77; Patricia Brady, *Martha Washington: An American Life* (New York: Viking, 2005), 52.
3. Martha Dandridge Custis to Cary & Company, August 20, 1757, Martha Washington: A Life, https://marthawashington.us/items/show/101.html; Martha Washington to Frances "Fanny" Bassett, September 29, 1794, "Coverture, Colonial Family Ethic, and Widowhood" lesson plan, https://mtv-main-assets.mountvernon.org/files/resources/coverture-colonial-family-eithic-and-widowhood-lp.pdf.
4. George Washington, last will and testament, July 9, 1799, Founders Online; Martha Washington, last will and testament (no date), "The Will of Martha Washington of Mount Vernon," George Washington's Mount Vernon, https://

www.mountvernon.org/education/primary-source-collections/primary-source-collections/article/the-will-of-martha-washington-of-mount-vernon.

5. Brown silk gown, 1790–1800, George Washington's Mount Vernon, W-1523, https://emuseum.mountvernon.org/objects/1308.
6. Martha Washington to Mercy Otis Warren, December 26, 1789, The Huntington Digital Library, https://hdl.huntington.org/digital/collection/p16003coll21/id/2406/.
7. Martha Washington to Frances "Fanny" Bassett Washington, October 23, 1789, George Washington's Mount Vernon, https://www.mountvernon.org/education/primary-source-collections/primary-source-collections/article/letter-martha-washington-to-fanny-bassett-washington-october-23-1789.

WILL THE REAL MARTHA WASHINGTON PLEASE STAND UP?

Teaching the Founding Mother in the Twenty-First Century

LAURA J. PING

In 1873, a Philadelphia socialite and great-granddaughter of Benjamin Franklin, Elizabeth Duane Gillespie, had her photograph taken portraying Martha Washington (see fig. 1).[1] Gillespie chose the most recognizable portrayal of Martha Washington: the elderly, maternal matron. The portrait shows Gillespie looking away from the camera, wearing a version of Washington's signature mobcap and kerchief. Reminiscent of Gilbert Stuart's 1796 "Athenaeum" portrait, Gillespie's imitation of Washington was part of a celebration that she and the Women's Centennial Executive Committee hosted in commemoration of the hundredth anniversary of the Boston Tea Party. Committee members all wore caps and kerchiefs honoring Washington, and attendees drank tea from specially ordered cups and saucers.[2] These "Martha Washington Tea Parties" continued to be held as fundraisers by the Women's Centennial Executive Committee for the 1876 Centennial Celebration of the Declaration of Independence in Philadelphia.

For Gillespie and her colleagues, however, dressing as Martha Washington was about more than just canvassing for money. They had a political agenda. The Women's Centennial Executive Committee insisted that a portion of the money raised be used to sponsor an international women's pavilion at the Centennial, which was dedicated to promoting women's rights through their labor.[3]

By Gillespie's account, the women's pavilion was a success, but not all women felt empowered by the celebration of female labor. Suffragist Elizabeth Cady Stanton criticized the Centennial organizers because the women's pavilion had

FIGURE 1. Elizabeth Duane Gillespie as Martha Washington, 1873. (Historical Society of Pennsylvania, Philadelphia)

been a late addition to the celebration, despite the fact that women did most of the fundraising for the event. Few of the women presenting their work within the pavilion owned their own business, she continued. And no one, Stanton claimed, mentioned that the same women being celebrated for their work paid taxes but were disenfranchised.[4]

In protest of "no taxation without representation," Stanton and her suffragist colleagues wrote the Declaration of Rights of the Women of the United States. This proclamation was read aloud during the national Fourth of July centennial celebration in Philadelphia's Independence Square, despite the women's having been told that there was no space for them in the event's program.[5] Stanton was adamant that the Declaration of Rights of the Women of the United States "become an historical part of the proceedings."[6] She would not take no for an answer.

Although Elizabeth Duane Gillespie and Elizabeth Cady Stanton viewed women's rights differently, both women's activism was justified in part by physical comparisons to Martha Washington. For Gillespie, depicting Martha Washington was about embracing the legacy of the American Revolution. For Stanton, who a few years earlier had been described by multiple publications as resembling Martha Washington, presumably because of her white curls and matronly appearance, comparisons were intended to feminize transgressive behavior.[7] These examples show that during the nineteenth century, Martha Washington's legacy was seen as belonging to all American women. But by evoking her physical image to represent personal political agendas, Martha

Washington, and by extension women of the eighteenth century in general, became one-dimensional. The real Martha Washington and her complex viewpoints and experiences were obscured.

While most Americans may think of Martha Washington as the white-haired matron depicted by Gillespie, it is likely that fewer people would be able to describe anything about her beyond being George Washington's wife. This was by design. At the end of her life, Martha Washington burned her personal correspondence, leaving historians and the public with as many questions as there are details about her life. As a result, Washington has not been quoted with the frequency of some of her contemporaries. While Abigail Adams and the Schuyler sisters have made their way into twenty-first-century popular culture, Washington is noticeably absent from dramatizations about the founding generation, even those in which her husband is featured. Yet Martha Washington's life offers a window onto the ways in which many elite women experienced the Revolutionary era and juxtaposes her with women outside her race and social class. By focusing on the nuances of Washington's life—including her appearance, the objects she owned, and enslaved persons in her possession—educators can guide students in understanding the varied experiences of women who lived during the eighteenth century.

Martha Dandridge was born in 1731 in Virginia, the eldest of eight children. Her family were middling planters, meaning that they were comfortable but not wealthy. Her father owned five hundred acres and fifteen to twenty enslaved persons. While the family could likely afford some luxuries, most of what they relied on for daily life would have been produced in the home by members of the Dandridge family. Education also took place at home. Martha Dandridge was taught to read—a privilege linked to race and social class. But unlike her brothers, who received more formal schooling, she was also taught tasks oriented toward making her marriageable: fashion, dancing, setting a table, and learning to hostess.[8]

Although by all accounts Martha Dandridge was beautiful and social, her parents were not wealthy enough to expect that she would marry a rich man. With so many children, the Dandridges could not provide Martha with a large dowry. Eighteenth-century marriages were more about land and social class than love, making them economic transactions. Perhaps it was a surprise, then, when eighteen-year-old Martha married thirty-eight-year-old Daniel Custis, one of the richest planters in Virginia. Custis owned almost eighteen thousand acres of land, spanning six counties, and enslaved three hundred people. As wife to one of the planter elites, Martha Dandridge (now Custis) was responsible for hosting formal dinners and balls, furnishing the Custis home with fine goods, and overseeing the labor of an enormous enslaved population.[9]

Shortly after her marriage to Daniel, Martha Custis also became a mother. She gave birth to four children in five years, although only two would live to adulthood. Death characterized Custis's life, as it did for many people of the era. In 1757 Daniel Custis also died. At twenty-six years old, Martha Custis was a widow with two small children. From this experience, historians can piece together bits of her personality.

During the eighteenth century, women's legal identities were dictated by English common law. The common-law system's principle of coverture categorized single women as "feme sole." That meant that a woman could buy or sell property, make contracts, and sue or be sued in court. When a woman married, however, her status shifted to "feme covert," which meant that her legal identity was covered, or subsumed, by her husband's. The law recognized only the husband's ability to complete property transactions, create legal documents, or represent the family in court. The law assumed that men would ethically protect the interests of their wives, though many women found this not to be the case. A widow, however, had many of her legal rights restored and once again became feme sole. When Daniel Custis died without a will directing how his estate should be settled, Martha Custis inherited one-third of his estate (including enslaved persons) per English common law. This was known as the dower share or widow's third. The other two-thirds of the inheritance was held in trust for their children.

While we can infer that Martha Custis grieved Daniel Custis, her role as a widow also launched her as a businesswoman. She chose not to appoint a trustee to manage the Custis estate and instead did so herself. This level of independence was unusual for colonial Virginia and provides a useful exercise in explaining to students how race and social class affected lived experiences.

To help break down these complicated identities so that I can explain them to my students, I draw on legal scholar Kimberlé Crenshaw's definition of intersectionality and its link to power. Intersectionality asks important questions about the ways in which social categories, such as race, class, and gender, create privileges or disadvantages. These markers of identity may overlap but can also be independent. For example, how might a White woman experience a situation? How might a Black man experience that same circumstance? In what ways would a Black woman's experience be the same or different from the previous two examples? Each person may experience a set of advantages, based on race or gender or other identities, or may be discriminated against because of them. The important thing to note is that there is no single perspective shared among historical actors. When discussing the history of race and gender, it is important to emphasize that women in the past did not have a universal experience. For upper-level classes, I show a TED Talk by Crenshaw that simplifies the methodologies of intersectionality and serves as a jumping-off point to discuss why Martha Custis's experience as a widow was unique.[10]

Custis's race and social class provided her with a level of independence denied other widowed colonial women. For an enslaved woman, there was no bereavement period, for instance. The law did not recognize enslaved marriages, and enslavers were unlikely to offer any type of mourning period. A grief-stricken enslaved woman would have been forced to keep working. A poor White woman may have had to resort to begging to feed her family and likely would have had to send her children to live with friends or family. Her children may have also been apprenticed. A woman of the middling class might have taken over her husband's business. Even other planter's wives would have had to answer to a male trustee.[11] Martha Custis had none of these limitations. She negotiated with her husband's business associates in Virginia and London and made it clear that she expected the same respect—and prices paid for tobacco—that they had shown her husband.

Although sources indicate that Martha Custis was talented in business, she would not remain a widow for long. In 1759 she married Virginia planter George Washington, to whom she would be married for forty years, throughout the American Revolution and her husband's two terms as the first president of the United States. In remarrying, Martha Custis (now Washington) once again became a feme covert, relinquishing her legal status to her husband. It typically baffles my students that a woman would give up financial and legal independence for marriage and is a good opportunity to discuss setting aside our modern viewpoints and contextualizing the past. Women, I explain, were pressured to marry. In the case of George and Martha Washington, however, historian Patricia Brady argues in her 2005 biography *Martha Washington: An American Life* that Martha Washington fell in love with George Washington.[12] Sometimes, I explain to my students, the answer to historical questions is not complicated.

What is more complex is helping students understand the next phase of Martha Washington's life—that of a political wife. Although Washington held no formal political office and informed her niece in 1788 that "I do not conscern myself about" politics, her role as the President's "Lady" and the nation's hostess linked her with a political identity. To have a political identity is different from being politically active, however.

I often begin my history courses with the question "What does it mean to be political?" As an example, I ask students to volunteer political terms that come to mind when they think of the American Revolution. Students typically offer "liberty," "freedom," "taxes," and "All men are created equal." They have little to offer, however, when I ask what women's political experiences were like during the Revolutionary era. Perhaps this reflects depictions of women and the American Revolution in popular culture—such as in Lin-Manuel Miranda's 2015 musical, *Hamilton*, where the character of Angelica Schuyler sings, "And when I meet Thomas Jefferson, I'ma compel him to include women in the sequel!" Such portrayals capture women's application of Revolutionary-era ideas without noting that they gained no new legal rights as a result of independence or the newly established republican government.[13] One of the challenges in teaching gender and the eighteenth century is pushing back against these popular-culture representations of proto-feminism to help students interpret the evolution of women's rights from the eighteenth century to the nineteenth. It is also important to guide students in understanding that suffrage was not an organized movement until the nineteenth century, and while many women supported it, other women opposed suffrage. Both groups used visual depictions of Martha Washington to support their positions.

Like Gillespie, many nineteenth-century Americans looked to Martha Washington as an example of a political woman. For critics of the women's rights and suffrage movements, like Gillespie, Martha Washington represented a female political identity that was comfortable because she also symbolized domesticity. Authors, editors, and artists explained that Washington had been indirectly political through her husband, but she was also primarily a wife and mother. She ran a household. As a result, visual representations of Washington as the traditional, nonthreatening political wife proliferated during the nineteenth-century women's rights movement. Historian Allison Lange explains that "the features of [Washington's] face mattered less than the ideas her portrait represented."[14] This created a historical memory that was not entirely linked to fact.

Scholars have defined historical memory, or collective memory, as the way a community associates a narrative with a particular time.[15] These memories are often shaped to meet the political identity of a group but are not always concretely rooted in fact. For example, Elizabeth Duane Gillespie viewed Martha Washington as representing polite political womanhood, while Elizabeth Cady Stanton's supporters suggested that Washington would have encouraged the organized suffrage movement. Showing Gillespie's portrait as Martha Washington is an easy way to begin discussion. By letting students guess first who is in the portrait and next who she is dressed as, I can test how familiar they are with the common images of Martha Washington and whether they realize that photography did not exist during her lifetime. And then we discuss women and politics.

There is always at least one student who is familiar with Abigail Adams's request to her husband, John, to "Remember the Ladies." Although the admonition was exceptional for its time, it has given the public the impression that Adams and, by association, her female contemporaries were feminists. The term "feminist" did not come into use until the early twentieth century, but more to the point, women in the founding era, including Adams, did not view women's rights the same way that later generations would. Women who pushed for equality did so through education and republican motherhood. The premise of republican motherhood was that girls should receive the same education as boys because one day, as mothers, these young women would be accountable for ensuring that their sons received the prerequisite education to become responsible voting citizens. Republican mothers were not supposed to engage directly in politics, but their duty to oversee their sons' early education was viewed as important to the future of the nation. However, republican motherhood was also impractical for most women, whose household duties were labor-intensive and time-consuming. Black and Indigenous women were barred from the educational opportunities available to White women. Yet as an aspirational role for women, republican motherhood linked women's political contributions to traditional gender roles, theoretically eliminating the need for women to vote.[16] The Nineteenth Amendment, giving women the federal right to vote, would not be ratified for more than a century.

So how does one help students tease out the nuances of women's political experiences in eras before women in the United States could vote or run for political office? I begin by asking students to consider how one might protest without a sign or banner. Students offer suggestions, and if no one brings it up, I mention clothing. Students are then asked to consider how they chose the outfits they are currently wearing. How do they choose their work clothing?

Do they wear a uniform? How might what they wear to a party differ from what they wear to school or work? This exercise is often hit-or-miss. Some students understand it immediately, while others claim that they choose their clothing based on what is clean and on top of the pile. To further demonstrate the point, I look for a student wearing a school logo (or wear one myself). I then ask the class to consider what it means to show membership in a community through clothing. We discuss what it meant to wear certain styles of clothing in the Revolutionary era. Clothing, the students learn, is replete with meaning.

In her 2011 book *The Politics of Fashion in Eighteenth-Century America*, historian Kate Haulman explains that during the Revolutionary era, Patriot women adopted homespun, or homemade, clothing to show that they were boycotting British textiles. In contrast, Loyalist women continued to wear colorful British fashions to show their loyalty to the Crown. We can similarly analyze Martha Washington's politics through her clothing.[17]

Prior to becoming Lady Washington (the term "First Lady" did not yet exist), Martha Washington wore elaborate garments and jewelry. She loved garnets. On her wedding day to George Washington, she wore a yellow silk brocade gown and purple satin slippers. One of her most fascinating gowns from the 1780s featured fifty-eight insects and flowers painted on silk taffeta by hand. This was not a novelty design for Washington. Historians Zara Anishanslin and Alexis Coe theorize that Martha Washington loved the natural world, as evidenced by certain of her possessions; she kept a book entitled *12 Months of Flowers* from her first marriage and spent years sewing (with the help of enslaved women) twelve seashell-patterned cushions.[18] But those fashion choices were made before George Washington became the first president of the United States of America.

As Lady Washington, it was important that Martha Washington communicate through her clothing the republican ideal of virtue. And so, while her clothing remained luxe, the style was simplified. Her contemporaries noticed these details. In 1789 Abigail Adams described Washington as "plain in her dress, but that plainness is the best of every article."[19] George Washington also praised his wife's style. In a letter to the historian Catharine Macaulay Graham, George described how Martha's wishes "coincide with my own as to simplicity of dress, and everything which can tend to support propriety of character without partaking of the follies of luxury and ostentation."[20] President Washington understood that anything he wrote to Macaulay might later be printed in a publication, and his words about his wife's garments were carefully curated to ensure that there could be no comparison between his family and the showy British aristocracy. Americanness was synonymous with simplicity.

Martha Washington's clothing offers a tangible example of how she created her political identity. However, I also want my students to understand that Washington's life was not representative of most women. To illustrate this point, I show students an image of Martha Washington's punch bowl.

Washington likely acquired the punch bowl when she was married to Daniel Custis and brought it with her to Mount Vernon after she married George Washington. It is Chinese porcelain, which serves as another example of Washington's affluence. The punch bowl is elaborately embellished with pink and blue patterns, peonies, chrysanthemums, pheasants, and other birds. While decorative, it was also likely functional, because wealthy Virginians often served alcoholic punch from bowls such as this. The punch, typically made from liquor, lemon or lime juice, sugar, nutmeg, and other spices, was indicative of the global economy that the planter class participated in and the elaborate get-togethers that Washington would have organized as the hostess of Mount Vernon.[21] This object—the image of which is available through Mount Vernon's website—has a narrative to tell.

As a teaching exercise, I show an image of the punch bowl to the students and let them analyze it based first on what they see. Once we have described the colors and patterns, I ask the students to consider what the bowl was used for. Students typically guess that it was used for some type of serving, which then leads me to the question, "Who used this punch bowl?" This allows me to bring up the idea that the people drinking the punch were not the only ones who used it. Who made the punch? Who poured the punch? Who served the punch? Who washed the bowl? Why might this punch bowl have survived? These questions all have the same answer: the enslaved population of Mount Vernon. This creates a segue to another question: What can this object teach us that we might not learn otherwise? By analyzing the punch bowl, the students and I can examine the story of women who did not leave written records, the enslaved women living at Mount Vernon. This is also an example of how intersectionality shifts the historical narrative. Not everyone experienced a party at Mount Vernon in the same way. The enslaved laborers might have been taken for granted by the White partygoers drinking from the punch bowl, but they were nonetheless a significant part of the event and of the Washington family history.

The punch bowl and the expensive clothing reflect Martha Washington's role as an enslaver. She was the daughter of an enslaver and wife to two men who were enslavers. As a matriarch, she protected her children's and grandchildren's enslaved inheritance. Slavery was integral to her daily comforts and wealth, and Washington relied on the institution throughout her lifetime. This is something that has only recently begun to be noted in popular culture. For example, James Ijames's 2018 play, *The Most Spectacularly Lamentable Trial of Miz Martha Washington,* puts Washington's role as enslaver front and center.

Ijames's play opens in 1802, with Martha Washington on her deathbed. George Washington had been dead for three years, and the ailing Martha was under the care of Mount Vernon's enslaved community. In the play, the enslaved are aware that per George Washington's last will and testament, they will be freed when Martha Washington dies. They have no idea whether Martha's will includes a similar stipulation.[22] In fact, only the enslaved persons owned by the Washington estate were freed (George Washington had no legal power to free the enslaved laborers owned by the Custis estate). Scholars have established that the elderly Martha Washington freed the enslaved attached to her husband's estate for fear that they would kill her to hasten their manumission.

Ijames explores the process by which a fictionalized Martha Washington, plagued with fever dreams, decides to free the enslaved people. Yet Ijames's Martha Washington remains steadfast in her belief that she had been kind to the enslaved population of Mount Vernon, even as she struggles to accept evidence of the rampant sexual abuse of enslaved women at the hands of their male enslavers.[23] Ijames's reimagining of Martha Washington's last days asks important questions about scholars' roles in holding historical figures accountable for actions that our modern society condemns. His play also pushes back against the memory of Martha Washington as a saintly, irreproachable mother figure in order to highlight her role as an enslaver.

Fictionalized versions of historical figures, such as Ijames's Martha Washington, satisfy a human need to understand the personalities and motivations of people in the past. Unfortunately, historians rarely have the sources to provide the kinds of details that playwrights and novelists can imagine. How, then, can educators explain to students why historical figures participated in institutions we abhor today, such as enslavement? Instead of speculating on Martha Washington's behavior, psychoanalyzing, excusing, or condemning her, I ask students to consider that multiple facts were true simultaneously. Martha Washington was a devoted wife. She was a loving mother. She was also an enslaver. To illustrate this point, students in my classes examine the advertisement seeking the recapture of Martha Washington's maid Ona Judge, who claimed her freedom in 1796.[24]

Without giving the students prior information, I hand out copies of the advertisement from the *Philadelphia Gazette and Universal Daily Advertiser* seeking Judge's recapture. I teach college students, so many can read the font used in the original newspaper advertisement. It is also important for them to recognize that the advertisement for Judge's return appears on the same page as advertisements for sugar, salt, and coffee. For younger students, however, a transcription may be more effective.

> **Advertisement**
> ABSCONDED from the household of the President of the United States, ONEY JUDGE, a light mulatto girl, much freckled, with very black eyes and bushy black hair. She is of middle stature, slender, and delicately formed, about 20 years of age.
>
> She has many changes of good clothes of all sorts, but they are not sufficiently recollected to be described—As there was no suspicion of her going off nor no provocation to do so, it is not easy to conjecture whither she has gone, or fully, what her design is;—but as she may attempt to escape by water, all masters of vessels are cautioned against admitting her into them, although it is probable she will attempt to pass for a free woman, and has, it is said, wherewithal to pay her passage.
>
> Ten dollars will be paid to any person who will bring her home, if taken in the city, or on board any vessel in the harbour;—and a reasonable additional sum if apprehended at, and brought from a greater distance, and in proportion to the distance.
>
> Frederick Kitt, Steward.
>
> May 23

Students are asked to read silently for a few moments. I then open discussion by asking students what they have learned about Ona Judge from the advertisement. Many begin with her appearance.

The advertisement describes Judge as "a light mulatto girl, much freckled, with very black eyes and bushy black hair. She is of middle stature, slender, and delicately formed, about 20 years of age."[25] As a class we discuss why appearance would be so important in such an advertisement. We then move on to the line that reads, "She has many changes of good clothes of all sorts, but they are not sufficiently recollected to be described."[26] I encourage the students to interrogate what it might mean that Judge had so many changes of clothing. How did she acquire these textiles? Who sewed them? Why does the advertisement detail that she had "many" items of clothing?

The advertisement also specifies that the Washingtons offered a ten-dollar reward for Judge's return. Additional compensation could be claimed if Judge was returned from outside the local area. Students are asked what it might mean that such a large dollar amount for the time was offered. At this point I offer biographical information about Judge.

Ona Judge (sometimes called Oney) was born at Mount Vernon around 1774. Her mother, Betty, was an enslaved seamstress on the Washingtons' plantation. Her father was a White tailor employed by the Washingtons between 1772 and 1784. Ona Judge became Martha Washington's personal maid at age ten. Perhaps this had to do with her skills as a seamstress. It may have also had to do with her light skin tone. As a maid, Judge would have helped Washington bathe and dress, washed and repaired her clothing, cared for her personal belongings, and tended to anything else that Washington asked. When George Washington became president, the fifteen-year-old Judge traveled with the Washington family to the nation's temporary capital at Philadelphia. Slavery, however, was no longer fully legal in Pennsylvania. The state had passed a gradual emancipation law in 1780 specifying that any enslaved person who lived in the state for six months could sue for their freedom. As a result, the Washingtons rotated their enslaved workers every six months, including Judge. In Philadelphia, however, Judge became acquainted with the free Black community and recognized an opportunity to escape.[27]

On May 21, 1796, Ona Judge took her freedom. The Washingtons were preparing to return to Virginia for the summer, and as Judge later recalled, she knew that if she accompanied them, she would never be free. She left the Washington home while the family was eating dinner. Despite George Washington's attempts to recover Judge through advertising and a bounty hunter, she was never re-enslaved. Decades after the deaths of George and Martha Washington, Judge (now Ona Judge Staines) was asked by an interviewer if she regretted her decision. "No," she told them, "I am free, and have, I trust been made a child of God by the means."[28] Judge had spent her adult life as a free woman in poverty, but it was preferable to being enslaved by a wealthy woman.

Once the context of Ona Judge's relationship to Martha Washington has been summarized, I ask the students to read the advertisement again. Again, we begin with Judge's appearance. The point in beginning with the advertisement, and not biographical information about Judge, is to let students consider what the details within the advertisement mean on their own. Then they can consider whether these details take on a different meaning with relevant context. This lesson serves as an exercise both in how context matters and in deducing information about a person who did not leave their own written sources.

To further explore Ona Judge's story, the next part of the lesson juxtaposes the advertisement with a letter written by Martha Washington to her niece Frances Bassett Washington (Lear) on May 24, 1795. Writing exactly one year before the advertisement for Judge's capture was published, Washington noted that "the Blacks are so bad—in thair nature that they have not the least Gratatude for the kindness that may be shewed to them."[29] How might that feeling be reflected in the advertisement for Judge's return? I ask students to pull key words from the advertisement that might be interpreted as the Washingtons' viewing Judge as ungrateful. Students typically note that Judge is described as having "many changes of good clothes of all sorts" and that "there was no suspicion of her going off, nor no provocation to do so."[30]

From here we discuss historical methodology and return to intersectionality. How did two women living in the same household experience life differently? Next, as students of history, how should we interrogate these sources? Who was the intended audience of each of these sources? How might that have changed how the author composed them? How were Martha Washington's ideas about the enslaved representative (or not) of other people in the late eighteenth century? This question can be tricky, because I never want to imply that we should excuse behavior simply because it is in the past. It leads to another interesting question about how we can align popular ideas of Martha Washington—the country's symbolic founding mother—with her identity as an enslaver.

Exposing Martha Washington as an enslaver can be upsetting for some students. While they may not have thought much about her before, the idea that she was racist by our modern standards threatens the belief that our nation was based on the tenets of equality. In recent years, my students have initially wanted to condemn her. In condemning historical figures, however, we erase uncomfortable but necessary conversations. And so we begin our discussion by considering whether two things can be true at the same time. Can I love flying in an airplane but also be concerned with climate change? Is it possible that Martha Washington was a loving wife and mother and a cunning enslaver?

To help students digest the complexities of Martha Washington's identity, I introduce them to the four truths established by South Africa's 1995 Truth and Reconciliation Commission, which followed the end of apartheid. The four truths are forensic, personal, social, and restorative. The first, forensic truth, is based on factual evidence, or the who, what, where, when, and how, of a traumatic event or mass atrocity. Next, personal truth is based on the individual narratives and personal experiences of those who lived through the atrocity. In class discussions we connect personal truth to primary sources. Social truth encompasses the interactions between participants in the trauma, but for teaching I broaden it to include public or historical memory. Lastly, restorative truth refers to how society can prevent future occurrences of trauma. I explain to students that this might be creating commemorative plaques that expose truths excluded from historical narratives and textbooks, such as historical markers acknowledging sites of slave auctions. It could also be challenging historical memory, such as depictions of Martha Washington as a simple wife and mother. Many historical sites, including Mount Vernon, have modified their tours and educational materials to acknowledge the legacies of injustice in American history, particularly those related to enslavement.[31]

Just as I simplify Crenshaw's explanation of intersectionality, I use the four truths to establish definitions that students can use as a foundation to understand complex and often uncomfortable parts of history. This framework is something they can carry forward from my class and apply to other subjects or use as a structure to understand modern global issues. I do not elaborate on the context of apartheid. Instead, I explain that the commission was organized to investigate human rights violations and that the resulting findings can help historians establish an outline for accountability when analyzing difficult topics. In this way, I can contextualize figures such as Martha Washington without erasing the history of women like Ona Judge. We conclude our discussion of Martha Washington and women of the eighteenth century by discussing the concept of restorative truth. This empowers students to make modern connections between the past and present. For those students who may have complex feelings about Martha Washington, challenging them to consider how they can practice restorative truth is also empowering.

Ask someone what image comes to mind when they hear the name Martha Washington, and they are likely to describe a woman who looks a lot like Elizabeth Duane Gillespie in costume or photographs of an aging Elizabeth Cady Stanton. We can only speculate what Martha Washington might have thought of Gillespie using her image as a fundraising tool or of Elizabeth Cady Stanton being physically compared to her. Likely, the answer would be "it's complicated"—much like Washington herself. In teaching the "real" Martha Washington's life, educators must challenge romanticizing portraits of the founding mother and allow for contradictions to emerge. In doing so, a more complete story of women's lives during the eighteenth century takes shape, one in which Martha Washington represents wife and mother but also businesswoman, political wife, and enslaver.

Notes

Citations of Founders Online documents do not include individual links, as each source can be found by searching the site at https://founders.archives.gov/.

1. To view the cabinet card of Elizabeth Duane Gillespie in Martha Washington costume, see F. Gutekunst, "Elizabeth Duane Gillespie as Martha Washington," Historical Society of Pennsylvania Digital Library, https://digitallibrary.hsp.org/index.php/Detail/objects/179.
2. E. D. Gillespie, *A Book of Remembrance* (Philadelphia: J. B. Lippincott, 1901), 283–84. Historian Allison Lange argues that throughout the antebellum period, portraits of Martha Washington represented traditional forms of political womanhood. Many of these portraits were made in response to the organization of the women's rights movement. Although the Gillespie example postdates Lange's study, Elizabeth Duane Gillespie likely chose to represent Martha Washington because her image was more associated with traditional femininity, and the organization wanted to distance themselves from radical women's rights reformers. See Allison Lange, "Picturing Tradition: Images of Martha Washington in Antebellum Politics," *Imprint* 37 (Autumn 2012): 22–39.
3. Gillespie, *Book of Remembrance*, 327. There was no suffrage exhibit included in the Women's Pavilion, and suffragists protested outside.
4. Elizabeth Cady Stanton, *Eighty Years and More* (New York: T. Fisher Unwin, 1898), chap. 19, https://digital.library.upenn.edu/women/stanton/years/years.html#XIX.
5. Elizabeth Cady Stanton et al., *History of Woman Suffrage*, vol. 3 (Project Gutenberg, 2009), 28.
6. Stanton, *Eighty Years and More*, chap. 19. Although Elizabeth Cady Stanton was one of the writers of the Declaration of Rights of the Women of the United States and corresponded with event organizers about reading the document at the Centennial Celebration, she was not in attendance on July 4. The doc-

ument was read aloud by Susan B. Anthony, who walked uninvited onto the stage following the reading of the Declaration of Independence.

7. Allison K. Lange, *Picturing Political Power: Images in the Women's Suffrage Movement* (Chicago: University of Chicago Press, 2020), 78.
8. Patricia Brady, *Martha Washington: An American Life* (New York: Viking, 2005), 25–27.
9. Brady, *Martha Washington,* 32, 38, 41.
10. Kimberlé Crenshaw, "Intersectionality," The Big Idea, The Institute of Art and Ideas, November 18, 2021, https://www.youtube.com/watch?v=-BnAW4NyOak.
11. Brady, *Martha Washington,* 52.
12. Brady, *Martha Washington,* 58.
13. Lin-Manuel Miranda, "The Schuyler Sisters," from *Hamilton: An American Musical,* 2015.
14. Lange, "Picturing Tradition," 25.
15. For information on historical memory studies, see David Blight, *Race and Reunion: The Civil War in American Memory* (Cambridge, MA: Harvard University Press, 2002); Michael D. Hattem, *The Memory of '76: The Revolution in American History* (New Haven, CT: Yale University Press, 2024).
16. For information on republican motherhood, including classroom activities using primary sources, see "Republican Motherhood," Women and the American Story, New York Historical, https://wams.nyhistory.org/building-a-new-nation/navigating-the-new-government/republican-motherhood/.
17. Kate Haulman, *The Politics of Fashion in Eighteenth-Century America* (Chapel Hill: University of North Carolina Press, 2011).
18. Alexis Coe, "Why Martha Washington's Life Is So Elusive to Historians," *Smithsonian Magazine,* March 2021, https://www.smithsonianmag.com/history/martha-washington-life-elusive-historians-180976983/.
19. Abigail Adams to Mary Smith Cranch, June 28, 1789, Founders Online.
20. George Washington to Catharine Sawbridge Macaulay Graham, January 9, 1790, Founders Online.
21. Punch bowl, 1735–1757, George Washington's Mount Vernon, W-2100, https://emuseum.mountvernon.org/objects/1656/.
22. James Ijames, *The Most Spectacularly Lamentable Trial of Miz Martha Washington* (New York: Dramatists Play Service, 2018), 12.
23. Ijames, *Most Spectacularly Lamentable Trial,* 11–14, 22, 59.
24. The original newspaper source and transcription can be found at *Encyclopedia Virginia,* Virginia Humanities, https://encyclopediavirginia.org/primary-documents/advertisement-for-the-capture-of-oney-judge-philadelphia-gazette-may-24-1796/.

25. Frederick Kitt, advertisement for the capture of Oney Judge, *Philadelphia Gazette and Universal Daily Advertiser,* May 23, 1796.
26. Kitt, advertisement.
27. Jessie MacLeod, "Ona Judge," in *The Digital Encyclopedia of George Washington,* George Washington's Mount Vernon, https://www.mountvernon.org/library/digitalhistory/digital-encyclopedia/article/ona-judge.
28. MacLeod, "Ona Judge."
29. Martha Washington to Frances Bassett Washington (Lear), May 24, 1795, in *The Papers of Martha Washington,* ed. Jennifer E. Stertzer et al. (Charlottesville: University of Virginia Press, 2022), 287.
30. Kitt, advertisement.
31. Special thanks to Tramia Jackson for making me aware of the four truths and for discussing with me how the concept can be used in the classroom. The Smithsonian Institution has created a pamphlet that describes actions taken by the organization to practice restorative history. See "Restorative History [Explained]," Center for Restorative History, The National Museum of American History, https://americanhistory.si.edu/sites/default/files/Restorative History-explained_2.pdf.

PART V

SHARING GEORGE WASHINGTON AND THE FOUNDING ERA WITH VARIED AUDIENCES

"THE FATHER OF HIS COUNTRY"

George Washington and the Constitution in College Classrooms

KATE ELIZABETH BROWN

George Washington was not a lawyer. Yet most of the luminaries of the founding era were, like Alexander Hamilton (New York's premier corporate litigator), Thomas Jefferson and James Madison (elite southern-gentleman lawyers), James Wilson and John Jay (Supreme Court associate and chief justices, respectively), and Edmund Randolph (first US attorney general). Washington never received a formal education, let alone a legal education, and as a result, the lawyers tend to loom large, overshadowing Washington's primary role in the creation, ratification, and interpretation of the US Constitution. Madison earned the nickname "Father of the Constitution" (a slight to his fellow convention delegate and jurist James Wilson, to be sure). Hamilton was, as I have dubbed him, the "Father of American Law" for his contributions to the development of US federal law, but Washington received the broader, vaguer moniker of "Father of His Country."[1] To be the father of the whole country is to be at least a step removed from the particulars of the constitutional law, judging, federal administrative law, and the business of actually governing. But, in reality, Washington was essential to all of it.

Though not formally trained in law, Washington was involved throughout his life in extensive litigation surrounding the western lands he owned. Though he did not propose the vaunted Virginia Plan or give multiple lengthy speeches at the Philadelphia Convention, Washington presided over the drafting of the Constitution. Though his constitutional opinions have not been consecrated by Supreme Court case law, Washington's steady, cautious legal judgment was essential to the success of his presidency. For these reasons, in my college classrooms, I teach my students about George Washington's essential place in the development of constitutional law. Reconsidering Washington's influence on constitutional law can help K–12 teachers ground early republican history, civics, and government for their students, too.

George Washington was essential to the process of drafting and ratifying the Constitution because his political philosophy helped shape the document and because he, the indispensable man who secured American independence, approved of it.

During the Revolutionary War, General Washington developed political ideas that helped shape the new nation, particularly the push to create a stronger national government under the Constitution in 1787–1788. His views aligned with those of other nationalists, who, during the debates over ratifying the Constitution, cleverly called themselves Federalists. Washington, like Hamilton, Jay, Wilson, and Madison (before his later turn to the Jeffersonian faction), thought that the central government established under the Articles of Confederation was largely impotent. The Articles, which established a compact among the sovereign states, denied the Confederation Congress all but a handful of foreign affairs and war-making powers. Domestic national power was virtually nonexistent. Furthermore, the threshold for amending the Articles—unanimity among the states—was impossible to achieve, at least in the 1780s.

Washington did not usually put quill to paper to diagnose or suggest solutions to constitutional issues, but in this case, he did. In his 1783 Circular Letter to the States, discussed by Scott E. Casper in his essay for this volume, Washington offered the states his advice about the nation's current problems, pitfalls to avoid, and suggestions for working together successfully. But, like feuding, jealous siblings, the states just could not make it work.

Since Washington's polite lecture did not have the intended result, extra-constitutional measures were in order. While the Philadelphia Convention of 1787 was technically authorized only to amend the Articles of Confederation, the master political strategist James Madison was not going to let a prime opportunity to fix the nation's problems and power imbalances go to waste. After he and Henry Knox coaxed a reluctant Washington from retirement at Mount Vernon, convention delegates unanimously elected His Excellency, wearing his old military uniform, to serve as president of the proceedings. Washington did not participate much in the convention's debates and was undoubtedly suffering mightily while locked indoors during that stiflingly hot Philadelphia summer, but none of this mattered. What mattered was that George Washington, the only man whom the entire nation trusted, respected, and even revered, approved of the proceedings, signed his name to the document, and therefore authorized the direction the republic was taking under the Constitution. The Father of His Country approved of the nation's new framework for government.

Of course, the real fight was still to come. Although nationalists like Washington thought the Constitution was an improvement over the state-centered Articles, there was plenty of political opposition to the perceived centralizing and "consolidating" tendencies of the proposed Constitution. The political theory of the US Constitution then, and now, is this: the people are sovereign. But in the US constitutional republic, the people vest their power to govern and make law with their agents, be they their elected president, representatives, or senators. Even appointed judges act as agents of the people, protecting the people's sovereign will from legislative or executive encroachment through the power of judicial review. Of course, the Constitution also limits what these agents can do to protect the people's sovereignty. This complex system, which we often shorthand as "checks and balances," is an intricate and mostly effective way of keeping the people's agents from usurping liberty or accumulating too much power.

The people's agents operate on two main levels: in the national government and in the states. This arrangement of dividing and sometimes sharing power between the national government and the states is called federalism and it, like the Constitution itself, is a primary mechanism for protecting liberty by dividing power. Under the Articles of Confederation, the division of power weighed heavily in favor of the states; under the US Constitution, the national government received a sizeable allocation of power. The catch, however, was that national power is limited by the text of the Constitution. This enumeration of authority sometimes granted robust power (taxation, for example), sometimes limited power (see Article I, Section 9, a list of prohibitions on what Congress can do), but always was confined to the contours of the written text (even in questions about power that seemingly go beyond the text, like the Hamilton-Jefferson disagreement over the bank).

Under the US Constitution, the national government does not have limitless power and, especially in the first decades of the early republic, its authority paled in comparison to the power reserved to the states. The Constitution ditched the confederacy framework and the Articles' specific provision that the states were sovereign, but the states remained relative powerhouses. According to Alexander Hamilton, under the Constitution, "the State governments would clearly retain all the rights of sovereignty which they before had" except in certain narrowly specified circumstances.[2] In other words, but for the specific prohibitions set out for the states in Article I, Section 10, the Constitution left state power nearly untouched.

Nevertheless, a potent political opposition formed to block the ratification of the Constitution. Under its own Article VII terms, nine states had to ratify the Constitution before it took effect; the Anti-Federalists, led by revolutionary luminaries like Patrick Henry and even Convention delegates like George Mason, organized to block ratification. Those who favored ratification, the Federalists, mobilized in response.

The first five states to hold ratification conventions were heavily in favor of the Constitution, and ratification occurred quickly. Then came Massachusetts, where the vote was too close for Federalists' comfort, and things got interesting.

Although delegates to the Massachusetts ratification convention ultimately voted in favor of ratifying, they recommended that the national government amend the Constitution with a bill of rights to ensure that certain liberties remained off-limits from congressional meddling. Even though many Federalists, including leaders like Madison and Hamilton, insisted that no additional bill of rights was needed because the Constitution itself was a bill of rights, the idea of recommending changes—or even requiring amendments as a condition of ratifying—gained traction in other states.[3] Still, the biggest political fights were yet to come.

Virginia was the largest, wealthiest, most populous, and symbolically important state to the new republic, and its ratification convention teemed with Anti-Federalists. If Virginia, the home of George Washington and Thomas Jefferson, did not accept the Constitution, then the future of the constitutional union would have been seriously imperiled. Fortunately, Washington let it be known that while he urged candor and honest debate about the proposed new government, he stood firmly on the side of ratification. His brilliant lawyer allies—Alexander Hamilton, James Madison, and John Jay—simultaneously launched a side project, writing articles to assuage fears surrounding the Constitution and explain how it really worked to New Yorkers, many of whom shared Virginians' skepticism about the proposed government.

Washington did not attend Virginia's ratification convention, but his support for the Constitution was widely known. He stayed in contact with Madison, who coordinated the Federalists in the Virginia Convention and defended the Constitution in his correspondence. Washington's persuasive words may have been decisive for Virginian ratifiers; the state narrowly ratified the Constitution, by a vote of 89 to 79.

In June 1788, New Hampshire became the ninth state to ratify, and Virginia followed suit just a few days later. New York ratified, also by a very close margin, in July. Only North Carolina and Rhode Island held out as the nation's problem children, failing to ratify until late 1789 and May 1790, respectively. Like any dad patiently waiting for his kids to get in line, President Washington withheld his visit to North Carolina and Rhode Island when he made his tours of the states, unwilling to reward their obstinacy until they relented and officially joined the constitutional family.

The history narrated above has proved, for me, tricky to teach. The Philadelphia Convention and the ratification process following it is one big contingent, transitional moment; it is fun to unpack as a historian or teacher, but confusing and even boring to students who might be thinking, "Okay, get to the end result already!" This history is messy, too, with drafters and ratifiers grappling with multiple difficult issues simultaneously—and students can easily lose track of concepts and debates surrounding them. Furthermore, teaching the specific *legal* history surrounding the Constitution—for example, what the text means—can be even more challenging. In some ways, the law resembles a foreign language; it has its own precise vocabulary, and some of its methods and interpretations can seem stilted, defying common sense, or even inequitable or unjust. It can be a real problem.

I have found a way to teach this challenging constitutional history that embraces the contingency and complexity of the 1780s debates, and luckily, it does so with minimal lecturing and maximum student engagement. It is called Reacting to the Past.

Reacting to the Past is an alternate pedagogy developed out of Barnard College that I often use to teach about Washington and his world. Developed first by historian Mark Carnes and subsequently by scores of faculty from around the world, the Reacting to the Past experience is about flipping the classroom (students role-play the past), exploring historical contingency (the idea that no significant historical event was ever predestined to turn out the way it did), and playing out the past through primary source analysis, teamwork, competition, and persuasive writing and debating.[4] This is what Reacting is, formally;

informally, it is exhilarating, loads of fun, and students love it. They tell me, semester after semester, that it makes history come alive to them and that they learn so much more through Reacting than they do from my lectures. (I am not offended by this.)

As an experienced Game Master (the teacher's role—usually to facilitate certain events through the roll of the dice), I have played games about the Protestant Reformation in England, the French Revolution, the Glorious Revolution, and the Imperial Crisis/American Revolution. But the game that prominently features George Washington is called *The Constitutional Convention of 1787: Constructing the American Republic* by John Patrick Coby, and through it, students negotiate the drafting of the US Constitution.[5] The lucky student who plays Washington presides over the convention and must demonstrate leadership to stay above the partisan politics. She or he emerges from the game truly understanding the balancing act Washington faced as a leader wrangling so many partisans and producing a workable blueprint for a new republican nation. Economic issues are discussed—such as commerce and the slave trade—but most of the game is about the political questions surrounding nation building, including the extent of presidential power and the nature of representation. It's a great game and a refreshing way for students to learn about early American history (or the histories of many other places throughout the ancient, medieval, and modern worlds through other games).

Though the Reacting curriculum is aimed primarily at the college classroom, slight modifications to the games can make them accessible to high school and middle school students. In fact, I know current high school teachers (and former students of mine) who have adapted their experiences playing the *Constitutional Convention* game for their high school classroom. It is an innovative pedagogy and rewarding on many levels. The immersive role-playing experience is yet another helpful tool for integrating a complex picture of the past into your American history classroom.

Because I know that Reacting to the Past makes a lasting impression on students who engage with its immersive gameplay, I asked one former student of mine, Coe Campbell (who graduated from Western Kentucky University in 2020 with a major in history), to reflect on his experience playing *Constitutional Convention* and, most importantly, on inhabiting George Washington's role as president of the convention.

First, I asked Coe where his love for American history and George Washington came from. I then asked him about his experience as George Washington. His answers were surprising—and revealing.

> I love George Washington for many reasons, but the start of this affection goes back to his donkeys. Donkeys? Yes! I grew up on a small hobby farm here in South Central Kentucky. My family moved to this area from Virginia in the late 1700s. The first reported date of my ancestors abiding here is in 1795. I have a picture of my great grandmother in the 1930s on a large mule at the old family homestead. This picture has always been one of my favorites. This large mule is a product of a mare (female horse) and a male donkey, more specifically, an American Mammoth Jack stock (AMJS).
>
> The AMJS is an American heritage donkey breed created at the start of our nation's history. I raised AMJS for many years, and still have my first Jennet, who is approaching her twenty-first birthday. The American frontier was cultivated, logged, and traversed by the hard work of millions of mules. The AMJS is the father of the American working mule. I was fascinated by this, and devoted hours of study to the development of this breed and the origins of it. It was during this time I discovered that Charles III, the King of Spain, gifted George Washington with two large Jacks. Following this, he began breeding and letting his Jack stand at stud. Eventually Washington was also gifted large stock from Malta. The breeding program for the AMJS had begun.
>
> George Washington is great in my eyes due to his ability to envision great possibilities from common beginnings. The Jack stock is an example of this. Washington took simple, common, working colonists and rallied them to accomplish a feat that the British Empire could not defeat. He taught us that we can all shape a better future for ourselves.
>
> Being chosen as George Washington in the convention game was a task I absolutely did not feel qualified for. I was completely shocked. In this role, I presided over the convention. I heard from each faction and had to take everyone's perspectives into account. This was especially challenging due to the fact that I was a part of a faction, with rigid ideas [the Nationalists]. I had to simultaneously be true to what I felt was best but also accept the ideas of all others and attempt to work with each group to form a constitution for all. I attempted to do as Washington

> would. I remember that in my classroom game notebook, I wrote a few notes down to remind myself each gameday:
>
> 1. You are George Washington
> 2. Talk slowly and do not make faces when you disagree
> 3. Disagreement is not disrespect
> 4. We left a king, don't act like one
> 5. We aren't fighting each other; we are creating something new.
>
> These were the sentiments I tried to keep in the back of my mind while playing the game. Washington, I think, held these same ideals.
>
> The most important thing I took away from the game was that the founding fathers were not on the same page with just about anything. They all disagreed about the government's role in nearly every aspect of life (how familiar does this sound?). The *one* thing, however, that everyone agreed on, was the creation of a new and better system of government. I had a preconceived idea that every founding father agreed about everything. I assumed every patriot thought alike. How wrong I was! I learned that George Washington assumed a role I'm not sure he really wanted, but a role he knew he could fulfill.

After sharing his experience with the game, I then asked Coe what he learned about the Constitution and what we can learn from George Washington:

> As embarrassing as it is, I felt the creation of the constitution was a grand, noble meeting where everyone sat down and unanimously agreed on these sacred American tenets. That was not the case. I learned each clause in the constitution was added with much thought, debate, and conviction. It is a living and breathing document while simultaneously being stoic and unvarying. Its creation and endurance are a miracle.
>
> George Washington can teach us a few things:
>
> 1. Leaders can be created; it isn't necessarily a born talent. It often is simply unwavering devotion with uncompromising conviction
> 2. Never mistake humble beginnings for a common end. A gifted donkey sparked a revival in agriculture that changed the course of a civil war (literally, I mean that)
> 3. Just do what you are supposed to do, and what you know is right and let the consequences follow

4. It is better to work with those whom you disagree with entirely and find common ground, than to rally yourself with like-minded people and have a group of bloated idealists.

Although Coe and I played the game in class over six years ago, it is a testament to the power of the pedagogy that so much of the experience of debating great constitutional issues and channeling George Washington stuck with him. This is the reason I devote weeks in the semester to Reacting to the Past games; they really do have a pedagogical impact that is second to none.

George Washington, though not trained as a lawyer or constitutional scholar, had an essential role in the development of early constitutional law. Even so, the complexities of the Constitution and Washington's executive prerogatives might be challenging for younger students. But this does not mean that K–12 students are too young to engage with George Washington and the Constitution.

iCivics is a teaching pedagogy, like Reacting to the Past, that brings important events like the Philadelphia Convention into your classroom in an accessible, age-appropriate way. The iCivics curriculum is available for elementary, middle school, and high school learners. In the *Constitutional Compromise* iCivics game, students do not inhabit a single role, like my former student Coe did when playing George Washington, but they are still immersed in the complex problems and possible solutions with which the framers grappled. Your students' goal is to debate various topics, like the scope and nature of government, executive functions, and the transatlantic slave trade, and then draft the Constitution through compromises. They are also limited in their options by the realities of late eighteenth-century sectional and ideological politics. The curriculum plays out through online games (though there are no-technology-needed options too), lesson plans, optional Spanish-language materials, and additional resources that are all free and available through the iCivics Education website.[6] I hope you try this tool to bring George Washington and the Constitution into your classroom. And when engaging with iCivics, may your students channel the judicious wisdom of Washington as they plot the course for the new nation.

The pedagogical value of these Reacting to the Past and iCivics curricula are that they immerse students into the messy, contingent world of the late 1780s. George Washington's Mount Vernon also offers a teaching tool to immerse middle- and high-school-aged students in role-playing decision-making through its Be Washington Interactive Experience.[7] *Be Washington,* a first-person interactive game that can be played remotely or on site at Mount Vernon, puts players in the scenarios that Washington faced, such as whether he should call out troops to suppress the Whiskey Rebellion or ally with France during the "neutrality crisis" of 1793. Students consult with Washington's advisors—who offer advice based on primary source evidence—but they have only limited time to act. After the student makes a decision about how to respond to the crisis at hand, they are shown the outcome and rationale that Washington chose when he was faced with the same decision. Through these programs, students understand the issues, trade-offs, and political realities of creating and then ratifying the Constitution. But what happened next? In 1789, with the Constitution drafted and ratified, the easy part was over. Now the hard part began. Americans had to implement their constitutional republic.

It is a truism that leaders in the young American republic aimed to avoid the trappings of monarchy after declaring their independence. This is true enough when it comes to the states, where legislators wrote constitutions during the late 1770s that eschewed executive and judicial power (both of which harkened back to monarchical power) in favor of legislative dominance. But, as legal scholar Saikrishna Prakash describes, this is not so for the executive power vested in the president under Article II of the Constitution.[8]

If Americans were so opposed to monarchical power, then Article II is curious. While the short article has a few enumerated powers listed for the president to exercise, Article II avoids the laundry lists of enumerated powers that govern how Congress can operate or not (see Article I, Sections 8 and 9). Instead, Article II bestows the *entirety* of executive power, in general, in the president. It reads: "The executive Power shall be vested in a President of the United States of America." Wow. That is potentially a lot of power. As Prakash argues, the sum total of what "executive power" meant in the eighteenth century amounts to a cache of powers that intentionally formed a limited monarchy.[9] Executive power, in its eighteenth-century conception, was limited by some constitutional restraints, but it also endowed the president with a general grant of largely unenumerated power.[10] It is a good thing that the Constitution's framers, ratifiers, and the first electoral college assumed that George Washington would be the first president—otherwise, who else could Americans possibly trust to wield so much monarchical power responsibly?

These are the enormous stakes of Washington's presidency. This is why I think he is so important to constitutional law. Washington sets the precedents for executive judiciousness and restraint when he sits on a kingly cache of power that could be claimed and then used irresponsibly or even detrimentally to the new nation. While other precedents he set as president are important, too, especially for symbolic reasons—things like addressing the president as Mr. President, refusing to share executive papers with Congress (the birth of executive privilege), Washington's levees (upscale meet and greets)—these precedents did not carry massive downsides for America if Washington got them wrong. But mishandling this enormous amount of power—the entire executive power vested in Washington alone—could have produced a constitutional crisis.

Washington's most important influence over the development of constitutional law, therefore, is the cautious, judicious approach he took to exercising his executive power. Below are three examples of this cautious restraint. Two are more familiar to the standard US history curriculum, and one emerged from my research on Alexander Hamilton's legal practice. These episodes reflect how Washington, although vested with power fit for a republican king, ended up wielding it like a wise, restrained judge.

The first big constitutional question to face Washington's administration arose over the constitutionality of Hamilton's proposed central bank. It was a doozy, causing debate in Congress, dividing Washington's cabinet, and leaving Washington with a constitutional question: To veto or not to veto?

Alexander Hamilton had proposed that Congress charter a central bank, modeled after the Bank of England, to be a financial engine for the bankrupt national economy. The bank was not part of Hamilton's controversial funding and assumption plans—where he proposed to pay back Revolutionary War debt (national *and* state debts combined) at par (face) value with federal customs duties revenues. But the proposed Bank of the United States would help restore and maintain the public credit by facilitating interest payment on the debt to creditors around the nation. More importantly, a big bank with a big capitalization could make a lot of loans—and that seed capital would, in time, help kick off a market revolution. The bank was a clear economic winner.

What was not so clear was whether Congress could charter the bank, since Article I, Section 8, enumerated a list of powers that did not include the power to create a bank or charter a corporation. To the Jeffersonian faction, this was a deal-breaker. Was this not a government of enumerated powers? If the Constitution included no power to create a bank, then Congress could not charter one, Jefferson and his allies argued. Hamilton, then secretary of the treasury, disagreed with this assessment. To Secretary Hamilton, the language (including the "necessary and proper" clause) and spirit of the Constitution allowed for Congress to create the bank. Hamilton's Federalist allies managed to pass the bank bill through Congress. But when it landed on Washington's desk, ready to be signed into law, Washington hesitated.

This is why Washington's judiciousness is so important. Here we have the nation's first domestic constitutional test. As the executive wielding his prerogative veto power, Washington could have just played the role of partisan and signed it into law because the bank was Hamilton's financial policy, and it formed the bedrock of Washington's domestic agenda during his first term in office. But President Washington did not want to do the partisan thing; he wanted to do the right thing, as authorized by the Constitution. So Washington asked Secretary of State Jefferson and Secretary Hamilton to write briefs arguing their respective positions on the constitutionality of the bank.

Jefferson argued that the Constitution did not explicitly authorize the creation of a bank.[11] To rebut the more flexible constitutional language of Article I, Section 8's necessary and proper clause, however, Jefferson argued that the United States could get by without a central bank and thus it was neither necessary nor proper. (He was correct about this; banks chartered by the states could do the same tasks as a central bank, though less efficiently.) Hamilton, offering his broad interpretation of the necessary and proper clause, argued that the bank was both necessary and proper because chartering it was not prohibited by Article I, Section 9, and the bank helped facilitate the enumerated powers of Article I, Section 8 (like collecting taxes and borrowing money).[12]

I always remind my students that either constitutional interpretation—Hamilton's or Jefferson's—was equally plausible, especially because this was a case of first instance, that is, the first time the constitutional question about broad versus narrow interpretation arose. Nevertheless, the question offered a crossroads for constitutional interpretation. The Hamiltonian option would allow for broader federal government power, while the Jeffersonian alternative would constrict the federal government's power now and in the future. The decision, therefore, was momentous, and only Washington's to make.

Washington sided with Hamilton's constitutional interpretation and signed the bank bill into law. But he did so not because he fell in line with the Federalist faction's policies but because, when he considered all arguments, Washington agreed with Hamilton. The point, however, is that Washington took the time to consider, first, before he wielded his executive discretion to sign the bank bill into law. Hamilton's bank comported with Washington's constitutional vision of a national government exercising meaningful power; also, the young nation's economic problems were tough enough to warrant a bold plan like this to restore and maintain America's public credit. Washington would carry with him this considered, thoughtful approach to vetoing or sanctioning congressional policy through both terms in office.

Another discretionary power vested in the president is the power to pardon. Like the veto, this prerogative power cannot be checked by the courts, and it represents an obvious throwback to the British king's prerogatives. Characteristically, Washington approached this discretionary executive power cautiously, aiming to be sure that he granted pardons in equitable and just ways.

One case arose from a mistake made by Samuel Dodge, who, while working for the Treasury Department as a customs inspector, unloaded cargo in violation of the 1790 Collection Act. Dodge did not know of the act's provision (Congress had just recently passed the law), and so though he was indicted for violating the law, he petitioned Washington for a pardon.[13]

Dodge's situation did not just raise an issue of whether President Washington would bestow mercy on a man who simply made a mistake. There was a rights-related issue involved, too. Under the Collection Act, the informer who reported Dodge for incorrectly unloading cargo was owed half of Dodge's punitive fine. If Washington pardoned Dodge, was he then depriving the informer of his statutorily guaranteed right to the bounty?

Alexander Hamilton did the legal research to present Washington with the best constitutional arguments with which to make his decision. Hamilton asked Edmund Randolph, then the attorney general, and Richard Harison, the first US attorney for the District of New York, for their advice. They recommended that Washington could issue the pardon, but Dodge would still have to pay the half fine to the informer. Washington's pardon should not interfere with the informer's vested right to a statutory award. By carefully exploring the consequences and possible limits of his pardon power, Washington exercised the mercy inherent in the pardon power for Dodge while upholding the vested rights of the informer.

Finally, President Washington was forced to consider the constitutionality of remaining neutral in an Atlantic world riled by the French Revolution and France's subsequent declaration of war against Great Britain. No one in Washington's cabinet thought it was a good idea to enter this war and, as a statement of the administration's intention to keep the United States out of it, Washington issued the so-called Neutrality Proclamation in April 1793.[14] This was an executive decision, but a contested one. The American public clamored to help their former revolutionary allies, the French people, in their struggle against King Louis XVI, an entitled aristocracy, and the power of the Catholic clergy.

But Washington's wise proclamation in favor of staying out of war did not just arise from foreign policy considerations; it came from constitutional reasoning. Hamilton defended Washington's reasoning in a series of public essays under the pen name Pacificus, where Hamilton explained that President Washington considered himself to have a legal obligation to keep the peace since Congress, the body responsible for declaring war, had issued no such declaration. And, to fulfill that constitutional responsibility, President Washington "must necessarily possess a right of judging what is the nature of [his] obligation."[15] In other words, Washington must exercise discretion, in this case in determining whether remaining at peace violated the 1778 Franco-American Treaty of Amity and Commerce. Washington did this by issuing the proclamation. If the American people did not want to remain neutral, then they should lobby Congress to declare war. Until then, Washington was duty bound to maintain the peace.

These episodes demonstrate Washington's thoughtful consideration of the constitutionality, legality, and consequences of his use of executive power. He was judicious, conscious of the precedents he set each time he exercised that power. He could have been less careful, more eager to wield prerogative power, but Washington did not want to be king, even if the Constitution could be interpreted as creating for him and his successors a limited republican form of monarchy. Washington's judgment and consideration of constitutional law and legal rights makes him an important figure in the development of constitutional law. He not only provided the example for how to act like a president, but he also set the precedent for wielding executive power like a responsible leader rather than an imperious king. Washington's legal judgment was thus crucial for the success of his presidency and for the trajectory of the young republic.

Notes

Citations of Founders Online documents do not include individual links, as each source can be found by searching the site at https://founders.archives.gov/.

1. Kate Elizabeth Brown, *Alexander Hamilton and the Development of American Law* (Lawrence: University Press of Kansas, 2017), 1.

2. Alexander Hamilton, *The Federalist,* no. 32, January 2, 1788, Founders Online.
3. Alexander Hamilton, *The Federalist,* no. 84, May 28, 1788, Founders Online.
4. See Mark C. Carnes, *Minds on Fire: How Role-Immersion Games Transform College* (Cambridge, MA: Harvard University Press, 2014); "Reacting to the Past," Barnard College, https://reacting.barnard.edu/.
5. John Patrick Colby, *The Constitutional Convention of 1787: Constructing the American Republic* (Chapel Hill: University of North Carolina Press, 2022). For related game materials, see Reacting Consortium, https://reactingconsortium.org/games/concon1787.
6. iCivics Education, *Constitutional Compromise* and *Race to Ratify,* https://ed.icivics.org/constitutionalcompromise and https://ed.icivics.org/node/2599424/resource.
7. See the Be Washington Interactive Experience, George Washington's Mount Vernon, https://www.bewashington.org/.
8. Saikrishna Bangalore Prakash, *Imperial from the Beginning: The Constitution of the Original Executive* (New Haven, CT: Yale University Press, 2015), 27.
9. Prakash, *Imperial from the Beginning,* 3–5, 13.
10. Prakash's catalog of typical eighteenth-century meanings of executive power is described in *Imperial from the Beginning,* 28–30.
11. Thomas Jefferson, "Opinion on the Constitutionality of the Bill for Establishing a National Bank," February 15, 1791, Founders Online.
12. Alexander Hamilton, "Final Version of an Opinion on the Constitutionality of an Act to Establish a Bank," February 23, 1791, Founders Online.
13. For details of the legal questions surrounding Dodge's pardon petition, see Brown, *Alexander Hamilton,* 29–31.
14. Neutrality Proclamation, April 22, 1793, George Washington's Mount Vernon, https://www.mountvernon.org/library/digitalhistory/digital-encyclopedia/article/neutrality-proclamation.
15. Alexander Hamilton, "Pacificus No. 1," June 29, 1793, Founders Online.

BRINGING THE EIGHTEENTH CENTURY TO LIFE FOR ELEMENTARY SCHOOL LEARNERS AND READERS

SHAWNEL PADILLA

My experience with the George Washington Teacher Institute (GWTI) began in 2018. I attended as a fifth-grade teacher from a Title I school. I knew I wanted to deepen my understanding of George Washington after spending the year teaching students about colonial America and the Constitution, and so I applied to the "George Washington and the Great Experiment" session. My goals were to expand my knowledge about Washington's world and to learn techniques for bringing Washington into my classroom. Greatly influenced by the demographics of my class, which was largely made up of English language learners (ELL), I realized that I was likely providing their first exposure to American history and civics education. Now I am my school's librarian, and I collaborate with educators in our elementary school by teaching library lessons that focus on George Washington at war, the Constitution, and developmentally appropriate aspects of Washington's personal life. As a librarian, I curate books about George Washington, teach students how to access and evaluate websites, locate digital resources, and co-teach lessons on Washington to all grade levels.

Why focus on George Washington? For starters, he is a recognizable historical figure to many American schoolchildren. We can scaffold our teaching about early America on his presidency, military career, slave ownership, and farm management as students progress through school. If we want students to develop higher-level thinking skills in middle and high school, we need to first familiarize them with historical events and people in elementary school. Exposure is important as we plant the seeds of historical knowledge and engage students in developing those ideas over time. I want students to strengthen their social studies knowledge and to ultimately emerge from high school as civic-minded adults. Studying Washington's life and his contributions to American history can also strengthen a student's understanding of modern-day politics and current events.

During a discussion about the three branches of government, a student raised his hand and explained that his mom was studying for the US citizenship test, so he was familiar with some of the civics vocabulary I used in class. He was able to make a connection from what we were learning in school to his home life, and that had a significant impact on me as a teacher. It was a light-bulb moment for me when I realized I had helped a student move beyond memorizing facts and find real-world linkages to the school curriculum. This moment of growth in my student's life was also a moment of growth for me as an educator. It was then that I decided to expand my knowledge of history to increase student learning. What began as a routine professional development opportunity—spending a week at the GWTI—turned into an eye-opening journey emphasizing the importance of integrating social studies into other academic areas at the elementary level. Elementary education is the foundation of social studies instruction.

Social studies skills and awareness should be elevated to the level of importance usually bestowed on reading, writing, and arithmetic. Being an elementary librarian and former classroom teacher has afforded me the opportunity to collaborate with teachers to integrate social studies into other areas of instruction, to ensure that students learn civics and social studies, even if through their math lessons. The pressure on today's elementary teachers to stick to the core lessons of English language arts and math leaves little time for the other disciplines, such as social studies, science, or social and emotional learning (SEL). Teachers are often given little support in teaching social studies to elementary school children. It is usually relegated to one day a week and taught in isolation, but we could make a bigger impact by integrating social studies into other academic areas. Elementary schools are the foundation of civics education, and students benefit when exposed at an early age to historical figures and events. We need to get our students excited about history, and one way to do this is by teaching them about figures such as George Washington.

A study published by education scholars Adam Tyner and Sarah Kabourek highlighted the benefits of social studies instruction on reading scores. Their results found that girls and students from lower-income households increased reading growth scores in the first through fifth grades with increased social studies instruction in the classroom. Their study also reported that students from lower economic backgrounds received less instructional time in social studies than those from upper economic backgrounds. Tyner and Kabourek concluded, "On average, students who receive an additional thirty minutes of social studies instruction per day (roughly equivalent to moving from the tenth to the ninetieth percentile of social studies instructional time) in grades 1–5 outperform students with less social studies time by 15 percent of a standard deviation on the fifth-grade reading assessment, even after controlling for multiple measures of kindergarten reading ability and a host of student, school, and teacher factors."[1]

Studies such as these underscore the importance of integrating social studies into the elementary curriculum to benefit all students, but this approach is especially important at our lower-income schools. This is what prompted me to change how I teach social studies and to find ways to incorporate it into the classroom and library settings.

Social studies is one of my favorite subjects to teach, as it encompasses so many programs within the education field. Lessons can easily be combined with the core subjects tested the most: reading, writing, and mathematics. When I was in high school, I often thought of social studies as just history class. But as a teacher, I came to realize that the study of past and present civilizations expands students' critical thinking ability. Our duty as teachers is to develop the idea of civic duty by incorporating the arts, history, civics, religion, economics, and more into the lives of our students. Today's students are more globally integrated, and so it is more important than ever for them to be critical thinkers.

History is complex and can be difficult to teach and explain at the elementary level, but primary sources such as paintings and photographs of objects are especially useful and engaging in the earlier grades. Luckily, there is no shortage of accessible, digitized resources about George Washington's life and the world of early America. For example, I often use Mount Vernon's Archaeology Online and Museum Collections websites to create virtual gallery walks and bring the eighteenth century into the classroom.[2] I "hook" students by displaying images of artifacts such as a marble, a piece of clothing, a chamber pot, or a sword to pique their interest about the lives of the people of the eighteenth century. It's a starting point for conversations about the people who once called Mount Vernon home.

From there we investigate additional sources to further explore eighteenth-century lives. There are many useful images on the Mount Vernon Education Collection of Secondary Sources and the Library of Congress Digital Collection. The gallery walks spark curiosity, engagement, and higher-level thinking skills as students evaluate images of individuals who were important during the eighteenth century but may not be known to them, especially at the elementary level. Even young students can answer questions about what they see and want to know more about. Gallery walks of paintings are useful for helping young students explore the roles that enslaved individuals, women, Indigenous peoples, and children played during the eighteenth century. Images can familiarize students with a foundational group of important people in history beyond the elite.

Popular images of George Washington, such as in *Washington Crossing the Delaware* by Emanuel Leutze (1851) or *Signing of the Constitution of the United States* by Howard Chandler Christy (1940), often highlight elite men from the past, but we cannot forget to introduce students to other figures in history who also made substantial impacts. It can be difficult for young students to comprehend historical time, but I can use digital images of artifacts to help students make connections to the eighteenth century. Exploring images from the websites, paired with corresponding literature, usually leads to an increase in book checkouts about this time in history (usually biographies or books about weapons and war), which is the goal of any librarian. Additionally, knowing that I have visited George Washington's estate brings a sense of realism and inquisitiveness to the lessons. I share personal photographs that I took during my time at Mount Vernon, because students are excited to know that I have visited historical places and stood in the same spot as famous historical figures. I also try to follow each of these lessons with a read-aloud to tie all of the academic areas together.

A read-aloud is another engaging way to start a classroom discussion about Washington. I use picture books at all elementary grade levels, because having a visual image available to students deepens their understanding of the civics or social studies content featured in the day's lesson. Last year I read *I Am George Washington* by Brad Meltzer (2016), which tells the story of George Washington through his presidency and includes historical facts at the end. After reading this book to a group of students for Constitution Day, a second grader at our school checked out every book we have about George Washington, including biographies. Planting the seed of knowledge with a good book helps build a love of learning. A read-aloud is also an effective way to pique students' interest in history and develop critical thinking skills at all grade levels.

In addition to using pictures for a gallery walk, or a slideshow with an interactive presentation tool, I also use digital resources from Mount Vernon's interactive website to bring George Washington into my classroom. Mount Vernon's website offers a collection of visual primary sources that are searchable and valuable for students at all elementary grade levels. Given our geographic location in Alaska, the digital resources from Mount Vernon might be the closest my students ever get to the East Coast. In fact, when I was first accepted to the GWTI, I took my students on a virtual tour of the Mount Vernon mansion. They were not only excited for me to visit in person but also eager to explore the website—which enabled them to learn about Washington's life for themselves. Mount Vernon's virtual tours are interactive, which allows students to fully immerse themselves in the past and experience places that might not be possible for them to visit in person. As the school librarian, I use technology integration, exploration, and evaluation to prepare elementary students to better navigate technological resources in high school as they tackle more complicated historical subjects.

Many contributions by Indigenous or Native Americans in the eighteenth century are overlooked or misunderstood. Elementary school educators can help address this problem for rising generations through age-appropriate discussions combined with rich literature, images, and artifacts. In particular, elementary school students need to know that not every Native American held the same perspective about the Revolutionary War. For example, Native American nations supported different sides in the conflict. I want my students to understand this diversity of perspectives.

I introduce leaders such as Joseph Brant, or Thayendanegea, who was a Mohawk warrior, tribal leader, and diplomat, to highlight the complex relationships between Native nations, Great Britain, and the United States.[3] At the elementary level, I do not dive into too many details, but I know it is important to preview them. As students progress through school, teachers will continue to add those details back in, gradually inserting historical nuance into their lessons. The elementary level is a good time to introduce this history and the overall concept of different perspectives of people associated with George Washington.

Focusing on spies active during the Revolutionary War is another great way to engage students in literature and science. I read the books *Nathan Hale, America's First Spy* by Aaron Derr (2018), *A Spy Called James: The True Story of James Lafayette During the Revolutionary War* by Anne Rockwell (2016), and *Redcoats and Petticoats* by Katherine Kirkpatrick (1999) to my fifth graders. After reading and discussing these books about Revolutionary War spies, I have students look at pages from the Culper Code Book used by General Washington and his ring of Culper spies to decode secret communications.[4] After putting these sources together, I ask my students guiding questions about why George Washington needed spies—and secret codes! Students then share their answers in small groups, followed by my lesson on how to make invisible ink. Together we create messages for classmates to decipher. By incorporating STEM (science, technology, engineering, and mathematics) elements into the classroom—making invisible ink—I am making connections between historical activities from the eighteenth century with science. I am also providing a hands-on, curiosity-sparking activity that will hopefully conjure a love of history in students. STEM activities connecting history and science can open doors to students wanting to explore different careers.

SEL lessons with a focus on friendship are common at the elementary level. Integrating an SEL lesson with history makes it more relevant to student learning. For example, an image of George Washington's lock of hair can initiate a conversation about friendship. George and Martha Washington were both known to send locks of hair to close family members and friends, sometimes as a sign of mutual affection. George Washington wrote to Catharine "Kitty" Livingston, the daughter of New Jersey's governor, while at Valley Forge after she requested a lock of hair from him. He enclosed his lock of hair, as a token of friendship, in the letter to Livingston.[5] Students can easily evaluate these primary sources, and the letter makes an explicit connection between friendship and the realities of war. Additionally, incorporating a primary source into the classroom, like a letter written by Washington, brings the great general to life while making him seem more human to students. And showing a picture of a lock of hair, an artifact perserved at Mount Vernon, kindles interest in the past, which is our goal when teaching history.[6]

Animals offer another engaging way to generate excitement in children. George Washington was known to have a large collection of farm animals and hunting dogs at Mount Vernon. We can bring Washington to life by discussing his beloved dogs with our students.[7] After introducing Washington's pets to the students, I then discuss presidential pets throughout history. These personal stories about families or pets stick with young students and humanize historical figures.

As the school librarian, I work with classroom teachers and specialists in music and art to integrate social studies into my lessons at all grade levels. Collaboration creates meaningful, active, and integrated social studies instruction, especially at the elementary level. Using an image of a young drummer boy sparks conversations about what students see, think, or wonder.[8] This is one way I integrate images with other academic areas, such as music and art. The Mount Vernon website also has a music archive that I use when discussing the Revolutionary War and teach about the fifers and drummers.[9] Students are amazed to learn that drummers were often young boys following their fathers into war. Some students make a personal connection during this lesson, because they might have a family member in the military or one who plays an instrument. We then watch and listen to videos showing how drums were used as military symbols. Asking guided questions about music during the Revolutionary War compared to modern times helps students understand the necessity of and importance of communication during times of war, no matter the century.

Many of the resources and methodologies I use to teach about George Washington are also what I use to teach Alaska geography and history. When teaching local history, I use a combination of resources, such as historical photographs, videos, art, and soundscapes, to foster inquiry and to model critical thinking skills. These resources include Alaskan Native art and photographs from people in history and the present, as they offer an authentic engagement opportunity for students to understand the historic conflict over natural resources waged between Alaska's Native peoples and European explorers.

These source-based activities help students develop a deeper understanding of Alaska's Native culture and historical events, and they can then apply those critical thinking skills in other areas of their lives as well. One such lesson I used to teach was about the relocation of the Unangax̂ or Aleut people from the Aleutian Islands to southeast Alaska during World War II. By the end of the school year, students would have examined maps and photographs and read testimony from survivors to better understand the hardships and experiences of the people who were ultimately forced to leave their homeland. I relate this bit of local Alaskan history to George Washington in wartime, as students can examine the relevant maps and correspondence surrounding the military expeditions of their respective times. Finally, studying military conflict and leadership throughout history allows students to examine current events through a critical lens.

By studying George Washington at war and as a politician, enslaver, farmer, and member of society, I teach my students that in order to understand our modern government, we need to understand our past. If we introduce students to historical figures such as George Washington and the foundation of civics educations in elementary school through interdisciplinary learning, they will be better prepared to tackle more complex subjects in high school and beyond. It is a privilege to be an educator to these students and a privilege to share with them in-depth knowledge of presidents such as George Washington.

Notes

Citations of Founders Online documents do not include individual links, as each source can be found by searching the site at https://founders.archives.gov/.

1. Adam Tyner and Sarah Kabourek, *Social Studies Instruction and Reading Comprehension: Evidence from the Early Childhood Longitudinal Study* (Washington, DC: Thomas B. Fordham Institute, 2000), 5.
2. "Archaeology Online," George Washington's Mount Vernon, https://www.mountvernon.org/preservation/archaeology/archaeology-online.
3. "Native Americans," George Washington's Mount Vernon, https://www.mountvernon.org/george-washington/native-americans.
4. "Culper Code Book," George Washington's Mount Vernon, https://www.mountvernon.org/education/primary-source-collections/primary-source-collections/article/culper-code-book.
5. George Washington to Catharine Wilhelmina Livingston, March 18, 1778, Founders Online.
6. "Hair as Historic Artifact," George Washington's Mount Vernon, https://www.mountvernon.org/blog/2019/02/hair-as-historic-artifact.
7. "Soldier, Statesman, Dog Lover: George Washington's Pups," George Washington's Mount Vernon, https://www.mountvernon.org/george-washington/facts/soldier-statesman-dog-lover-george-washingtons-pups.
8. See Edward Percy Moran, *The Hour of Victory*, ca. 1914, George Washington's Mount Vernon, M-4535, https://emuseum.mountvernon.org/objects/1784.
9. "Music in the Revolutionary War," George Washington's Mount Vernon, https://www.mountvernon.org/george-washington/the-revolutionary-war/music.

AUDIENCES AND OPPORTUNITIES

Teaching George Washington to the American Public

LINDSAY M. CHERVINSKY

I spend much of my time teaching adults, from graduate students to teachers to lifelong learners. I meet them through podcasts, opinion editorials, books, articles, radio interviews, television appearances, seminars, class visits, and invited talks. Most audience members, listeners, or readers have firmly held convictions about the United States and its history. Their preexisting ideas about George Washington offer an opportunity for teachers to embrace.

Engaging with public audiences rarely counts as teaching, at least in our conventional use of the word. These events are called lectures or speaking engagements—or simply labeled as entertainment. But the goal of discussing history with the public is always for the audience to leave with a better understanding of the past, just as it would be in a traditional classroom setting. Adult audiences make up the majority of the population, and interactions with adults constitute a huge portion of teaching opportunities.

Adult audiences present unique challenges and possibilities for the history or civics teacher. Attendees usually self-select, meaning that they bring a general interest in history to this public classroom. They often, though not always, have a base of historical knowledge informing the way they absorb a public talk, and adult audiences can usually sit contemplatively and patiently during a talk and ask thoughtful, critical questions afterward.

On the other hand, their perspectives can also be calcified. Public audiences do not always bring open minds to a discussion. Their views on history might be colored by their life experiences, politics, cultural trends, or previous education. In my experience, George Washington offers a rare opportunity to reach most audiences and engage in meaningful conversation. Most people have a basic knowledge of Washington, which can serve as a foundation for further exploration. And because his life overlapped with so many aspects of early American history, he can introduce audiences to a wide range of new subjects.

As a public historian and now the executive director of the George Washington Presidential Library at Mount Vernon, I consider Washington to be the indispensable man of the American Revolution and early republic. Washington and his contemporaries knew that as long as the Continental Army survived, so too would the cause of independence—and the Continental Army would survive as long as Washington was in command and avoided capture. Members of Congress understood that the troops were loyal to Washington first and foremost. In more candid moments, congressmen referred to the army as "Washington's army." After the nation won independence, Washington was again essential to the formation of a new federal government. His presence ensured that the Philadelphia Convention was a success, and the states would not have ratified the draft Constitution without his support. No other person could have served as the first president of the United States. He was the only man with the national stature, widespread respect, and trust of the American people to hold the powerful office. Finally, he willingly relinquished power twice, rejecting a monarchy.

Washington was also very much a man of his time. He held people in bondage and benefited from their forced labor. He separated families and ordered corporal punishment. He pursued the enslaved people who ran away and expressed disbelief that they had reason to do so. His ideas about gender, race, and equality feel foreign to us. And yet, as a product of his time, he also changed as he traveled, acquired new experience and expertise, and met diverse people. Washington's perspective on slavery began to shift during the Revolutionary War after he witnessed the heroic military service of Black soldiers and discussed slavery with abolitionists, including the Marquis de Lafayette. Situating Washington in the eighteenth century does not excuse his actions but does provide important context for his ideas and their evolution.

I have spent the last decade talking about Washington's contributions to the founding of the nation. My scholarship explores his command of the Continental Army, his leadership at the Philadelphia Convention, and his presidency. I discuss his essentialness—his unique stature, the importance of his presence at several key moments during the nation's founding, and his willingness to serve his country. I include his shortcomings or failures, but I am straightforward about my respect for his role and sacrifice.

By starting with Washington's contributions, I establish a foundation of trust. The audience understands that I am not trying to discredit their beloved founders. This trust is especially important in an age when the loudest and most radical voices receive the lion's share of attention. There are historians arguing in public that we should not talk about the founders because they have received enough attention over the last two centuries. Partisan actors have seized on that all-or-nothing approach to characterize all historians as radicals. That image undermines the rest of us trying to offer a nuanced approach.

After I finish my prepared remarks, I always leave time for audience questions. Attendees usually ask about the role of Vice President John Adams in Washington's cabinet, the public response to the cabinet, how Washington navigated the conflict between Secretary of State Thomas Jefferson and Secretary of the Treasury Alexander Hamilton, and why Washington retired after two terms. Public audiences generally seek a better understanding of the origins of our political institutions and how they evolved over two centuries. When you think of those often silver-haired people who make up the majority of public history audiences, these are the questions you might expect. You might not expect what comes next.

Audience members also inevitably ask about slavery, women, Native Americans, race, labor, inequality, and the limits of citizenship. They ask how they should grapple with slavery and Washington's role as the first president and "Father of His Country." They ask about his flaws, his temper, his treatment of enslaved individuals, what he thought of women, whether he was a loyal friend, and more. More often than not, these questions come early in our conversation.

Sometimes audiences want to know more about a specific person or how slavery worked at Mount Vernon. Sometimes they want to confirm a fact or story that they have already heard and whether it is a "good" or "bad" fact. At other times, they are checking to see if I will acknowledge less flattering aspects of Washington's life.

Almost always, these questions come from a place of deep unease with the complicated nature of American history. People who ask such questions are not rejecting the darker aspects of history. Instead, they are trying to acquire new knowledge while not abandoning everything they thought they knew. They want to know how to make sense of the good and the bad in one person, especially a historic person as beloved and revered as George Washington. They want to know if they can condemn slavery and still respect Washington's contributions to American lore—both the reality and the myths. They want to know how to balance contradictory aspects of his life.

I think that these conundrums represent a positive development for Americans and their history. They demonstrate that our society is grappling with the difficulties of our shared past. We are not sweeping our worst moments under the rug, and we are trying to develop our ideas about who counts as a citizen and who deserves space in the history books. It can be uncomfortable in the messy middle, but progress always is. I encourage these questions because I want readers, students, and audience members to consider these complex issues.

The same politicization emerges around the efforts to preserve the papers and estate of George Washington. Occasionally, these documentary-editing and preservation projects get pushback for glorifying Washington or spending precious resources on historic figures who have always been studied. These critics argue that the same level of attention or financial investment should be redistributed to cover forgotten or more obscure historic actors.

While it is true that women, the lower classes, and people of color have received less historical analysis than elite White men, in Washington's case, the attention and care to his papers and estate makes more expansive history possible. In the last several decades, archaeologists and historians of all stripes have made incredible archaeological discoveries and archival finds at the homes of founders and in their paper projects, including George Washington's Mount Vernon. These discoveries flesh out the lives of women, laborers, enslaved communities, and Native Americans. Many of those communities left few extant written or archaeological records of their own. Some of their members were illiterate; others did not have descendants who could ensure the survival of their records. Poorer neighborhoods often experienced higher turnover and development, destroying any remaining archaeological evidence of residents' existence.

Because generations of Americans have celebrated (and sometimes worshipped) Washington, they went to extreme lengths to save his papers and his home. Those efforts can yield surprisingly diverse perspectives. For example, in the spring of 2024, the archaeological team at Mount Vernon discovered thirty-five glass bottles containing preserved cherries and other berries. In the Washington papers, Martha Washington mentioned a recipe for preservation perfected by Doll, an enslaved chef.[1] While we do not have Doll's words describing her work process, the bottles, their contents, and the recipes reveal much about her daily life and expertise. The fruit was carefully snipped from the tree, meticulously cleaned, and bottled with such precision that the contents survived nearly 250 years later. Doll either completed this work herself or supervised the labor of other enslaved women or children. Martha's letter reveals a grudging respect for Doll's knowledge about cooking and food preservation, borne out by the product. Archaeological discoveries and paper projects make this knowledge possible. While our preservation and editorial efforts are more inclusive today, we can still be grateful that Washington's lofty place in American memory makes contemporary cutting-edge scholarship possible.

The lesson, therefore, is that teaching Washington's contributions or preserving his physical legacy does not obscure slavery, women, or working-class people. Rather, such efforts offer an opportunity to engage broader audiences on these important subjects. By establishing trust, we encourage our audiences to ask difficult questions and accept our answers.

There is no perfect answer to the tough questions Americans ask about George Washington and the nation's history. My approach is to embrace the full Washington story, highlighting the good while never denying the bad. When addressing the anxieties, unease, and hostility that audiences may have about Washington as an enslaver, I usually give a brief overview of the enslaved community at Mount Vernon and acknowledge that Washington knew slavery was wrong. I list some of Washington's more pernicious actions, including topics discussed by other contributors in this collection—such as sending the enslaved workers at the President's House in Philadelphia to Mount Vernon every six months to prevent their automatic emancipation under Pennsylvania law or his attempts to capture Ona Judge and return her to slavery. There is no doubt he benefited from enslaved labor, both economically and as an enhancement to his and his family's quality of life.

I also explain how Washington's will freed the enslaved people under his legal control upon the death of Martha Washington. This act was extraordinary for its rarity in the early republic. Yet Washington could have done more. He could have taken a stronger stand against slavery in his annual addresses to Congress or his Farewell Address. Even a few remarks in a letter that he permitted his friends to share publicly would have exerted an impact. In 1786, John Dickinson drafted abolition legislation for his home state of Delaware. The next year, he objected to the slave trade in the Philadelphia Convention. Dickinson's motion led to the clause in Article I, Section 9 of the Constitution that empowered Congress to prohibit the importation of enslaved peoples after 1808. Washington's words, either in the Philadelphia Convention or as president, would have carried enormous weight because of his stature.

Washington's failure to completely grapple with the moral problems posed by slavery was as true a part of his life and legacy as his prestige and his essentialness, that part of his life in which he sometimes single-handedly held the Continental Army together, gave up power twice, forged the presidency, and served as the indispensable man during the American Revolution and the early republic.

How then do we reconcile these competing legacies? The key is to accept that we must hold two complicated thoughts in our heads at once. Human beings are not an Excel spreadsheet that can be balanced or reconciled at the end of their lives. They do good things; they contribute to and cause harm. We cannot ignore either. We must tell their full story.

Audiences have proven to be incredibly receptive to this message. I have enjoyed thoughtful conversations with audiences across varied demographics, including groups of people we might not always expect to be open-minded. They don't leave, they buy my books, they sign up for my newsletter, and they attend additional events—even after hearing complex history that sometimes contradicts what they were taught in high school.

This nuanced approach to teaching supplements the valiant work done by teachers to bring complex history into the classroom. These strategies allow us to reach adults who need to hear about our past in all its messy complexity. Maybe they worry that historians are trying to censure their favorite historic figures or tear down remaining statues honoring what they perceive to be America's glorious past. Maybe they are wary that addressing American history by honestly grappling with race and slavery is inherently "woke." Maybe they fear that historians will tell them they cannot be proud to be an American or proud of the country's history. Often, they enter these conversations with predisposed ideas about a historian's agenda.

We should not write off this portion of the population. Of course there is a small segment that cannot be reached, but the great majority of people I speak to are open to my message because of how I deliver it. That doesn't mean we can't share facts or the full story. But maybe it is worth packaging that story in a way that has a better chance of being received, including Washington's contributions *and* his shortcomings—and how they often intersected. The goal should not be to make people mad or to make them feel guilty. Criticizing any audience never works well for persuasion purposes. They shut down and stop listening to what you have to say.

You might perceive my approach as asking for a concession to a "balanced" version of the past when some things—like slavery—are inexcusable. For some teachers or speakers, it will be. If they are able to launch straight into the hard history and be well-received by their audience, I applaud them. For other, more intransigent audiences, I think this small compromise is worth it if it leads to a meaningful conversation. I would rather get three-quarters of what I want than have the door shut in my face. My approach will not work for everyone, but there are three guidelines that might help other historians and educators develop their own authentic style.

Tone matters. What we say is just as important as how we say it, especially when the audience is voluntary. Adults are not forced to listen to podcasts, attend events, or buy tickets at museums. And yet historians, speakers, and public history sites depend on these revenue dollars and audience bums in seats. We must balance teaching with encouraging them to come back.

Accordingly, no one likes to be scolded. Unless they are in church, most people do not want to listen to a sermon. It doesn't matter if you are in kindergarten or one hundred years old. Nor do most adults like it when a teacher, guide, or speaker overdoes the dramatics. American history is action-packed enough to stand on its own.

Language matters. Nothing turns off public audiences faster than a bunch of jargon or language that grates on the ear or makes an audience member feel like an outsider, or worse, stupid. That does not mean we should use hurtful language. Consider two separate examples to explain the difference: "enslaved" versus "labor camp." I think we should always use "enslaved" to describe a historical worker, person, or community instead of "slave." "Slave" belittles the humanity of the people held in bondage. It erases their humanity. It causes harm.

On the other hand, is "labor camp" that much of an improvement over "plantation"? It might be the current trend in some circles, but I am not sure it is always more accurate. Furthermore, "plantation" does not erase humanity any more than "labor camp" does. In most cases, public audiences will snag on this description and spend the next few minutes wondering about or debating your word choice. In those moments, people missed the important information you shared. Worse, you might have alienated them such that they will resist your argument.

Of course, we should update our language when appropriate and thoughtful consideration dictates it; deference should be paid to the preferences expressed by experts and descendant communities. But if there is disagreement or a lack of consensus, we should also factor in how these words are received and whether they undermine the ultimate goal of sharing complex history.

Sharing history as a sandwich. Editors are taught to give a "compliment sandwich" when providing feedback on written work. You start and end with something positive so that the constructive feedback in the middle is received and heard. History cannot be taught as a compliment sandwich, because our goal should not be to compliment or criticize. But we can take a valuable lesson from this approach.

If we want audiences to hear the hard parts, don't start there. Start with parts of the story they might already know. For example, with Washington, it is helpful to start with his war service or the presidency. It welcomes the audience into the conversation, gives them confidence by confirming that they are not starting from scratch with their historical knowledge, and provides a solid foundation for further exploration. Then proceed to share the meat of your argument, whether it is a new approach, a controversial position, or information that challenges previously conceived ideas about cherished figures. The meat should include the hard history, or at least a mention of it, with an invitation for further discussion. Finally, conclude with an analysis that encourages audience members to retain both parts of your presentation. The new information should not erase the old but rather be held together as two pieces of the same story. This approach works for many touchy topics, not just those that apply to George Washington. It can be applied to other members of the founding generation, the Constitution, or any subject that has traditionally been swathed in a gauzy haze of reverence.

Teaching good history, and reaching a broad public, has never been more important. The founding era has become a tool in political battles, used to boost partisan arguments or tear down opponents. Increased awareness of the importance of history is to be celebrated, but its politicization can have dangerous outcomes. It is essential that Washington is neither ceded to conservative voices nor abandoned by leftists. Instead, his history can be used to open doors, start conversations, and include as many Americans as possible in a better understanding of our history.

Capturing this complexity can be a challenge when speaking in sound bites as a talking head. Most of my television appearances are five minutes. Canadian or British channels will give me seven or eight minutes. Radio interviews are ten minutes. If I'm lucky, a longer-form podcast will give me twenty to forty-five minutes. Sometimes I know the questions in advance, but more often I have a few bullet points detailing the topics, and the phrasing of the questions is a surprise. The host can also throw a curveball and ask me a question about a completely different subject. I can't ramble and I can't provide a ton of context and nuance for every subject. I can't always answer follow-up questions, and I rarely say everything on my mind.

But someone is going to answer those questions. Producers of all forms of news need someone to provide historical context, even if it is not the ideal forum. I would rather do my best to answer the question, help people understand where we have been, explain similar moments in the past, and highlight what is genuinely unprecedented about this moment than give up and cede that ground to those who speak in platitudes or present a uniformly dark or overly optimistic perspective. Anything I can do to meet people where they are and embrace history as an important part of understanding our current moment is worth doing, at least in my view.

This approach also informs my leadership of the George Washington Presidential Library. The Library shares a mission with the broader Mount Vernon community: to preserve and share the history of George Washington and his world. More specifically, we offer resources to researchers, support and facilitate cutting-edge scholarship, provide leadership workshops based on historical examples, and produce resources that encourage lifelong learning. We also have an incredible opportunity to explore Washington's presidential and constitutional legacy. We are the only presidential library not claimed by a political party, and we focus on the only president who established precedents for every other person to hold that office.

As the Washington Library moves into its second decade, my goal is for the institution to serve as a forum to discuss the big questions facing our nation based on George Washington's leadership example. We are the only presidential library or center in the Washington, DC, metropolitan area and can welcome global audiences from the policy, journalism, law, government, history, and education fields. Convening these groups follows Washington's model, as he welcomed difficult conversations and intentionally surrounded himself with different perspectives. Some things he got very right, like the peaceful transfer of power. In other moments, Washington struggled to align his principles with his actions. For example, through most of his career, he was adamant about the importance of civil control of the military. At the very end of his life, however, President Adams asked Washington to resume duty as head of the army. During this short tenure as commander in chief of the New Army, Washington undermined Adams's authority and came very close to destroying the civilian command he had worked so hard to create. If Washington struggled with civil-military relations, it is no wonder we still do today. The George Washington Presidential Library is not only a forum for public programming but also an opportunity to include teachers, researchers, students, and the public audience in this work. I hope you will join us.

Note

1. For the 2024 discovery, see "35 18th-Century Glass Bottles Discovered," George Washington's Mount Vernon, https://www.mountvernon.org/preservation/restoration-projects/mansion-revitalization-project/an-in-depth-look/sealed-18th-century-bottles-discovered. For the eighteenth-century discussion, see Martha Washington to Fanny Bassett Washington, May 24, 1795, George Washington's Mount Vernon, https://www.mountvernon.org/education/primary-source-collections/primary-source-collections/article/letter-martha-washington-to-fanny-bassett-washington-may-24-1795.

"WE ARE OUR HISTORY"

How Self-Reflection on Identities Informs Teaching

ERIC LOUÉRS-PHILLIPS

Educators do not enter the profession as blank slates. They carry with them experiences, histories, and identities that shape how they interpret the world and, by extension, how they engage with the curriculum they are handed and asked to teach. Instructional leaders and teachers, as agents of the state, are often tasked with implementing standards and delivering content that reflects dominant historical narratives. Yet their decisions about what to emphasize, how to frame complexity, and when to invite critique are intrinsically informed by who they are.

While state or district curricula may dictate common content, the lens through which teachers approach this material is uniquely shaped by their cultural backgrounds, lived experiences, and personal values. This perspective becomes especially significant when educators encounter historical content that raises ethical tensions, competing narratives, or political sensitivities. In such moments, teachers must navigate not only what is sanctioned by the state, and in turn their district, in some cases, but also what feels developmentally appropriate, just, and truthful for students.

As educational scholar Michael W. Apple explains, "Teachers are part of the ideological apparatus of the state, but they are also individuals who can resist, challenge, and reinterpret the curriculum in ways that reflect their own experiences, values, and commitments."[1] While teachers work within systems that reflect dominant power structures, they are not passive implementers of state mandates. Their decisions on what and how they teach reflect complex negotiations between identity, policy, and purpose. Recognizing this complexity is especially vital when engaging with foundational historical narratives that both unify and divide.

As part of the "apparatus of the state," it is crucial for educators to consider what aspects of history are taught as well as those that are omitted. The decisions surrounding what is included in history lessons—particularly regarding the events and individuals that have shaped our shared past—carry significant implications for how students understand the complexities of historical narratives and their own place within their communities, country, and history.

This is particularly evident when teaching and examining the legacy of George Washington. The historical narratives surrounding Washington often emphasize his role as a "Founding Father," his leadership during the Revolutionary War, his position as the first US president, and his embodiment of American ideals. However, when teaching this narrative, educators face critical decisions regarding the level of detail and time they will devote to exploring the complexities of Washington's legacy.

This raises critical questions for them. Beyond the prescribed curriculum, what influences my decisions about what to teach? What informs how much time I allocate to certain topics or content? Answering these questions requires educators to engage in purposeful self-reflection on why they choose to teach certain topics or content. Educator and scholar Christopher Day suggests, "Without routinely engaging in reflective practice, it is unlikely that we will be able to understand the effects of our motivations, prejudices, and aspirations upon the ways in which we create, manage, receive, sift, and evaluate knowledge."[2]

This essay examines the NOWW (Nature, Orientation, Worldview, and Workplace) framework as a tool for exploring how educators' identities and professional contexts shape their instructional decisions. Through illustrative scenarios involving the legacy of George Washington, it considers how reflective practice can help teachers hold space for historical complexity, personal responsibility, and inclusive civic learning.

By engaging in purposeful self-reflection on their identities and background, educators can uncover biases that influence both their interactions with students and their approach to delivering content. Examining how one's identities shape what one teaches can be achieved through two separate, deliberate steps: first, by contemplating those identities, and second, by carefully noting how those identities affect decision-making in educational contexts.

To better understand how the various factors that inform my identities affect my teaching practices, I find it most beneficial to use the Four-Layer Model of Diversity, which provides a framework for examining the different dimensions of identity in professional settings.[3] This model identifies four key dimensions, or layers, of one's interconnected identity: personality, internal, external, and organizational. These layers are the basis on which the NOWW framework is built and offer a structure for educators reflecting on how various aspects of their identities influence their pedagogical choices.

When guiding educators on the application of these layers to deeper self-reflection, I first find it helpful to model the process through my own experiences. Educators often form a deeply personal connection with their work, and vulnerability is essential when examining one's "why" in relation to instructional practices. Such in-depth self-reflection requires educators to confront aspects of their identities that may be uncomfortable or previously unexamined. Embracing this vulnerability fosters a deeper understanding of one's biases and influences and models a growth mindset for students and colleagues.

A part of my personality is my reserved, introverted nature. Growing up, I was often uncomfortable in situations involving conflict. I tended to withdraw from arguments, especially during my teenage years, and when disagreements became overwhelming or I believed my voice was not being heard, I would leave the exchange and go on a solitary walk. This nonconfrontational aspect of my personality persists today. I prefer finding peaceful resolutions to conflicts. This trait has, at times, influenced my teaching—especially when addressing potentially controversial or challenging topics in history. Reflecting on this aspect of my personality has helped me recognize the importance of engaging in difficult discussions more openly and constructively in my classroom.

Another key aspect of my identities is my learning disability, diagnosed in elementary school—an internal layer of who I am. I have a phonetic reading disability, which can make spelling and reciting unfamiliar words challenging. I received accommodations, my family supported me and expected me to perform well, and I was also driven to want to do well. Once I became a classroom teacher, for many years, I was self-conscious about spelling in front of students. I eventually found the courage to share my struggles with them. This vulnerability became a defining feature of my teaching philosophy: my commitment to teaching with accuracy and clarity, and to modeling perseverance in the face of challenges, reflects my desire to provide students with the tools to succeed despite difficulties.

In addition to my personality and the internal layers of my identities, such as my learning disability, my external experiences have also shaped my teaching philosophy. From fourth grade through high school, I lived in a diverse community where it was evident that many of my neighbors practiced different faiths. I learned that respecting others' beliefs was crucial and saw people in my community working toward being good neighbors. This formative experience taught me the value of understanding diverse perspectives, a lesson I carry into all my classrooms. Whether teaching social studies or another subject, K–12 or graduate school students, I am committed to presenting multiple viewpoints and helping students appreciate the complex ways in which individuals shape our shared history. I use that same approach in my professional and social interactions.

Moreover, my twenty-eight-plus years of experience as an educator—including roles as a classroom teacher, school administrator, and district leader—have broadened my perspective. These organizational positions have provided me with opportunities to collaborate with diverse staff and members of various communities and advocate for causes I was unable to address earlier in my career. Yet I also have blind spots. Having not taught in a K–12 classroom for over a decade, I cannot fully comprehend the daily demands faced by today's teachers. In my current role as an associate superintendent in a mid-Atlantic school district, I observe, converse with colleagues, and make decisions that impact staff, but I must acknowledge the limitations of my perspective. This awareness is crucial before offering advice to current educators on presenting complex historical narratives.

The Four-Layer Model of Diversity (personality, internal, external, and organizational) offers a structured way to examine how personal identities shape teaching practices. To personalize this model, I have developed a reflective framework called NOWW: Nature, Orientation, Worldview, and Workplace. This framework, when mapped onto the Four-Layer Model of Diversity, helps me consider how my identities across each of these dimensions inform what and how I teach—including complex historical figures such as George Washington. The acronym NOWW serves as a continual reminder to reflect on who I am and to take action *now,* ensuring that my instructional practices, as well as those I teach others to employ, are thoughtful, are reflective, and uphold the teaching of our history with fidelity.

Nature (personality dimension). This dimension encompasses a person's preferences, values, and beliefs, which are often formed during early childhood. When considering this layer in relation to purposeful questioning on instructional practices, teachers can use the following questions for self-reflection: How do my personal values and preferences affect the way I engage with historical narratives, including about the American Revolution and founding of the nation? How do my personal beliefs inform how I plan for the delivery of information about individuals and/or groups that I do and do not identify with? In what way does my communication preference inform my willingness to engage in discussions that could be viewed by some as controversial or contentious?

Orientation (internal dimension). Some aspects of how one identifies are beyond their control, such as age, ethnicity, gender, race, and physical or mental ability. To explore how these internal aspects shape teaching practices, consider the following reflective questions: How does my racial identity shape my approach to teaching sensitive topics, such as protections for the institution of slavery in the US Constitution or race- and gender-based discrimination as practiced in the eighteenth century? How do I respond to historical narratives in which individuals or groups that I identify with have committed actions that have caused harm to others? Do I consider the perspectives and experiences of individuals from different abilities, ethnicities, gender, and racial groups in my instruction, as distinct from my own identity? How do I understand the diversity of perspectives and experiences within groups I identify with?

Worldview (external dimension). After considering the internal layers of identity, which are often beyond our control, we now turn to external layers. These aspects of one's identities can change over time and may be influenced by personal choices and experiences. Reflecting on external factors is crucial for understanding what influences one's teaching practices and philosophy. Reflecting on the following questions can help educators understand how these factors shape what they believe about teaching: How do I take into account the socioeconomic backgrounds of my students when designing lessons on historical events? Am I aware of how my communication style affects my willingness to teach topics that may be viewed by some as controversial? How might my schooling, faith-based beliefs, and political views inform the historical narratives I choose to exclude or teach, including about the founding era and leading historical figures such as George Washington?

Workplace (organizational dimension). The final layer focuses on the cultural elements present in an individual's professional environment and their role and experiences. Reflection in this area provides teachers with the opportunity to consider how their experiences working in particular schools and districts influence both what and how they are expected to teach. The following questions can help educators examine how their professional identities shape their teaching practices: How does the curriculum or school policy shape my teaching decisions, especially when addressing complex figures like George Washington? What influence do I have in addressing gaps in the curriculum or resources when key aspects of historical figures' lives, including George Washington's, are omitted because they might challenge or complicate the dominant historical narrative? What is my ability to explain and justify the teaching of historically factual figures and actions that some might view as casting a negative light on the ideals upon which our country was founded?

To illustrate the practical application of the NOWW framework, the following three instructional scenarios highlight how educators and leaders can use reflective inquiry to navigate identity-informed decision-making. In each case, examples of self-questioning across the four dimensions—Nature, Orientation, Worldview, and Workplace—demonstrate how educators might engage in intentional, identity-informed decision-making. Following reflection on each dimension, a corresponding instructional or leadership intention is articulated.

Scenario 1. Teaching land conflict and Indigenous histories in elementary social studies. In this scenario, students in an upper elementary social studies class investigate the relationship between George Washington's presidency and Native nations, focusing specifically on early land conflicts. The teacher's multifaceted identities inform decisions about how to present content that is developmentally appropriate, historically accurate, and inclusive. The NOWW framework supports the teacher in considering how personal values, cultural affiliations, external influences, and institutional contexts shape both the delivery and the substance of instruction.

Nature (personality). In this case, the teacher's personal beliefs are shaped by stories from their own upbringing, which portrayed George Washington as a fair and noble leader. As an educator, they value teaching students to respect historical figures—believing that such respect includes a commitment to honesty and nuance. A core aspect of the teacher's personality is a strong preference for harmony in the classroom. Consequently, they are concerned that introducing Washington's role in authorizing violence against Indigenous nations may unsettle students and, by extension, their families. There is a worry that students might feel disillusioned or confused when confronted with this lesser-known aspect of Washington's legacy.

However, the teacher is also a natural storyteller and draws on this strength to make complex content accessible. They intentionally use storytelling as a pedagogical tool to introduce multiple perspectives and moral questions in an age-appropriate and reflective manner.

Teaching intention. The teacher will use clear, honest, and developmentally appropriate language to explain that George Washington—like many historical figures—made decisions that caused harm, including to Indigenous communities. This approach encourages students to begin exploring concepts such as fairness and justice, even when discussing admired national leaders.

Orientation (internal dimension). The teacher recognizes that they do not share the background or lived experiences of Indigenous communities. This awareness prompts a commitment to avoid speaking for these communities or reducing their histories to narratives of victimhood or erasure. Addressing the harms committed by a long-celebrated national hero elicits an emotional response, but the teacher also acknowledges that omitting such truths serves to protect the comfort of some while perpetuating the marginalization of others. Knowing that their classroom includes students from Indigenous and other historically marginalized communities, the teacher is committed to ensuring that these histories are presented not as peripheral but as integral to the American story.

Teaching intention. Whenever possible, the teacher will incorporate resources created by Indigenous educators and storytellers. They will affirm that Indigenous peoples are not only historical figures but living communities with ongoing stories. The teacher commits to approaching the topic with humility, care, and a sense of ethical responsibility.

Worldview (external dimension). The teacher's educational background did not include instruction about George Washington's military campaigns against Indigenous nations; their training largely emphasized patriotic narratives. Since entering the profession, they have actively sought to unlearn and relearn through independent study and critical engagement with diverse historical sources.

Awareness of their community reinforces the importance of perspective-taking. The teacher knows that their students come from a range of cultural and economic backgrounds. For some students, this lesson may be the first time they hear that a celebrated leader was involved in acts of harm; for others, it may be the first time their ancestral histories are acknowledged in the classroom. The teacher's professional experience supports a belief that elementary students are capable of engaging with complexity when it is framed in accessible ways—through concepts such as fairness, truth-telling, and responsibility.

Teaching intention. The teacher will use questioning to anchor the lesson in familiar moral and civic concepts, helping students move beyond simple judgments. Guiding questions include: What does it mean to be fair? Can someone make harmful choices and still be considered a good leader?

Workplace (organizational dimension). In their district, the elementary curriculum introduces George Washington primarily as a "Founding Father" and national hero, with little attention to his policies toward Indigenous peoples. As a result, the teacher will need to find creative ways to extend and enrich the lesson beyond the standard materials.

Additionally, there is an implicit expectation to maintain a "positive" tone in early grades, in part to avoid potential pushback from families. The teacher, however, believes that positivity should not come at the expense of historical accuracy or inclusion. As the grade-level team lead, they are in a position to advocate for the integration of Indigenous perspectives in early US history units and to share aligned resources with colleagues.

Teaching intention. The teacher will connect the lesson to civic values such as truth, fairness, and democratic inquiry, emphasizing that learning full and inclusive histories supports critical thinking rather than division. Supplemental materials, including primary sources and children's literature authored by Indigenous voices, will be used to extend and deepen the curriculum.

Scenario 2. Confronting slavery and patriotism in eighth grade. In this scenario, a teacher prepares to engage eighth-grade students in an examination of George Washington's role as an enslaver, focusing specifically on his active efforts to circumvent Pennsylvania's 1780 gradual abolition law. By rotating enslaved people in and out of the state to avoid their legal manumission, Washington sought to preserve their bondage while maintaining appearances. The teacher, raised to speak out against injustice, now works in a politically polarized community with strong and divergent views on patriotism and slavery.

Nature (personality). The teacher's upbringing instilled a belief that silence in the face of injustice is a form of complicity. This conviction generates a sense of moral urgency in their teaching and a strong commitment to historical truth-telling. When others—including colleagues or students' families—respond with resistance or discomfort, the teacher can feel disheartened, even frustrated, by what they perceive as a lack of shared commitment to justice. Their communication style is direct, but they also recognize that meaningful dialogue often requires strategic pacing and relational care. They understand that clarity does not always come through declaration alone but through purposeful, empathetic engagement.

Teaching intention. The teacher will bring their convictions to the classroom with integrity but will also employ strategies that meet their community where it is. Their goal is to teach boldly and truthfully while also creating space for students and families to engage with historical complexity at a pace that supports learning and reflection.

Orientation (internal dimension). For this teacher, the history they teach is intimately connected to their own identity. They carry a generational awareness of what was taken, lost, and fought for, which they view as a powerful lens for instruction. At the same time, this awareness brings emotional weight—particularly when histories of marginalized people are dismissed, minimized, or deemed "too political." This internal positioning allows the teacher to bring depth and authenticity to the classroom, but they also acknowledge that their passion may, at times, unintentionally alienate students or families who hold different worldviews. Their aim is to foster critical engagement without foreclosing dialogue.

Teaching intention. Rather than moralizing, the teacher will ground their instruction in historical evidence and ethical inquiry. They will affirm the humanity of those affected by enslavement while guiding students to critically examine the choices and beliefs of historical figures—including George Washington—in a balanced and thoughtful manner.

Worldview (external dimension). From an early age, the teacher was encouraged to challenge sanitized narratives of history. They view confronting historical myths as a civic responsibility and a way to prepare students for democratic participation. In their current community, interpretations of patriotism vary widely. Some associate it with loyalty to national symbols and tradition, while others demand transparency and full historical accounting. The teacher sees their role as both educator and translator: helping students understand how past injustices continue to shape present-day realities and showing how engaging with complexity can deepen, rather than diminish, civic identity and responsibility.

Teaching intention. The teacher will draw connections between historical events and contemporary themes such as justice, labor, and resistance. Students will be guided through inquiry-based questions, such as the following: Whose freedom was prioritized? Whose was not? What does that tell us about the founding ideals of this country? Do you see any parallels today?

Workplace (organizational dimension). In the district's curriculum, George Washington is celebrated for his leadership in the American Revolution, but little attention is given to his evolving views on enslavement or his direct involvement in the institution over time. The inclusion of this dimension of his legacy may be seen by some colleagues or families as divisive or unpatriotic.

Teaching intention. The teacher will prepare in advance to communicate with administrators and families about why a fuller historical account is necessary—not to tear down Washington but to more accurately understand the complexities of American history. They also see opportunities to collaborate with colleagues across grade levels to build a more inclusive and layered curriculum that reflects the diverse experiences of the nation's past.

Scenario 3. Leading gender-inclusive curriculum development. In this scenario, an instructional or curriculum leader seeks to inform standards and support instruction that highlights the histories of women in early America, with particular attention to the contrast between George Washington's public legacy and the relative invisibility of women in his personal, political, and economic world. This includes examining figures such as Martha Washington and Ona Judge and investigating the broader legal and social status of women in the early republic. The leader serves in a politically diverse and divided community, where some families view gender-based critiques as "political," "revisionist," or aligned with contemporary cultural agendas.

Nature (personality). Since childhood, the leader has seen themselves as a unifier—committed to building consensus and fostering inclusion. They believe that history must be taught with integrity, even when doing so causes discomfort. In their role, they work to ensure that curriculum feels inclusive and community-supported.

Though their instinct is to bridge divides, they have also come to recognize a personal tendency to overlook gender unless it is the explicit focus. This awareness has led them to acknowledge that absence is a form of erasure; silence communicates who does and does not matter in the stories we tell. Their impulse to "soften" controversial content for the sake of community buy-in is something they now interrogate. They recognize that courage and clarity are vital components of educational leadership, especially when advocating for representation.

Leadership intention. The leader will approach curriculum decisions with honesty and humility. They will model how to examine foundational figures like Washington within the context of systems that excluded women from political power and public recognition, resisting both erasure and hero-worship.

Orientation (internal dimension). As someone who identifies as a woman, the leader has long felt a disconnect between dominant national narratives and their own sense of historical belonging. The stories they encountered growing up rarely positioned women as leaders, thinkers, or agents of resistance—instead casting them as supporters of male greatness. This narrative absence shaped their early understanding of power and contribution.

They are particularly attuned to how intersectional erasures compound this invisibility. Women of color, women in poverty, and women resisting subjugation were often completely absent. The leader believes it is essential that students learn about women like Ona Judge—who resisted enslavement—and Martha Washington, whose experience reflected both constraint and privilege.

Leadership intention. The leader will support curriculum that treats women's experiences and perspectives not as add-ons or side notes but as central to understanding the founding era. Instructional materials will illuminate the choices, constraints, and contributions of women in ways that resist caricature and embrace complexity.

Worldview (external dimension). Before their professional training, the leader accepted simplified historical narratives, where the "Founding Fathers" were presented as unproblematic heroes and the women in their lives were peripheral. Conversations about gender equity in education now often feel politicized in the community they serve. But the leader believes that when grounded in historical evidence and primary sources, these conversations become academic, not ideological. Their commitment to telling fuller histories stems from a desire to honor women who have been erased, who resisted oppression, and who shaped the nation—regardless of whether they were formally recognized in their time.

Leadership intention. By guiding educators and administrators to reframe gender inclusion as essential to historical accuracy—not a political add-on—the leader aims to embed this work into curriculum development. Key guiding questions include the following: Whose freedoms were deferred so others could be celebrated? Whose labor supported Washington's success?

Workplace (organizational dimension). State and district standards often prioritize military and political narratives, marginalizing the economic, legal, and social experiences of women. The leader believes that with intentionality and courage, this narrative can shift. In their community, some families view discussions of gender as "modern issues" and argue that such content belongs at home, not in the classroom.

The leader, however, sees the inclusion of women's histories as foundational, not fringe. To foster understanding and reduce defensiveness, they will use historical evidence to demonstrate how gender shaped the early republic. They also recognize that teachers often feel unprepared to teach about women in early America.

Leadership intention. The leader will provide instructional models, coaching, and resources to help teachers confidently integrate gender-inclusive content into the core curriculum—not as a sidebar or special month but as central to how students understand citizenship, nation-building, and power. They will support staff in building community trust and professional confidence around this work.

While these three scenarios each use the NOWW framework to reflect on teaching and leadership practices related to George Washington and early

American history, the insights and strategies presented are broadly applicable across topics, grade levels, and roles. The NOWW framework invites educators at all levels to pause and examine how their identities, values, and institutional contexts shape not only what is taught but also how it is taught. Whether addressing race, gender, labor, or resistance, these scenarios underscore the importance of reflective, intentional practice in advancing historical understanding and fostering inclusive civic education.

Modeling a willingness to question the "why" behind what is taught or omitted encourages a classroom culture of openness, critical inquiry, and personal responsibility. Through reflective practices like these, educators can better understand the roles their identities play in shaping the content and delivery of their lessons, ultimately enhancing their teaching and fostering a deeper learning environment for students.

This important self-reflection should shape how we—as citizens, educators, and scholars of the early American republic in the twenty-first century—perceive and learn from the life and world of George Washington. It is imperative that students of history, broadly, understand all facets of Washington's legacy, including the complexities that make him both what many view as an embodiment of American ideals and a figure with significant flaws. It is not only the "good" that makes certain figures from our past worthy of imitation but also their faults, shortcomings, and weaknesses. There is much to learn by examining the moments when those we hold in high esteem failed to live up to the ideals they espoused. Their successes, strengths, failings, and shortcomings contribute to our past and inform our present. As James Baldwin stated, "History is not the past. It is the present. We carry our history with us. We are our history."[4]

To teach the history of George Washington with authority and credibility, we must incorporate and carry into our instruction all of the layers of his life and identities. As we prepare to teach about every aspect of his life, we must also engage in meaningful self-reflection about our own identities as educators. We cannot disregard our own identities, the identities of our students, or the identities of those we teach about.

Ignoring or omitting key aspects of Washington's life—such as his treatment of Indigenous populations, his role as an enslaver, his relationships with enslaved people, and his evolving views on slavery and abolition—does not erase these elements of history. The absence of these discussions in the classroom does not make them any less real or impactful. Just as we can learn from the successes of our past, we must also recognize the lessons embedded in our historical shortcomings, failures, and mistreatment of individuals and groups that have been marginalized. Both the triumphs and the failings of our history shape our present and our future.

With all this in mind, a critical question for self-reflection is: Do I know myself—and the reasons behind what and how I teach—at least as well, if not better, than I know historical narratives and figures such as George Washington? This self-awareness is essential, as it shapes the how and why of what we teach. The practice of purposeful self-reflection, however, extends beyond educators and their teaching methods; it can be applied more broadly. We are living our history today, and a clear understanding of it informs how we will shape tomorrow.

Notes

1. Michael W. Apple, *Ideology and Curriculum,* 3rd ed. (New York: Routledge, 2004), 58.
2. Christopher Day, "Researching Teaching Through Reflective Practice," in *Researching Teaching: Methodologies and Practices for Understanding Pedagogy,* ed. John Loughran (London: Falmer Press, 1999), 215–32 (quotation at 229).
3. The Four-Layer Model of Diversity was originally presented by Marilyn Loden and Judy B. Rosener, *Workforce America! Managing Employee Diversity as a Vital Resource* (New York: McGraw-Hill, 1990), and developed by Lee Gardenswartz and Anita Rowe, *Diverse Teams at Work: Capitalizing on the Power of Diversity* (Alexandria, VA: Society for Human Resource Management, 2003).
4. James Baldwin speech, December 10, 1986, in Arica L. Coleman, "James Baldwin Documentary *I Am Not Your Negro* Is the Product of a Specific Moment in History," *Time,* February 24, 2017, https://time.com/4680673/james-baldwin-documentary-history/.

PART VI

EIGHTEENTH-CENTURY SOCIETY AND CULTURE

GEORGE WASHINGTON AND EIGHTEENTH-CENTURY VALUES

LORRI GLOVER

In the pantheon of Revolutionary-era leaders, George Washington died young. He was only sixty-seven when he took that long wintry ride around his farms that turned fatal. Benjamin Franklin, Thomas Jefferson, and James Madison all lived into their eighties, and John Adams died shortly after turning ninety years old.[1]

If premature, it might also appear poetic that George Washington died in the last month of the last year of the eighteenth century. His values were decidedly ill-suited for the nineteenth century, with politicians openly competing—"running" became the new term—for public office. Washington's longer-lived contemporaries lamented the growing democratization of American politics, the expanding political factions, and the coarse men often elevated to positions of power.[2] John Adams, for instance, complained about rhetoric and reason collapsing under the weight of partisanship: "[E]very Man in our public assemblies will vote with his party, and his nose is counted before he takes his Seat." As for the voters, they appeared to have "contempt of Wisdom and Virtue and overweening Admiration of fools and Knaves!"[3] Aging revolutionaries also criticized the rising generation, which they found self-involved and disreputable—a far cry from the virtuous citizens the founding generation envisioned as essential to the survival of the republic. Jefferson, for example, was devastated when he learned that his idealistically planned "academical village" erupted in a student revolt in 1825. He vented his frustrations to a friend: "I have been long sensible that while I was endeavoring to render to our country the greatest of all services, that of regenerating the public education, and placing our rising generation on the level of our sister states . . . I was discharging the odious function of a physician pouring medicine down the throat of a patient insensible of needing it."[4] George Washington certainly saw cause for concern in the 1790s, both among his sometimes wayward young relatives and within his wobbly young country, but his relatively early death spared him from the chain of regrets for the American republic that Jefferson, Adams, and others chronicled in late-in-life correspondence.

Washington was a thoroughly and quintessentially eighteenth-century man. He lived out the central values of the eighteenth-century Anglo-Atlantic world, which makes him an ideal subject for learning about that history.

It can be quite challenging to foster student engagement with and understanding of eighteenth-century cultural values. The Anglo-Americans seem so different from us, with their wigs and knee-breeches and corseted dresses, their long-winded version of the English language, and their higgledy-piggledy capitalization and spelling. The cultural terms we teachers are supposed to clarify can seem intractably opaque. There is the Enlightenment, and refinement and gentility, and all the "isms": patriarchalism, nationalism, deism, republicanism.

George Washington, as he did so often in his unparalleled career in public service, provides an example, a path forward for understanding these centuries-old cultural values. The conduct guide he crafted in his boyhood reflected models of English-style refinement that influenced him across the decades. He developed early on and maintained throughout his life a keen interest in reputation. He grew up—and grew old—consistently pursuing Enlightenment ideas. At the height of his renown in the Revolutionary era, he embodied republicanism. Simultaneously, he and his carefully manicured estate, Mount Vernon, epitomized the patriarchalism of Virginia planters and enslavers. This essay samples surviving records of Washington's life—his writings, belongings, and home—to ground these abstract, sometimes perplexing concepts.

Washington's personal temperament and qualities certainly shaped his leadership, too. Other contributors to this collection explore those personality traits in greater detail, as writers emphasize Washington's courage, perseverance, ambition, and forward-looking attitude, particularly toward political ideals and economic practices, as well as his reserve and occasional hot-temperedness. This essay emphasizes not his personal qualities but how Washington reflected and embodied eighteenth-century cultural values. Of course, the two can blur. But it will be useful for readers of this essay to focus on the wider context of George Washington's life.

The earliest and most persistent eighteenth-century cultural value Washington embodied was refinement: an elaborate code of how to speak, walk, dress, eat, and generally act in public. Refinement was a core value among elite Anglo-Americans—in fact, it is hard to understand eighteenth-century Americans' language, material culture, society, or even their politics without appreciating its importance. Refinement, sometimes referred to as gentility, can seem abstract, but Washington's writings, lifestyle, and estate provide a clear, strong grounding.

At around age fourteen, George Washington used the English translation of a French conduct book to define for himself "Rules of Civility and Decent Behaviour in Company and Conversation." Such books were commonplace in the colonial era, as young people learned how to act in society from self-styled experts and often copied their advice to polish penmanship. Much is unknown about this part of Washington's earliest writings: When did he write the list? Under whose direction? Why did he make edits? Where did he get the English translation of the French book? One thing is clear: Washington cared deeply about acting the part of a refined young man. Throughout his life, he followed the general guidance to always control his actions in society, and he hewed to many of the specific rules.[5]

Washington's "Rules of Civility," sometimes called "110 Precepts," covered everything from eating to hygiene, facial expressions to attire, and the document vividly captures eighteenth-century ideas about refinement. It also shows how rigorously people judged each other's behavior.

Washington's rules—do not raise one eyebrow higher than the other, hum in public, laugh too loud, blow on your soup, or "play the peacock" with your clothing—are easy to visualize. Some can seem silly today, especially the ones about social rank and how to sit, stand, walk, and talk with prominent people. We no longer think it appropriate to avert our eyes from anyone richer or more distinguished (#37). Cleaning one's teeth with a tablecloth (#100), thankfully, does not come up very often. But other rules remain important. "Sleep not while others Speak" is still considered polite—and required of students. Keeping your promises and avoiding interrupting others remain good qualities to cultivate (#82, #74). Mocking people with disabilities is still despicable. It remains unwise to immediately believe gossip (#50). And, with COVID-19, #12 gained renewed urgency; it recommends against speaking so closely that you risk spreading saliva droplets.

The first, foundational rule was the one Washington followed the longest and most closely: "Every Action done in Company, ought to be with Some Sign of Respect, to those that are Present." Washington understood, from his boyhood, that how he acted would determine whether others viewed him as refined and genteel and therefore a person worthy of their time and respect. People who failed to live up to these ideals, he also knew, would lose respect. Being perceived as unrefined limited a man's opportunities for friendships, in courting women, with business partnerships, and for winning election to public offices.

Surviving artifacts of Washington's life also allow students to see and understand Washington's desire to act the part of a refined man. Throughout his life, Washington chose clothes and shoes and a hairstyle that signaled his refinement. His portraits display the fabrics, fashions, and body language of a refined, genteel man, and they can easily be analyzed in classrooms on all educational levels. Students can take virtual tours of Mount Vernon, too, and see up close how refined families lived. Everything from the crown molding to the paint colors, the candle holders to the bed canopies, was stylish and elegant—all carefully chosen symbols of the Washingtons' taste and gentility. George and Martha paid the greatest attention to presenting the right kind of image in the public parts of the mansion; the kitchen and outbuildings along the south lane are far more functional. And virtual visitors can see the stark contrast between how the Washingtons lived and how the people they enslaved lived.[6]

George's marriage to Martha Dandridge Custis in 1759 enabled him to purchase many symbols of a refined lifestyle. Martha was a twenty-seven-year-old widow when she began to accept George's romantic overtures. She was not just any young widow, though; she was extraordinarily rich and well-connected. Her first husband, Daniel Parke Custis, died seven years into their marriage, leaving Martha with two young children and a vast estate that included over seventeen thousand acres of land and nearly three hundred enslaved people. Once the newlyweds settled in at Mount Vernon, they assumed they would lead an unexceptional life as genteel British Americans. In the early years of their marriage, they spent like mad to eat, dress, entertain, and live in a house that signaled their refinement. The Revolutionary War interrupted George and Martha's plans, but they continued to prioritize refinement and gentility long after he became renowned.

The Washingtons, like all genteel British Americans, bought from England the belongings that signaled their refinement. George and Martha used a London-based firm, Cary & Company, as agents for the varied business interests of the Custis plantations and Mount Vernon. Martha's first husband, Daniel, had used that firm, and Martha continued her business relationship with Cary & Company after Daniel died. George followed suit when he and Martha married. Cary & Company marketed Virginia crops (usually on consignment) and shipped goods from England (usually on credit or charged against tobacco and other agricultural commodities). George and Martha sent shopping lists, which they called invoices, to Cary & Company. These sources, available at Founders Online, are fascinating and revelatory. Just a few months after they married, the Washingtons sent a swatch of wallpaper to Cary & Company and requested "fashionable" blue or blue and white curtains to complement the color and design. They also ordered a matching bedspread and enough fabric to upholster four chairs "in order," George Washington wrote, "to make the whole furniture in this room uniformly handsome and genteel."[7] They also bought a set of six silver-plated, ivory-handled carving knives and forks, specialty glassware, and fifty pounds of spermaceti candles. Enslaved laborers at Mount Vernon could and did manufacture candles. But these imported candles, made from a substance found in the heads of sperm whales, were a new technology and luxury item. They lasted longer and burned more cleanly than ordinary tallow candles, giving more light after sunset. The manufacturing process was complicated and the candles expensive. Only rich people could afford them, and only well-connected North Americans knew to acquire them in 1759. Spermaceti candles were one of countless goods the Washingtons bought that other people, paying close attention in their home, could see as a reflection of their stylishness, good taste, metropolitan connections, and wealth—their refinement.

The food the Washingtons ate and served to their guests also reflected their genteel, refined lifestyle. In the early fall of 1759, they sent to Cary & Company a long list that included everything from a pair of white satin shoes to several barrels full of nails. The food they bought showcased their immersion in global markets, wealth, and sophistication: anchovies, capers, and olives; mangoes from India; a wheel of Cheshire cheese; green tea; raisins and almonds.[8] The couple entertained a lot, in high style and for large parties, and they ordered in 1760 a great deal of what we today call barware: a dozen beer glasses, eighteen punch (cocktail) glasses, and twenty-four wineglasses. Washington clarified here, and often in invoices, that he and Martha wanted their goods "all of the newest Fashion."[9] Studying even one of the Washingtons' many shopping lists, such as the one from September 28, 1760, given in the appendix at the end of this essay, allows present-day readers to envision their lifestyle.

Every list also reveals the lives of enslaved communities at Mount Vernon. George bought fabric for their annual clothing allowance and tools for their endless labors. Who was using the dozen thimbles or the six hearth brushes or the nearly 250-foot-long fishing seine he ordered in September 1760? And all the purchases, from the anchovies to the silk shoes, were paid for with their labor.

Washington's careful attention to his every public behavior was intricately connected to his lifelong concern about his reputation. His deep understanding of eighteenth-century Anglo-American values convinced him that others would judge how he acted, every time, and in every public setting. Their opinions of his conduct would determine his reputation. And reputation was of paramount importance in Washington's world. A good reputation was difficult to build and fragile, whereas a bad one was nearly impossible to change. Washington corresponded with many young people over his life, and he told all of them that they needed to be careful about how they acted to establish and protect their reputation, which he sometimes called "character." He used the term not to mean personal qualities, as we often define character today, but rather how others perceived public behavior. "Your future character and reputation," he cautioned one nephew, "will depend very much, if not entirely, upon the habits and manners which you contract in the present period of your life . . . [and] can never be effaced."[10] Washington held the same concerns for the new American republic. Right after the Revolutionary War, he reflected: "We are a young Nation & have a character to establish. It behooves us therefore to set out right; for first impressions will be lasting, indeed are all in all."[11]

Washington's concern for reputation—both his own and the country's—shaped his conduct in the war, his actions during his presidency, and his decisions to retire (twice). His hesitancy about attending the 1787 Philadelphia Convention provides a great example. Though Washington heartily supported creating a stronger central government, he felt apprehensive about attending the meeting. He feared that the convention might fail or generate widespread reproach, which would damage his hard-earned reputation. And there was another sticky issue related to his reputation. Washington was president of the Society of the Cincinnati, and the organization of veteran officers of the Continental Army was scheduled to meet in Philadelphia in early May 1787. Washington publicly declined attending in October 1786, listing a host of reasons. Among them were "the peculiar situation of my private concerns; the necessity of paying attention to them; a wish for retirement & relaxation from public cares, and rheumatic pains which I begin to feel very sensibly." But he confided to close friends other, more pressing motivations, namely, that the organization, with its hereditary membership and fancy medallions, was drawing increasing criticism for elitism. Washington did not want to damage his reputation by attending the national Society of the Cincinnati meeting, and he did not want to insult members by attending the Philadelphia meeting in the same city at the same time.[12]

Washington weighed these personal reputational concerns against the imperative to solve the young country's problems and save its reputation. "Without some alteration in our political creed," Washington wrote James Madison in the fall of 1786, "the superstructure we have been seven years raising at the expence of much blood and treasure, must fall. We are fast verging to anarchy & confusion!" "Thirteen Sovereignties pulling against each other, and all tugging at the federal head, will soon bring ruin on the whole," he predicted. But, he added, "a liberal, and energetic Constitution, well guarded & closely watched, to prevent incroachments, might restore us to that degree of respectability & consequence, to which we had a fair claim, & the brightest prospect of attaining."[13]

As Washington deliberated, his friends begged him to attend the Philadelphia meeting. Madison wrote in early December 1786 that "it was the opinion of every judicious friend whom I consulted that your name could not be spared from the Deputation to the Meeting in May in Philada." Mindful of Washington's concerns about the Society of the Cincinnati, he followed up on Christmas Eve: "I still am inclined to think that the posture of our affairs . . . would prevent every criticism on the situation which the contemporary meetings would place you in." Madison, keenly aware of the magnitude of reputation, decided he needed to underscore the high stakes and urged Washington to set aside "every consideration, but that of our national existence or safety."[14]

George Washington's concern over reputation is evident in matters great (the 1787 Philadelphia Convention) and small (his clothes). In 1791, when he took his southern tour in hopes of binding the nation together, President Washington adopted a specific routine, reflective of his near obsession with reputation. He traveled between March 21 and June 4, in carriages and on horseback over rough and varyingly muddy or dusty roads, on boats and ferries, through swampy interiors and sandy shores, enduring winds and rains and even some of the heat and humidity he tried to avoid with the spring start. The 1,700-mile journey was, in short, a physical ordeal. But Washington refused to let it show. When his entourage approached a destination point—and communities across the Southeast had spent months planning welcomes—everyone stopped. Washington changed his clothes and mounted his well-groomed horse to ride into town clean and stylish, safeguarding his and the country's reputation. President Washington's entrances, into balls and legislative halls, marketplaces, and churches, were always carefully orchestrated and the source of conversation and admiration. Every time he entered a room, he thought about how others would judge him and, by extension, the country he led.

The Washington Papers on Founders Online are filled with opportunities to study Washington's concerns about reputation: his reaction to the Newburgh incident; struggles with his grandson, George Washington Parke "Washy" Custis; crises during his presidency; the design of his estate; what others said about his dancing, conversation, and body. It is, in fact, difficult to find a part of the record of Washington's life bereft of close attention to reputation.

Washington's life bore the deep imprint of the Enlightenment, too. The Enlightenment was an intellectual and cultural movement in the seventeenth and eighteenth centuries emphasizing the use of reason, empirical observation, and scientific inquiry to expand knowledge and improve society. Enlightenment thinkers promoted science and rationalism, opposed superstitions, and supported natural, individual rights. That is a lot of abstraction for learners of any age to process! Furthermore, the Enlightenment included many variations, unfolding across Europe and in North America at different times and in different contexts. And so much Enlightenment thinking persists today that we can slip into thinking of the mindset as timeless: supporting human rights, trying to improve society, studying science to understand the world.

Washington's life and his writings were grounded in Enlightenment ideals. His advice to young relatives on love and marriage, for instance, is all about observing closely and thinking rationally about a good match rather than falling victim to dangerous passions. Love, he explained to his granddaughter Eleanor Parke Custis, "ought to be under the guidance of reason." He gave her a detailed list of questions to consider: "When the fire is beginning to kindle, and your heart growing warm, propound these questions to it. Who is the invader? Have I competent knowledge of him? Is he a man of good character? A man of sense? For be assured a sensible woman can never be happy with a fool. What has been his walk in life? Is he a gambler? a spendthrift, a drunkard? Is his fortune sufficient to maintain me in the manner I have been accustomed to live, and my sisters do live? and is he one to whom my friends can have no reasonable objection?"[15] Note his concern about her reputation—what friends would think—as well as her ability to continue to live a refined lifestyle.

Washington's farming innovations at Mount Vernon are easy-to-understand examples of eighteenth-century science in action and the pursuit of new knowledge. He was always experimenting, including with a shift away from tobacco, constructing a treading barn, testing crop rotation and fertilizers, and expanding the gristmill and distillery. Washington's farm books recorded his observations about weather patterns, and he corresponded with many other innovative "book-farmers" who used scientific methods to improve farming. Washington's correspondence with his friend Samuel Powel is witty and informative and showcases their shared love of agricultural pursuits. They discussed chestnut trees, grapevines, wheat varieties, and cheese-making methods—just about anything that might be produced on a farm. Powel was president of the Philadelphia Society for the Promotion of Agriculture, and when Washington learned of the organization, he celebrated the mission of advancing innovations: "No measure, in my opinion, will be more conducive to the public weal than the establishment of this Society." And he wished "that each State would institute similar ones; & that these Societies when formed would correspond regularly & freely with each other."[16] During his presidency, Washington became an honorary member of the society and wrote about his enthusiasm for such work: "As no one delights more than I do in the objects of your Institution, so no one experiences more real pleasure from every proof of their progress." President Washington also kept in close contact with his farm managers at Mount Vernon, who sent him long reports of the work undertaken at his five farms.[17]

Unlike his well-recorded scientific approach to farming, Washington's religious views have been difficult for historians to document. He kept those thoughts private. His contemporaries gave conflicting accounts of Washington's actions in religious matters. Records show that for many years he financially supported and served as a leader in the Pohick Church, though he attended sporadically and often declined to partake in communion. Washington was, however, clearly committed to religious freedom, and he offered a significant public reflection in a 1790 letter to members of a Jewish congregation. It is worth quoting at length for Washington's understanding—and admiration—of freedom of religion and Enlightenment ideals:

> The Citizens of the United States of America have a right to applaud themselves for having given to mankind examples of an enlarged and liberal policy: a policy worthy of imitation. All possess alike liberty of

> conscience and immunities of citizenship. It is now no more that toleration is spoken of, as if it was by the indulgence of one class of people, that another enjoyed the exercise of their inherent natural rights. For happily the Government of the United States, which gives to bigotry no sanction, to persecution no assistance requires only that they who live under its protection should demean themselves as good citizens, in giving it on all occasions their effectual support.[18]

From his views on religious freedom to his approaches to farming to his family relationships, George Washington was clearly a product of the Enlightenment. The Enlightenment shaped Revolutionary-era leaders' views on government, too. By now, readers likely perceive how these eighteenth-century cultural values intersected and overlapped. The Enlightenment influenced some of young Washington's 110 precepts. Washington's estate reflected his scientific approach to farming as well as his affinity for refined consumer goods—and his republican and patriarchal ideals, too.

It is easy, when studying Washington's extraordinary achievements in the military and governance, to overlook the fact that he was, throughout his life, a typical eighteenth-century southern planter-patriarch. As other authors explain in greater detail, Mount Vernon was a Black majority community, with enslaved residents consistently outnumbering White residents by over ten to one. The year of George Washington's death, 317 enslaved people lived on the estate alongside 5 members of the Washington family and 17 White employees and their families.[19]

Slaveholding enabled not only Washington's lifestyle but also his long service to the country. He was able to be gone for months and years at a time, including periods of commanding the Continental Army and serving as president of the United States, because he was independently wealthy, owing to his lifelong exploitation of enslaved laborers. Slavery underlay his civic values—and those of other leaders among the founding generation. Virginia planter-patriarchs were the primary architects of republican ideals expressed in the Virginia Declaration of Rights (George Mason), Declaration of Independence (Thomas Jefferson), and US Constitution (James Madison). They were also all lifelong enslavers. They envisioned a republic grounded on freedom and equality—for White men.[20] The Constitution that Washington believed would secure the future of the United States repeatedly sanctioned racial slavery, though the framers of the document, concerned about their reputations in history, carefully avoided ever using the words "slavery" or "slaves." Instead, they tried to use obscuring language that one delegate charged was "an Endeavour to conceal" from future generations of Americans "a principle of which we are ashamed."[21] But everyone in the eighteenth century certainly understood what "all other persons" meant and that the Constitution would preserve the country's racial order and the foundation of much personal wealth, including George and Martha Washington's.

Mount Vernon displayed the intersection of refinement, patriarchalism, and republicanism. Slaveholding planters such as the Washingtons believed that their vast estates allowed them to pursue, as George put it, the "republican style of living." Mount Vernon and similar estates that spread across Virginia and other southern states communicated civic ideals: independence, community, order, and racial hierarchy. At the same time, none of the stylish homes and scenic grounds existed without slavery. Enslaved adults and children ran the workshops, cleaned the parlors, toiled in the fields, and maintained the houses.

After 1776, George Washington grew increasingly troubled about how being an enslaver might hurt his reputation—both in the eighteenth century and in history. He knew all about the rise of antislavery societies and networks in the mid-Atlantic and New England states and the laws passed by some state legislatures to gradually abolish slavery. Many of his friends began to condemn human trafficking, and others, including Lafayette, directly urged Washington to emancipate the people he enslaved. Instead of acting, he fell silent on the topic in nearly all his correspondence to avoid leaving a permanent record of his thoughts. As he wrote his will in the summer of 1799, George wanted to fulfill his republican ideals and protect his reputation. He also wanted to ensure that Martha would remain at Mount Vernon, living a refined and racially powerful lifestyle. So, except for William Lee, George Washington's will freed no one immediately. Instead, he set up an emancipatory program to begin upon Martha Washington's death. George is often mistakenly credited with freeing the people he enslaved in his will. But Martha did that in January 1801. George Washington died as he lived: an enslaving planter-patriarch.[22]

The most important concept for understanding the American Revolution—and George Washington's career in public service—is republicanism. Historians have long debated the origins, variations, nuances, and effects of American-style republicanism, so it can be a tricky concept to understand. But there are some basic ideas that leading members of the founding generation shared. They decided that the best form of government was not a monarchy or aristocracy or democracy but a republic, where power rested with citizens' representatives. It worked this way, ideally: a constitutional republic, with clearly defined laws equally applied to all citizens, would balance individual liberty with governmental power. Citizens would check the tendency of governments to become corrupt and exploitative; governments would prevent citizens from falling into disorder and anarchy. Educated citizens would choose worthy representatives and, through regular elections, limit those representatives' ability to amass power and become corrupt. Well-chosen representatives would reason together to make the best decisions to advance the common good. And, critically, both citizens and leaders would practice civic virtue, often shortened to simply "virtue."

Virtue was the cornerstone of these ideals of republicanism, and, in the eighteenth century, virtue had a specific meaning, different from our more generic uses of the term today. Exercising civic virtue required putting the good of society above self-interest, sacrificing personal desires for public needs. No one in the Revolutionary era was more widely perceived to uphold civic virtue than George Washington. His countrymen saw him as the paragon, the very embodiment, of republican values, starting with civic virtue. (Republicanism intersected with Enlightenment ideas. Washington's views on government reflected his dedication to pursuing knowledge, rationally reasoning through problems, defending natural rights, and embracing innovation, with confidence in humanity's ability to pursue improvement.)

Washington earned an unparalleled reputation—always important, but now with a new political meaning—for sacrifice and service during his 1775–1783 command of the Continental Army. He led an all-volunteer army to defend an abstract, radical set of ideas. He had no navy and no means of mass-producing or buying munitions. The British military was the most sophisticated, skilled, battle-hardened fighting force in the Western world. And Britain was only the primary opponent; Washington also needed to coax along an ambivalent public. There were strong pro-British pockets across North America, and a good percentage of the overall population did not want to take sides. Even men enthusiastic enough to volunteer to serve in the military remained deeply parochial. Many Continental Army volunteers thought of themselves as Pennsylvanians or New Yorkers or South Carolinians, not Americans, and were reluctant to fight and die outside their state. The state militias were considerably worse.

Furthermore, the Continental Congress was crippled by an ineffectual structure that left General Washington's forces chronically deprived of munitions, uniforms, and even food. In September 1776, one year into the war, Washington wrote a relative: "I am wearied to death all day with a variety of perplexing circumstances." "In short," he confided, "such is my situation that if I were to wish the bitterest curse to an enemy on this side of the grave, I should put him in my stead . . . I do not know what plan of conduct to pursue."[23]

For the fledgling republic he served, Washington persevered. With all the odds stacked against him, he held firm to the idea of an independent American republic. His conduct in the war cemented his unrivaled reputation for upholding republican ideals.

When the war ended, Washington did something both essential for the future of the American republic and unprecedented in history. His duty to the republic fulfilled, he resigned his command to Congress. The language he used on December 23, 1783, is worthy of close consideration: "Having now finished *the work assigned to me,* I retire from the great theatre of Action." Washington's command of the Continental Army had not been, as he made clear, about his interests or his power. Rather, he had served under and answered to the elected legislature, the representatives of citizens. The point was so important, he repeated it: "[B]idding an Affectionate farewell to this August body *under whose orders I have so long acted,* I here offer my Commission, and take my leave of all the employments of public life."[24] Kings and oligarchs did not retire. There was no tradition in the Western world of a man with the power Washington held willingly laying it down. He embodied so fully the ideals of republican government and civic virtue that even King George III said that Washington's actions made him the greatest man in the world. As news of his resignation spread, so did Americans' admiration of Washington as a model of republican values. He understood what was at stake for the upstart country, and he met the moment.

A private citizen for the first time in over eight years, Washington spent Christmas 1783 at Mount Vernon. His retirement did not last long, however. Within a few years he found himself pulled back into public service: in 1787 at the Philadelphia Convention and in 1789 as president of the United States. This power, too, he willingly resigned. (There were no term limits at the time, so Washington could have remained president for life.) Both in 1783 and 1797, Washington felt keenly responsible for publicly enacting the surrender of power, and both events were deeply important to Washington's reputation—in his own time and in ours—as a model of republican values.

Throughout the war, in the fits and starts of designing republican governments in the 1770s and 1780s, and during Washington's presidency, local and regional loyalties often collided with national interests. Americans struggled to sort out what, exactly, constituted their country: Was it their state or the union?

Washington was, from the earliest stages of the war, throughout his career, and in retirement, a consistent nationalist. Usages of the term "nationalist," like "virtue" and "reputation," have evolved over time, and today it carries a particular politicized meaning. Washington was an eighteenth-century nationalist: a citizen whose principal allegiance was to the nation at large. Washington believed that local biases, what he often dismissed as parochialism, eroded civic life. He believed that the fate of the American people depended on the strength of the United States as a single nation. He consistently thought about his country being the United States, and he did all he could to ensure that state biases and localistic interests would not undermine the greater good of the nation. That commitment drove his enthusiasm for revising the Articles of Confederation—and his concern about thirteen sovereignties pulling against one another—as well as his support for the Constitution. It shaped his desire to foster nationwide networks for agricultural improvement and his actions throughout his presidency, including touring the states. Just a few days before he died, Washington wrote a letter that started with his self-identifying as "a Citizen of the United States" and closed with his hope that citizens across the nation would set aside "local interests, destructive Jealousies, and inveterate prejudices."[25]

What can bring this all together for students? Education! George Washington never received an extensive formal education, but he was, to use a modern term, a lifelong learner who cared deeply about education. His hope for a national university presents a terrific opportunity to see the intersecting influences of eighteenth-century values—of refinement and reputation, the Enlightenment, and republicanism and nationalism.

In the spring of 1795, President Washington said that he felt "indescribable regret" watching young Americans travel abroad for university educations and study in places "not congenial to republicanism." "The time is therefore come," he reasoned, "when a plan of Universal education ought to be adopted in the United States. Not only do the exigencies of public & private life demand it; but if it should ever be apprehended that prejudice would be entertained in one part of the Union against another; an efficatious remedy will be, to assemble the youth of every part under such circumstances, as will, by the freedom of intercourse and collision of sentiment, give to their minds the direction of truth, philanthropy and mutual conciliation."[26] Keep in mind that the "youth" he envisioned were elite boys and men. In his will, Washington reiterated his long-standing concern about future leaders of the republic going abroad for their college educations and "contracting, too frequently, not only habits of dissipation & extravagence, but principles unfriendly to Republican Governmt and to the true & genuine liberties of Mankind." As he considered the legacies he wished to leave via his will, Washington wrote that it remained his "ardent wish" to "see a plan devised on a liberal scale, which would have a tendency to sprd systemactic ideas through all parts of this rising Empire, thereby to do away local attachments and State prejudices."[27] And he added this long reflection, full of insights into eighteenth-century culture as well as that higgledy-piggledy writing style:

> my mind has not been able to contemplate any plan more likely to effect the measure than the establishment of a UNIVERSITY in a central part of the United States, to which the youth of fortune and talents from all parts thereof might be sent for the completion of their Education in all the branches of polite literature; in arts and Sciences, in acquiring knowledge in the principles of Politics & good Government; and (as a matter of infinite Importance in my judgment) by associating with each other, and forming friendships in Juvenile years, be enabled to free themselves in a proper degree from those local prejudices & habitual jealousies which have just been mentioned; and which, when carried to excess, are never failing sources of disquietude to the Public mind, and pregnant of mischievous consequences to this Country.[28]

The fact that we can read this revealing commentary on the power of education, along with tens of thousands of other pages of George Washington's writings, is a consequence of his eighteenth-century values. Most of the leading members of the founding generation, including Thomas Jefferson, James Madison, and John Adams, carefully preserved their writings during the Revolutionary era. Washington's recordkeeping long predated the American Revolution: he practiced refined penmanship and epistolary conversation as a boy, kept accounts of his reputable stewardship of the Custis children's inheritances as a young husband and stepfather, and cataloged his farming experiments. The recordkeeping took on greater urgency and vigilance in the Revolutionary War, when Washington began to perceive his and his new country's place in world history. He kept compiling materials for decades, preparing for posterity a record of his roles in creating the American republic, the nation he led and loved. The writings secured Washington's reputation across time, enabled later generations of architects and curators to re-create his refined, patriarchal lifestyle at Mount Vernon, and provided lasting lessons in republican leadership. Teams of scholars have been working on annotating and editing comprehensive records of the papers of George Washington and his contemporaries for decades—and they will continue to do so for years, perhaps decades, to come. The work of these documentary editorial teams so far is available on Founders Online: meticulously edited, word searchable, an absolute wonder. Mount Vernon—the historic mansion and grounds, the Presidential Library, and the ever-evolving website resources—also preserves an amazing array of sources, of every kind under the sun. So whatever deep dive you find inspiration to take, George Washington is waiting to show you his eighteenth-century world.

Appendix: George Washington (Mount Vernon) to Robert Cary & Company (London), September 28, 1760

[Mount Vernon] 28th Septr 1760
Invoice of Sundry Goods to be sent by Robert Cary Esqr. & Company for the use of George Washington—Virginia.

1 pair Crimson Velvet Breeches 1 pair black knit silk Ditto 1 pair Black ditto worsted ditto 1 pair light colo[re]d silk Shag Ditto to be made by the Measure Inclosd to Charles Lawrence 2 pieces Irish Holland @ 6/ 1 piece of Cambrick for Ruffles, or something else proper if Cambrick is not to be had 1 piece of Irish Linnen @ 2/ 4 Yds fine book Muslin @ 10/ 4 ditto fine white Gauze 1 piece of fine white Canting 1 piece of white Callico @ 40/ 1 piece of Bird Eye diaper for Towel 2 pieces best Nankeen with buttons & Mohair to suit ditto 1 white persian quilted Petticoat 2 Satten Bonnets

2 pr dble Channel pump 4 pr strong Shoes 2 pr very neat Stichd & bound Pumps from Mr Didsbury 12 rolls best Shoe Blacking 1 pr Womans black Satten Shoes 1 pr ditto white Ditto 4 pr neat black everlasting ditto all to be made accordg to the Meas[ur]e Sent 2 pr Womans black Everlastg Ditto & 2 pr strong leather ditto of large Sixes 6 pr Mens neat white Gloves 6 pr ditto of Norway Doe—above the middle Size—

Stichd Tops 6 pr Womans white Kid Gloves 6 pr ditto Mitts 2 pr colourd Gloves 4 pr ditto Mitts

1 Groce Shirt Buttons 1 pair Tabby Stays according to the Meas[ur]e 6 Knots & Breast Knots 3 Egrets 2 fashionable Fans 4 pieces Diaper Tape—fine 6 M Miniken Pins 6 M Short whites 6 M large Ditto 1 Comb trae, Combs & Powder Box 6 fine horn Combs, & Comb Brushes 2 Bottles westerns lowdried Scotch Snuff

1 dble bitted Bridle with two pair Reins 4 Circingles 6 Girths 3 Sadle Cloaths 6 Strong Snaffle Bridles 2 dozn Hempen Halters with flat Hea⟨d⟩ 6 Coach Whip Thongs 2 Chair Whip Ditto 1 dozn Horse Collars 1 Set of strong Waggon Harness for 5 middle Sizd Horses—-N.B. they may be strong but not heavy

1 dozn Beer and Cyder Glasses 1½ dozn Punch Ditto 2 dozn wine Glasses—all of the newest Fash. ½ dozn glass Milk Pots 6 China Mugs two of a Sort 6 ditto potting Pots, 2 of a size—none large 2 large Stone Churns, each to hold 10 Gals. 6 dozn earthen Milk Pans 1 dozn strong Mugs different sizes ½ dozn ditto Pipkins—2 of them to hold a galn each 2 a Pottle & 2 a quart 1 dozn Stone Chamber Pots 1 dozn ditto wash Basons 12 white Stone Butter plates

½ Rheam common writing Paper 2 quire large Dutch Paper & some pastboard 6 papers Ink powder 1 Box Wafers 1 Jar best Raisons 1 large Stone pot of Currts ½ Bushels Almonds in the Shell ½ lb. Nuts 4 Oz. Mace the same qty of Cloves & Cinnamon & 5 lb. Comfits different sorts 6 lb. Ginger 3 lb. Allspice 1 dozn bottles flower of Mustard

6 House Brooms 6 Hearth Brushes 1 piece black Ribbon for hair 2 Cloaths flaskets 1 large Tea Kettle 1 pr Backgammon Tables—large 2 fine hair Sifters 1 dozn Course Hair Ditto 25 Salt Petre 2 dozn Packs playing Cards A Tin Candle Box with a Lock to it 2 dozn strong course pewter Spoons 1 dozn horn Ditto 1 dozn brass Thimbles sorted 1 dozn Tin Sheets to bake Bread upon 1 dozn Tin Dish Covers sizd 1 pr neat dble bellows for dining Room 6 pieces of Beggars Tape

1 Forty fathom Sein—well Rigd—not to be above 8 Feet deep—to have spare twine and 150 fathom of Rope to haul her by 50 fathom of Line for Leading strings to be a size smaller than Bed Cords 50 fathom of Garden Line

A Very neat Pocket Book—7 Inches long & 4½ wide with several Vellom, or other Leaves that will bear writing thereupon with a Pencil, & rubbing out again—to have a Pencil therein, & a Pocket or two for Papers—to be inclosd and fastned by a Silver Catch 2 Nett Silver Pencil Cases, & spare Pencils for Ditto 2 dozn Common Pencils ½ dozn Mens fine worsted Hose large & long

50 lb. large Bristol Drop Shott 50 lb. bird Shott 70 lb. Small Mould Shott 1 Rundlet red paint Ground in Oyl 4 pair Stilliards midling large 4 large watering Pots 1 Wier Sieve for cleaning wheat 1 Iron Ditto for cleaning Indn Corn The case (which is now sent) to be filld with Pickles—among which let there be 3 bottles of French Olives—and none of other sorts One Cheese of 50 lb. 1 handsome glass Lanthorne for Passage—wt. Lamps & 10 Gals. Oyl for Do 2 pair hand Mill Stones 6 Blank Books for Accts from a very small to a midling size—N.B. not to be Ruld

1 Mahagony Case with 16 Square Bottles in it, each bottle holding a Gallon; and the case to stand upon a frame supported by 4 Legs from the foot of which to the Top of the case let be 2 feet 4 Inches N.B. let the Bottles be very Strong

Order 25 Sacks of Salt from Liverpool

50 lb. White Bisquet

Hartlibs Legacy of Husbandry—also a new System of Agriculture done by various hands, but collected chiefly from the Papers of Mr Hale

2 Bushels of Hop clover Seed An Assortment of Garden Seeds N.B. let these and the Clover Seed be fresh and good—and put into the Cabbin, or dont send any

3 dozn bottles Stouton's Bitters 4 Oz. Nitre a Dulcis 1 lb. Orange Peale 1 Quart Orange flower Water 4 Oz. Elixor of Vitriol 4 Oz. Spirits Sal Armoniac 4 Oz. Hartshorn 4 Oz. Salvolatile 4 Oz. Tincture of Myrrh 4 Oz. Jallop 4 Oz. Ipecacuana 4 Oz. Diascordium 4 Oz. Syrrup of Poppies 4 Oz. Conserve of Roses 4 Oz. Contra Irva 2 Oz. Matthews Pills 1 lb. Bark prepard 4 Oz. Tincture of Castor 4 Oz. Spirit of Vitriol—all in dble Flint Bottles

1 Hhd best Porter—or the same quantity of Porter in Bottles if the Ship Sails time enough to be here before the Weather gets too warm

1 Dozn Grindstones ½ dozn Grass Scyths 2 Briar Scyths 2 dozn large & strong Padlocks 6 Stock locks—all to have difft Keys 2 dozn handsaw files 2 dozn x cutsaw Ditto 1 dozn whipsaw Ditto 1 dozn

pair HL Hinges ½ dozn drawing Knives 2 dozn box Gimblets 2 Whipsaws—of the best kind ½ groce of course, cheap, sheathd Knives for cutting Tobo 10 M 4d. Nails 5 M 6d. Ditto 20 M 8d. Ditto 25 M 10d. Ditto 1000 half Crown Ditto

600 Ells Oznabrigs 350 Yards Cotton 4 dozn pair Mens plaid Hose 4 dozn pair Womens Ditto 2 dozn pair Boys & Girls Ditto 6 lb. brown thread 2 lb. whited brown Ditto 4 Oz. 12d ditto 4 Oz. 2/ ditto 6 Loaves of dble & 6 of Single Refind Sugar

A Light handy Circumferenter for Surveying Lands—the Dial plate to be large and well graduated—the Sights to let down by Hinges (and not to slip of as is common) a spare needle in case of accidents—A Load Stone Set—and a Chain to be strong & well fixd—Platting Instruments, nor nothing but what is here specified, is wanting

4 Oz. Gutte vite 1 pint of Daffes Elixor 4 Oz. Squires Elixor 2 Wig, or Hair Bags 10 yds light Shag course & strong for Negroe waiting Men's Breech⟨es⟩ 100 W. white Paint—cheap sort 1 large brass or Iron Lock for an Outer Door

Go: Washington

Notes

Citations of Founders Online documents do not include individual links, as each source can be found by searching the site at https://founders.archives.gov/.

1. Alexander Hamilton was the greatest outlier, killed in his duel with Aaron Burr at age forty-seven.
2. Gordon S. Wood detailed this attitude among leading members of the founding generation in *The Radicalism of the American Revolution* (New York: Knopf, 1992), part 3.
3. John Adams to Benjamin Rush, September 19, 1806, Founders Online.
4. Thomas Jefferson to Joseph C. Cabell, February 7, 1826, in *The Writings of Thomas Jefferson*, ed. Paul L. Ford (New York: G. P. Putnam's Sons, 1899), 10:373–74.
5. For more on Washington's "Rules of Civility and Decent Behaviour in Company and Conversation," see Jennifer Stertzer, "The Rules of Civility," Washington Papers, https://washingtonpapers.org/documents/the-rules-of-civility/.
6. Virtual Tour, George Washington's Mount Vernon, https://virtualtour.mountvernon.org/.
7. Invoice to Cary & Company, May 1, 1759, Founders Online.

8. Invoice to Cary & Company, September 20, 1759, Founders Online.
9. Invoice to Cary & Company, September 28, 1760, Founders Online.
10. George Washington to George Steptoe Washington, May 5, 1788, in *The Papers of George Washington: Confederation Series*, ed. W. W. Abbot (Charlottesville: University of Virginia Press, 1992–97), 6:263.
11. George Washington to John Augustine Washington, June 15, 1783, Founders Online.
12. George Washington to James Madison, November 18, 1786, Founders Online.
13. George Washington to James Madison, November 5, 1786, Founders Online.
14. James Madison to George Washington, December 7, 1786, Founders Online; James Madison to George Washington, December 24, 1786, Founders Online. Edmund Randolph wrote, too, begging Washington to serve as a delegate. "For the gloomy prospect still admits one ray of hope," Randolph insisted, "that those, who began, carried on & consummated the revolution, can yet rescue America from the impending ruin." Edmund Randolph to George Washington, December 6, 1786, Founders Online.
15. George Washington to Eleanor "Nelly" Parke Custis, March 21, 1796, Founders Online.
16. George Washington to Samuel Powel, July 19, 1785, Founders Online.
17. George Washington to Samuel Powel, February 21, 1790, Founders Online. Readers can take a deep dive into the many agriculture-related records Washington and his farm managers produced at the Mount Vernon Farm Reports and Plantation Records collection, The George Washington Presidential Library at Mount Vernon,https://catalog.mountvernon.org/digital/collection/p16829coll11.
18. George Washington to the Hebrew Congregation in Newport, Rhode Island, August 18, 1790, Founders Online.
19. A powerful visual representation of the people living at Mount Vernon in 1799 can be found in Jessie MacLeod's essay in this volume.
20. Edmund S. Morgan first traced this interconnection in his transformational *American Slavery, American Freedom: The Ordeal of Colonial Virginia* (New York: W. W. Norton, 1975).
21. John Dickinson, quoted in David Waldstreicher, *Slavery's Constitution: From Revolution to Ratification* (New York: Hill and Wang, 2009), 84.
22. For context, see Kathryn Gehred, "Why Did Martha Washington Free Her Husband's Slaves Early?," Washington Papers, https://washingtonpapers.org/why-did-martha-washington-free-her-husbands-slaves-early/.
23. George Washington to Lund Washington, September 30, 1776, Founders Online.

24. George Washington, address to Congress, December 23, 1783, Founders Online (italics added).
25. George Washington to William Thornton, December 8, 1799, Founders Online.
26. George Washington to Robert Brooke, March 16, 1795, Founders Online. For Washington's support of the Alexandria Academy, see William Serverian, "Alexandria Academy," in *The Digital Encyclopedia of George Washington*, George Washington's Mount Vernon, https://www.mountvernon.org/library/digitalhistory/digital-encyclopedia/article/alexandria-academy/.
27. George Washington, last will and testament, July 9, 1799, Founders Online.
28. George Washington, last will and testament, July 9, 1799, Founders Online.

HOMO ECONOMICUS

The Economic World of George Washington

KATE ELIZABETH BROWN

One challenge of teaching early America arises from the sheer complexity of the age. The American founding comprises many important events occurring simultaneously, with a full complement of noteworthy personalities contributing to independence and nation-building. Consequently, in order to cover the late eighteenth century's many moving parts, the cast of founding players can often be reduced to one-dimensional roles: Alexander Hamilton becomes the finance guy; Thomas Jefferson, the ideas guy; George Washington, the "Father of His Country" who presides over it all, detached from the rough-and-tumble of politics.

This compartmentalization extends to the economic history of the early republic as well. The traditional way of teaching early American history is to center the political narrative; I'm not referring just to the development of political factions or their ideologies but also to the foreign affairs and domestic business of government that become students' primary focus and set the chronology of key events. Women's history, legal history, material and cultural history—they all form offshoots of this primarily political narrative, occasionally taking center stage for an event or two (for example, you can't leave *Marbury v. Madison* [1803] out, or Abigail Adams admonishing, "Remember the Ladies"!), then receding into the background as political history reasserts itself. Economic history fares no better. It's a sideshow to the main government-and-politics events.

Because of this traditional approach, historical silos form around historical figures and events. In the early republic, for example, Alexander Hamilton stands out as seemingly the only person thinking about the national economy, because his plan to restore the public credit—funding the Revolutionary War debt at par value, assuming state debts, creating a central bank, and planning for robust American manufacturing—has become a standard element of the early republic's all-too-familiar political narrative. But that's about it. Where in the Advanced Placement US history curriculum, for example, is the overview of early American banking or the importance of the carrying trade to the early republic's economy?[1] The rampant land speculation or the tax cuts that states enjoy when Hamilton's funding and assumption plans take effect?[2] Sure, slavery gets attention, but more for the political problems it causes and moral compromises it demands than for its central role in the early American economy. My point is that students get short shrift on early American economic history, and this diminishes their knowledge of the complexity of the period. If, as modern politico James Carville famously quipped, "it's the economy, stupid," that is so central to America and its politics, then should we be paying more attention to America's economic past?

George Washington offers teachers a useful way to integrate more economic history into their lessons about early American history and therefore to provide a more comprehensive narrative about early America. Washington's economic world demonstrates, writ small, what the eighteenth-century national and transatlantic economies represented writ large. In addition to leading the "George Washington and the Economy of a New Nation" week at the George Washington Teacher Institute, I teach courses in colonial America, the American Revolution and early republic, and American legal history at Western Kentucky University. In all these classes and seminars, I include a version of the multilayered economic history analysis I describe below. My students and I find this way of exploring the complexities of early American economic history accessible and intelligible—and I hope you will, too.

This essay presents an approach to teaching early national economic history that imagines Washington's economic world through three overlapping layers (an economic "onion," as I call it): Washington's personal economy, centered at his Mount Vernon estate; the Virginia and national economies; and the economy of the Atlantic world. By zooming in on Washington's economic world, we gain the perspective to simultaneously gaze outward to larger economic developments of the colonial era and early republic.

The five working farms of Washington's Mount Vernon estate, as well as the careful records Washington kept of his planting and business interests there, showcase America's integrated economic world, connecting Washington's personal fortune and business decisions to Hamilton's macroeconomic public policies as well as the changing conditions of Atlantic-wide trade. In command of land, enslaved laborers, and capital, Washington navigated boom and bust markets while creating economic opportunities for his estate. In doing so, his active management of his working farms helps students understand how the American economy changed throughout his lifetime. From mercantilism to a freer international trade, from a single-cash crop plantation to diversified agricultural commodities and proto-industrial methods of production, all while relying on the cruelties of slave labor: Washington's Mount Vernon estate, itself the key primary source for Washington's economic world, provides a comprehensive view of how the early American economy operated.

When teaching the economic history of the early republic, distinct phases of American capitalism track with the biggest political developments of the age. While the American economy is always tied to capital investment in the pursuit of profit and future pecuniary gains, American independence coincides with a freer, less regulated market economy taking root in the colonies-later-states. The Revolutionary War is partly a cause of this transformation; wartime interrupted the old notions of fixed marketplaces and locally controlled prices, and when the cannon fire quieted, American merchants adapted to prices set by fluctuating supply and demand. The marketplace itself—long confined to specific spaces, like city squares, and limited within the British Empire—became an abstraction. Adam Smith's *Wealth of Nations,* published in 1776, encouraged perhaps the biggest break from the past of all: the deregulation of trade.

Smith's idea—that governments should not limit the individual's pursuit of self-interested trade—challenged the dominant economic philosophy embraced by European empires and applied to their American colonies: mercantilism. Mercantilism was not just a heavy regulatory scheme. It was a purpose-driven program that sought to balance trade, limit self-interested pursuits (ineffectively, it turned out), prohibit colonial manufacturing, and extract from colonies to economically benefit the imperial center. Great Britain began constructing its mercantilist scheme for its American colonies in the mid-seventeenth century, with the first set of Navigation Acts. These customs duties and trade regulations constructed a trade network that limited colonial trade by adding extra costs (e.g., inserting British middlemen at British port cities into the tobacco trade). They also limited access to foreign marketplaces for colonial exports and imports (e.g., forcing colonial exporters to ship to British ports or to other colonial ports within the empire and prohibiting free trade with foreign nations). While Navigation Act rules and procedures restricted some colonial exports more than others, the totality of the mercantilist system was to benefit the home economy. The colonies would see some benefit, of course, but never more than Great Britain did.[3]

George Washington experienced the constraints and benefits of mercantilism. When he inherited Mount Vernon in 1761, he understood that his economic fortunes would be tied to his new estate's lands. And so he set out to become a knowledgeable, expert steward of the land—and he aimed to acquire a lot more land, too.

Marrying Martha Custis transformed Washington's socioeconomic status, rocketing him into the top tier of Virgina's planter class, but this social elevation only served to exacerbate and make clear to Washington how Virginia tobacco planters were trapped on multiple fronts. First, they were trapped by the tightly regulated mercantilist rules: tobacco had to be shipped on British ships to British cities and sold by British merchants. Washington didn't have the option to go rogue, shipping his hogsheads of tobacco off to a foreign market of his own choosing or on a whim. Then, tobacco planters were trapped by the uncontrollable variables that make farming a difficult occupation: too much rain, too much drought, worms and beetles destroying good harvests, and the typical boom-and-bust cycles of the transatlantic economy. Finally, marriage made painfully clear to Washington how farmers, but especially wealthy, landed planters, could so easily succumb to the cycle of debt endemic in the mercantile system.

To be sure, debt is common to farming, period, whether the farmer is trapped in a mercantilist economic system or not. Much capital expenditure (for equipment, labor, seeds, soil additives) is required up front, at the beginning of a growing cycle and through the harvest. Farmers often need to borrow money to begin the season's planting and harvest. Return on this investment only comes once the crop or livestock is sold on the market—and weather, insects, booms, and busts all impact the size of the profit the farmer ultimately sees. The debt can only be repaid—if it can be repaid—once a successful harvest delivers revenue that covers these costs, so many months or even years after the initial debt was incurred.

All this uncertainty and debt was made worse by the mercantilist system. Because the British government regulated imports into the colonies and exports out of the colonies, Washington and his planter brethren had added burdens imposed on them. If Washington harvested only a small crop of tobacco, he didn't have the flexibility to shop around the global marketplace to find the highest price possible and lock it in—to purse a self-interested trade, as Adam Smith would describe it. Instead, he depended on a London agent, a middleman deliberately inserted into the mercantilist system to benefit British workers while costing colonial farmers a cut of their profits. Washington's agent, the prestigious Cary & Company firm of London, then shopped around for the best prices at which to sell Washington's tobacco. But did Robert Cary, factor for Washington, really have an incentive to work hard to find the absolute best price available? Though Cary was probably doing the best he could, Washington remained suspicious, and understandably so. The Navigation Acts deprived Washington of free-market trade, where he could ensure that he locked in the best prices for his tobacco.

Furthermore, mercantilism deprived Washington of the choice to import from nations that would sell him cheaper goods. Built into the mercantilist middleman system was the practice of importing British finished goods on credit while you waited for your factor to return the proceeds of tobacco sales. This practice only exacerbated planters' debts. What if you went shopping now, buying textiles, farm tools, silks, wines, and dishware, only to find out that your tobacco proceeds didn't cover your bill?

A few years into their marriage, as the Washingtons spent lavishly, George found himself in exactly this predicament. It shocked him. It also caused him to rethink this participation in the mercantilist system in the short term and, as the imperial crisis brought the colonies' grievances with Great Britain into focus, to prepare for freer markets in the long term.

When I teach colonial economic history, Washington's struggles within the mercantilist system feature prominently to showcase how this system worked, including the costs and benefits for colonial planters. Extant letters written by Washington open a window for students onto wealthy planters' lavish shopping sprees. In just one example, in October 1761, Washington ordered from the Cary firm a long list of items such as "1 dozn breakfast Cups & as many Sawcers of China" and "2 pair black Satten Shoes."[4] Washington's letters also vividly depict, in his own words, his frustrations with being trapped in the mercantilist system. In one letter to Cary, Washington complained about drought that had impacted his crop and thus made it difficult to pay back his outstanding debt.[5] Washington's colonial correspondence made concrete the real frustrations and limitations of an economic system that could otherwise feel abstract to students. But these letters also showcase the benefits of the mercantilist system: colonists had access to an empire-wide demand for their foodstuffs and raw materials and, through British merchants like Robert Cary, American colonists could import a wide variety of consumer goods. The American addiction to shopping was thus born.[6]

Washington is also a useful figure through which to demonstrate economic change over time, not only for his shift away from a single-cash-crop production farm but also, in the long run, for his orientation toward a market less encumbered by regulatory restrictions. The moment when Washington realized how much he owed the Cary firm occurred around the same time that Washington decided to move away from tobacco production and toward a more diversified portfolio of crops. The 1765 Stamp Act, which taxed colonists directly on everyday products and services such as newspapers and court documents, produced economic boycotts across the colonies. These boycotts accelerated Washington's transition away from tobacco. And so, between 1764 and 1766, Washington made the strategic decision to grow wheat as his main cash crop while he turned his ever-growing estate into a diversified farm.[7] While wheat would become one of Washington's main sources of revenue, the farms that constituted the Mount Vernon estate would shift from tobacco fields to cornfields, orchards, kitchen gardens, salted fish production, and fields dedicated to other crops like peas, flax, and barley.

Washington's decision to diversify his estate held several advantages. First, while Washington's tobacco was entangled in the web of Navigation Act regulations, wheat was less regulated, and it could be shipped to other colonial ports directly. Washington was involved in at least two shipping ventures where he sent his own ship (or a ship he invested in) to the Caribbean, carrying wheat and salted fish.[8] These two cash "crops," which enslaved laborers grew on Washington's five farms and fished out of the Potomac River every spring, supplied the sugar-producing islands in the Caribbean. On those islands, like Jamaica and Barbados, where every available acre was dedicated to growing and processing extremely profitable sugarcane, little food was grown to feed the local population (largely comprising the enslaved labor force doing the dangerous, laborious work of producing and refining sugar). Washington's new wheat and salted fish outfits found a steady demand for these staple goods that were less subject to the boom-and-bust cycles that plagued the tobacco market.

Washington's diversification scheme allowed him to service the local Virginian marketplace as well and thus escape the strictures of mercantilism completely. Virginians needed flour (ground to different specifications, from the more expensive refined flour to the cheaper whole grain) and they purchased wheat from Washington; Virginians then further enriched Washington's pocketbook by paying him to mill it through Mount Vernon's commercial gristmill. This arrangement began when Virginia was still a colony, but it remained in place for the rest of Washington's life.

Finally, by moving away from tobacco production, Washington insulated himself somewhat from the economic protests arising from the imperial crisis. The Stamp Act engendered colonial boycotts, but that was only the beginning of the colonies' economic protests. As the Stamp Act gave way to the Townshend Duties (1767), and then Parliament shocked the colonies by punishing Massachusetts with the Coercive Acts (1774), the British North American colonies ratcheted up their protests—largely in the form of economic boycotts. The 1774 Continental Association is the best example of this. This declaration, produced by the First Continental Congress, protested the Coercive Acts through colonial threats of nonimportation of British goods, nonexportation of colonial goods and raw materials, and the nonconsumption of British goods. As a member of the First Continental Congress, Washington supported this policy.

By this time, Washington had stopped growing tobacco on his Mount Vernon estate—relinquishing his dependency on one export alone for cash—and though nonexportation would limit his wheat exports, he could sell wheat to the local market around Alexandria. Also, Washington's enslaved labor force grew the corn and salted the fish that were the staple foods of their diet, and Washington found that he could temporarily make do without the silks and satin shoes he imported from London. Other Virginian farmers, who had not transitioned away from tobacco, were in a less flexible situation. Washington encouraged them to make the switch, however, and he advocated that farmers receive a few months' time before boycotts went into effect in order to begin the transition from tobacco to other crops.[9]

In the end, Washington—along with all American farmers—would be released from the bonds of British mercantilism when America declared its independence in 1776. The Revolutionary War created the opportunity for a new nation, experimenting with federalism and republicanism, to create a system of freer trade. The war had another consequence for farmers, planters, merchants, and tradesmen alike: it called into question the morality of slavery.

To paraphrase Samuel Johnson, What business did Americans have whining about taxation without representation (especially when its tax burden was relatively light) and calling the British Parliament and king tyrants for depriving them of liberty, when Americans in the North and South subjected human beings to chattel slavery? Americans, including George Washington, enslaved people and depended on their labor for their economic livelihoods—yet their fight for independence from Britain was inspired by the rhetoric of freedom from tyranny. The same war that would free Americans from mercantilist regulations could also deprive them of their property and the economic engines for their tobacco, cotton, and rice plantations—and in Washington's case, his wheat farm too.

The threat emerged early in the war. Although American law treated Africans and their descendants as chattel (personal property, no different than livestock), enslaved laborers were wise to the opportunities offered by a civil war occurring around them. Lord Dunmore, the last royal governor of Virginia, tried to capitalize on this with his famous 1775 proclamation offering enslaved laborers their freedom if they would, and could, fight on behalf of the British. It worked. As many as one thousand enslaved men and women flocked to Dunmore and other British officials during the war.[10] Washington did not lose any of his enslaved labor force to Dunmore's proclamation, but later in the war, seventeen people Washington enslaved escaped from Mount Vernon. Washington attempted to retrieve them at the end of the conflict.[11]

Other essays in this volume examine Washington's evolving and contradictory relationship to slavery, but here, as we explore Washington's illustrative place in the early American economy, slavery must be central to every lesson and every conversation about Mount Vernon's production and Washington's innovativeness as a farmer. Though it is true that Washington was in the vanguard of Virginia planters switching from tobacco to wheat, from tightly regulated trade to a freer marketplace, he was just making the decisions. Like a chief executive officer managing workers bustling on the factory floor, Washington made the executive decisions for the Mount Vernon estate while hundreds of enslaved men, women, and children carried out his plans. For every bit of Washingtonian innovation—from determining the best soil additives and figuring out ideal crop rotation schemes to adopting new technologies, like the sixteen-sided treading barn and new plow designs, and opening a merchant mill on the Dogue Run Farm—the women and men Washington enslaved contributed the labor that made all of this happen. Enslaved laborers were the human engines driving the productivity of the Mount Vernon estate (as well as underwriting Washington's lifestyle and free time to fight the Revolutionary War and serve as president).

While General Washington was away, keeping the Continental Army fighting while pestering the British redcoats into submission, Mount Vernon suffered wartime hardships. But when he retired from the army and returned to his beloved lands nestled on the Potomac River, he did so while eagerly anticipating the work of restoring Mount Vernon's productivity. Washington was, at heart, a farmer. Moreover, he held land stewardship as the highest priority—higher than profit margins. Now that a new republic was born, new economic opportunities awaited.

George Washington's engagement with the colonial mercantile economy offers students insights into early America, including the myth of salutary neglect, the costs and benefits of mercantilism, and the innovations of Farmer George (rather than General Washington or Mr. President). The Mount Vernon estate, with Washington at its helm, leads students into exploring the multiple layers of the early American economy, too.

When I teach the early American economy, I present it like an onion, with three layers to peel back and explore. The deepest layer, the core, is the local economy—for Washington, his Mount Vernon farms—which encompasses both sites of subsistence agriculture and large sites of cash-crop production. Washington innovates on the colonial plantation model by maintaining a cash crop but dropping the traditional tobacco to switch to wheat and other cereal grains like oats, rye, and barley (grains that, conveniently, are used to make whiskey; more on that later). Washington was a subsistence farmer, too, in that he diversified his farms to produce food for his family's consumption as well as for the carbohydrate and protein staples of the diets (corn and salted fish) of the people he enslaved.

Washington also participated energetically in the outermost layer of the economic onion, the transatlantic economy. Yet unlike the lucrative slave labor plantations in the Caribbean, which produced only cash crops like sugar and coffee, Washington's farms demonstrated how subsistence crops could be scaled up and sold as nutritious cash crops used to feed other parts of the British Empire.

After you peel back the transatlantic layer of the economic onion, and before you work down to its local core, a middle layer of economic activity exists: intra- and inter-colonial—and then state—trade. Washington participated in intra-colony/state trade, using the port at Alexandria to ship and receive domestic and foreign shipments, selling his wheat to Virginia farmers, and encouraging local neighbors to buy flour or grind their own at his merchant mill. Washington participated in intra-colony trade during the 1760s and early 1770s. But once the new American nation was born, and, not coincidentally, under Washington's own administration, national economic policy moved American merchants, farmers, and nascent manufacturers toward a market revolution of increasing commercial ties and economic production. Farmer George exemplified this national economic dynamic as well.

I once told a group of teachers at the George Washington Teacher Institute that I gave Washington some credit for the early republic's macroeconomic policy, that is, for Alexander Hamilton's combined Report on the Public Credit, Report on the Central Bank, Report on the Mint, and Report on Manufactures. The teachers had a good laugh—they knew that I am a big fan of Hamilton's.[12] But they also wanted to know why Washington should share credit in Hamilton's great policy accomplishment. Washington did not write any of those state papers, of course, and they were not his ideas: Hamilton deserves that credit, plus acknowledgment for doing the political wheeling and dealing necessary to get his funding scheme (paying the national debt back at par value) and his highly controversial assumption of state debts plan through Congress. Still, Hamilton and his macroeconomic policies benefited from Washington's immense reserves of political capital, and Washington also approved of Hamilton's brand of commercial capitalism—even signing the constitutionally questionable bank bill into law. Hamilton's financial program was the signature domestic policy of Washington's administration.

Washington's commercial and economic life also mirrored the intended effects of Hamiltonian policy. Just as Hamilton advocated a close relationship with the British through trade and a move toward industrial manufacturing, Washington embraced cooperation with Great Britain so that American farmers could benefit from what Washington considered to be superior British farming practices. The British "New Husbandry" movement—the late eighteenth-century style of farming and land stewardship that Washington adopted and implemented on his own estate—was the kind of British export that

Washington actively encouraged. Not only did Washington consider British farming methods to be excellent and implementable in the United States, but he also considered farming and trade to be the basis of peaceful, prosperous international cooperation.[13] Hamilton agreed.

In his Report on Manufactures, Hamilton implored Congress to use constitutional powers and fiscal policy to create a diversified American economy. Hamilton's vision included developing manufacturing at home, stable banks and capital markets, and a thriving commercial and carrying trade with domestic and foreign markets, all in addition to American agriculture. All these sectors, not just the banks and the monied interests, were essential for a productive commercial nation. Furthermore, Britain, as our primary trade partner and the first nation to industrialize, naturally played a key role in Hamilton's vision of commercial capitalism.

Washington, like Hamilton, looked to Congress to act. While Hamilton gets all the attention for his controversial (but effective) projects, Washington also asked Congress to legislate for his economic vision—to set aside funds to create a national board modeled after the British Board of Agriculture to teach and disseminate the New Husbandry techniques to American farmers. Unfortunately for Washington, Congress failed to act; nevertheless, he attempted to mobilize the nation to adopt his vision for efficient farming.[14]

In other, related ways, Washington's farming practices nod to Hamilton's manufacturing vision. Washington was keen to adopt new technologies whenever possible if he thought they would prove efficient and effective for their cost. For example, Washington adopted mechanized threshers on his River and Union Farm properties in 1797, thus adopting the most cutting-edge system for wheat processing.[15] In doing so, Washington's Mount Vernon estate anticipated the vertical integration that industrialized firms like U.S. Steel would employ a century later.

Vertical integration is the process by which a firm expands in size along its supply chain and production process. That is, the firm expands to acquire all or some of the raw materials, processing facilities, transportation fleets, warehousing, and consumer sale points involved in producing and selling the firm's products. Andrew Carnegie and John D. Rockefeller get much credit for vertically integrating their steel and oil corporations, but George Washington anticipated the efficiencies of vertical integration in the late eighteenth century.

Here's how Washington's vertically integrated wheat processing system worked (see fig. 1):

Vertical integration on the Mount Vernon estate

Raw material produced, extracted:

Grow and harvest wheat

↓

Initial processing:

Dry, thresh, winnow with mechanized thresher and sixteen-sided treading barn

↓

Refining:

Automated merchant mill and distillery

↓

Finished product to sell on local and international markets:

Fine/coarse flour; whiskey; brandy

FIGURE 1. Vertical integration on the Mount Vernon estate

Step 1: First, enslaved laborers planted, tended to, and grew wheat. When the wheat was ready to be harvested, enslaved laborers cut the wheat and brought it to production facilities on the estate for processing.

Step 2: The wheat berry (the part of the plant that is ground into flour) needs to be separated from the stalk and chaff (husk) surrounding it. For millennia, farmers threshed wheat with a handheld staff with a block at the end, but during Washington's lifetime, the first mechanized threshers were being invented.[16] Washington was aware of this new technology and adopted it on the River and Union Farms. He also used a less mechanized, but still advanced, technology to separate the wheat from the stalk and chaff on his Dogue Run Farm: the sixteen-sided treading barn (see fig. 2).

Washington built his sixteen-sided treading barn between 1792 and 1794 from his own design. The barn had two levels: a top level outfitted with floorboards separated just enough that wheat berries (with or without the accompanying husk) could fall from the top to the ground level, where enslaved workers

FIGURE 2. Sixteen-sided treading barn. (Courtesy of The Mount Vernon Ladies' Association)

could collect them. Before the barn-threshing began, workers laid cut and dried wheat on the floor of the top level of the barn and brought in a team of two horses (entering the second floor from a ramp) to trot around on the wheat. The repetitive up-down, up-down pounding of their hooves on the wheat did the mechanical work of separating wheat heads from the stalk, but only the berry plus chaff was small enough to fall down to the ground floor to be collected.

Step 3: After enslaved farm workers collected the wheat berries and any chaff not yet separated, they winnowed the remaining husks from the wheat berries in a sieve-like basket before transporting the wheat berries to Washington's in-house mill.

Step 4: In 1771, Farmer George constructed a merchant mill on his estate for him to use. Local farmers who needed access to a gristmill to process their corn and wheat could also use it. But in 1791, while in office, President Washington viewed the patent submitted to the US government for a fully automated merchant mill. Washington licensed the plans under the patent filed by the mill's inventor, Oliver Evans, and installed the Evans automated gristmill on the Mount Vernon estate (see fig. 3). Washington had the state-of-the-art gristmill outfitted with expensive French burr millstones that could produce the finest grade of white flour. In addition to the fine flour, Washington's mill also ground coarser flour and cornmeal to feed his enslaved workforce.

Step 5: The final stage in Washington's integrated farm-to-table production model included processing the finished product into shippable, final forms. For the fine and coarser flours, Evans's gristmill automatically ground, dried, and sifted the flour into barrels that just needed to be filled and sealed for shipment to Virginian or Caribbean consumers. But Washington could also transport

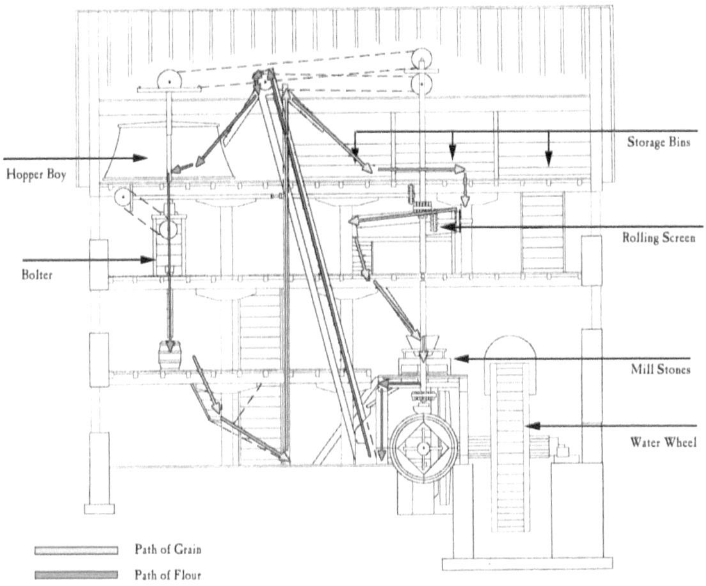

FIGURE 3. Inside Washington's gristmill. (Courtesy of The Mount Vernon Ladies' Association)

the grains grown on the Mount Vernon estate in liquid form, if he processed the wheat not in the gristmill but in the large distillery he built next door to the gristmill in 1797.

The Mount Vernon distillery, while run under the efficiency-oriented Farmer George himself, became the most profitable production center on the estate. It also connected the Mount Vernon farm to the local Virginian economy, as Alexandria's taverns sold Mount Vernon's unaged whiskey and brandy to locals and travelers alike.[17]

The wheat-production process described above demonstrates how the Mount Vernon estate reflected the larger changes occurring in the American economy in the late eighteenth and early nineteenth centuries. While not yet a part of America's first wave of industrialization, Washington's adoption of new farming techniques geared toward land stewardship (for long-term productivity), combined with his installation of new technologies that automated (the Evans gristmill) and efficiently scaled up grain production (treading barn), illustrate how commercial capitalism developed, reaching more domestic and international markets and adopting more efficient production methods. Alexander Hamilton's economic plans aimed to facilitate this expanding web of commercial capitalism as well as to encourage domestic manufacturing. While Washington's farms did not generate finished consumer goods, he did integrate proto-industrial technologies to manufacture commercially sold flour and liquor, and he sold them into an increasingly integrated web of marketplaces, near and far. In other words, Washington's Mount Vernon estate peeled back all the layers of the American economic onion.

George Washington's farms provide an excellent teaching tool for learning about economic history. The Mount Vernon estate demonstrates not only the interconnected layers of the early national economy—the local, intra- and interstate, and international layers of the economic onion—but also how Washington's decisions as chief executive farmer highlight mercantilism, the New Husbandry farming techniques, and freer market exchange. Washington's experience does not cover all topics involved with early American capitalism; Mount Vernon cannot replace discussion of the Lowell mills or the factory system, for example. Still, Washington's example does allow teachers to cover a lot of economic complexity and change over time through one familiar farmer. Washington's farms also allow for the grim but necessary conversations about chattel slavery and the essential fact that all of Washington's economic and political successes were underwritten by the labor of people he enslaved. As it goes for Washington, so it goes for all of early America.

Notes

Citations of Founders Online documents do not include individual links, as each source can be found by searching the site at https://founders.archives.gov/.

1. They are important topics. See Sharon Ann Murphy, *Other People's Money: How Banking Worked in the Early American Republic* (Baltimore: Johns Hopkins University Press, 2017); Douglass C. North, *The Economic Growth of the United States, 1790–1860* (New York: W. W. Norton, 1966).
2. See Michael A. Blaakman, *Speculation Nation: Land Mania in the Revolutionary American Republic* (Philadelphia: University of Pennsylvania Press, 2023); Max M. Edling and Mark D. Kaplanoff, "Alexander Hamilton's Fiscal Reform: Transforming the Structure of Taxation in the Early Republic," *William and Mary Quarterly* 61, no. 4 (2004): 713–44.

3. Jonathan Levy, *Ages of American Capitalism: A History of the United States* (New York: Random House, 2022), 9–38.
4. Invoice to Cary & Company, October 12, 1761, Founders Online.
5. George Washington to Cary & Company, June 20, 1762, Founders Online.
6. T. H. Breen, *The Marketplace of Revolution: How Consumer Politics Shaped American Independence* (New York: Oxford University Press, 2004).
7. The best and most comprehensive scholarly treatment of Washington as a farmer and an economic actor is Bruce A. Ragsdale, *Washington at the Plow: The Founding Farmer and the Question of Slavery* (Cambridge, MA: Harvard University Press, 2021), 41.
8. Ragsdale, *Washington at the Plow,* 65, 85.
9. Ragsdale, *Washington at the Plow,* 61.
10. Ragsdale, *Washington at the Plow,* 80–81.
11. Ragsdale, *Washington at the Plow,* 91–92.
12. See Kate Elizabeth Brown, *Alexander Hamilton and the Development of American Law* (Lawrence: University Press of Kansas, 2017).
13. Ragsdale, *Washington at the Plow,* 6.
14. Ragsdale, *Washington at the Plow,* 214–16.
15. Ragsdale, *Washington at the Plow,* 262.
16. Ragsdale, *Washington at the Plow,* 110.
17. "Ten Facts About the Distillery," George Washington's Mount Vernon, https://www.mountvernon.org/the-estate-gardens/distillery/ten-facts-about-the-distillery/.

A BITE OUT OF HISTORY

George Washington's Dentures and Teaching with Objects

LUCY SMITH

George Washington did not have wooden teeth. Yet the myth of the wooden dentures—like the chopping down of the cherry tree—remains ingrained in the lore of the early American republic. Unlike the apocryphal cherry tree, Washington's still-extant dentures raise complex questions about economics, medicine, the body, race, gender performance, and politics. Essentially, they reveal the mundane lived experiences of elites like Washington while connecting him to trans-Atlantic trade and international intellectual networks.

Tracing the production, consumption, and legacy of Washington's dentures illuminates the complex economic and cultural relationships connecting a Virginian planter to the vast eighteenth-century commercial world. This is the power of objects—to make the intangible tangible. While George Washington left an extensive formal written record of his political and military life, he did not leave an autobiography. Yet the objects of his life and the physical grounds of Mount Vernon act as an autobiography of sorts, documenting his choices about what to buy, what to wear, and how to live. Constructing an "object biography" of his dentures, now housed at George Washington's Mount Vernon, allows us to create what historian Karin Dannehl outlines as a "time capsule."[1] This essay uses Washington's dentures to model what kinds of questions objects can answer and how objects can be employed to understand the past and, ultimately, our present, with clarity.

Washington had poor dental health throughout his life. His iconic dentures (see fig. 1) were based on designs from France and England and crafted by

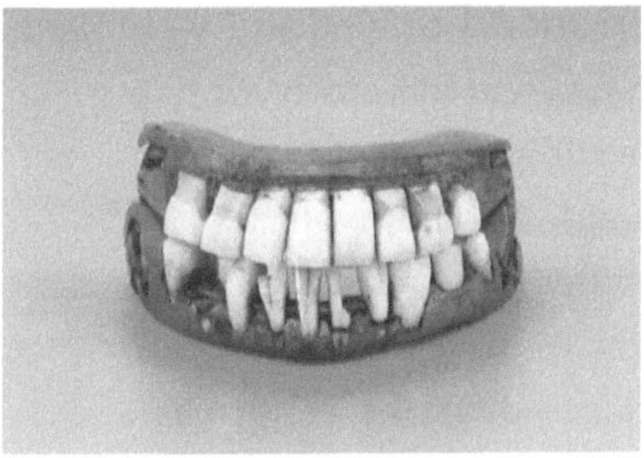

FIGURE 1. George Washington's dentures, created by John Greenwood, 1790–1799. (Photograph by Gavin Ashworth, courtesy of The Mount Vernon Ladies' Association)

American dentist John Greenwood in Philadelphia. The teeth were either human or carved from ivory, cow, or horse teeth. The top and bottom bases were made from a lead cast with a large groove in which to set the artificial teeth.[2] The teeth were attached to the base by drilling holes in each tooth and threading a brass wire that secured the teeth in place. The upper and lower sets were then connected with silver spring-loaded hinges designed to mimic the natural opening and closing of the jaw. Lead-based dentures weighed nearly a quarter of a pound, with sharp wires poking the inside of the mouth.

Washington's earlier dentures connected to his remaining teeth to stay in place so he could eat, drink, and speak. For example, the dentures worn during his inauguration in 1789—also made by John Greenwood—had a hole on the right side to allow the ivory-based dentures to slip over the remaining teeth to anchor the set.[3] However, Washington's final set of dentures could not rely upon his remaining teeth—by 1796, he had only one tooth left. In addition, the spring-loaded hinges required Washington to use his jaw to constantly clamp down on the dentures to keep them positioned. Thus, the famous Gilbert Stuart portrait—the image featured on the dollar bill—depicts a stoic and stern Washington with bulging jowls due to his firmly clamping his jaw to ensure that the spring-loaded hinges remained closed. Otherwise, Washington risked his mouth popping open and his teeth flying out—which actually happened to Charles Willson Peale while at a dinner party with Dolley Madison![4]

Ultimately, Washington's final dentures contained metals mined from South America, ivory from Africa, North American domesticated animal teeth, and human teeth, possibly from Europe, North America, or the Caribbean, based on designs and scholarship from Europe and crafted in New York City. In short, Washington held the Atlantic world in his mouth.

Washington's dentures had extensive international origins and were made possible by the rise and solidification of new connotations teeth had developed throughout the Atlantic world that are still present today. In the twenty-first century, teeth carry a series of meanings. The normalization of braces in the United States, for example, demonstrates how meanings of race, class, and country of origin are mapped onto teeth. We have been socialized to read teeth to organize and classify people. American politicians, celebrities, and executives alike have the bright, white, and straight Hollywood smile because Americans "read" their mouths and make assumptions about their individual character and class. The inverse is also true. In modern America, individuals with missing teeth lose income for every missing tooth, as moral judgment is applied to those who lack teeth.[5] This internalization of the connection between health, morality, and teeth makes many Americans recoil when they see missing, crooked, or yellowed teeth—which are all perfectly healthy, natural, and normal. However, within the western European tradition, teeth were not actively used to interpret (or judge) people and their bodies until the late seventeenth century.[6] Throughout the eighteenth century, systems of meanings were newly mapped onto teeth, making teeth and the mouth pivotal sites to interpret a person's body, moral character, and socioeconomic status.

Teeth gained this status through social and economic connections during the mid-eighteenth-century consumer revolution. At this time, luxury goods and cheap imitations alike flooded the Atlantic marketplace. This influx of products—from textiles to porcelain, furniture, books, and exotic foodstuffs—dramatically shifted social-class presentation and communication modes. Scholars Jennifer Van Horn, Elizabeth Kowaleski-Wallace, and Catherine Kelly examine how elites like Washington began to use health and beauty to distance themselves from the middling and lower classes through prosthetics and cosmetics as luxury goods.[7] When the expanded marketplace made more goods available to the lower classes, the corporeal body became a site on which to perform and prove elite respectability and gentility. Washington himself internalized this relationship with his body, performance, and gentility from a young age.[8] By sixteen, he had copied the highly popular "Rules of Civility and Decent Behaviour in Company and Conversation," 110 precepts that included lessons like "Shake not the head, feet, or legs roll not the eyes lift not one eyebrow higher than the other wry not the mouth, and bedew no mans face with your spittle, by approaching too near him when you speak" and "The gestures of the body must be suited to the discourse you are upon."[9]

Unlike the body, which could be held in a manner considered virtuous, teeth were manipulated and circulated throughout the eighteenth-century Atlantic world, illuminating more significant questions about economics, race, gender, and the physical self. Beyond the broader social trends spurred by the consumer revolution, there was also a radical shift in food production, consumption, and distribution. While Washington's dental troubles may have been exacerbated by genetics, tooth loss was common in the eighteenth century owing to increased life expectancy and the widespread consumption of sugar, tea, coffee, Madeira, and other enamel-eroding substances. Washington's dental troubles were shared by many; his concern over appearance and ability to afford dentures revealed his social status. The extensive and expanding sugar trade and ritual dining practices of consuming tea, coffee, and hot chocolate changed dietary habits across class lines. As diets changed, teeth started to rot. Elites consumed the most sugar—and had the most rotten teeth.

In the eighteenth century, as now, rotting teeth required intervention, and demand for dental expertise expanded along with sugar consumption. Some 740 treatises and dissertations concerning teeth, operations on teeth, management of teeth, or natural histories of teeth were published between 1723 and 1800.[10] This proliferation of medical texts reflects the rise of the dental profession, so medical knowledge and training became more standardized as it circulated throughout the Atlantic world.

In 1706, Pierre Fauchard published *Le chirugien dentiste, ou Traité des dents* (*The Surgeon Dentist or Treatise on the Teeth*), later translated into English and German, heralding a shift in dentistry from a craft to a profession.[11] Fauchard came to be known for elevating the reputation of dentists while cultivating elite clients and institutionalizing dental care in the French miliary. However, dentists, quasi-dentists, quacks, and charlatans alike all coexisted throughout this era in the medical-dental landscape, with different kinds of care and knowledge intermingling. Before the formal professionalization of dentists and the establishment of dental schools in the early nineteenth century, "tooth-drawers" and women's domestic knowledge were the main channels of dental care.

If the eighteenth century marked an era before formal dentistry, where did you go if you had a toothache? The short answer is the tooth-drawer. These quasi-professionals were often the last resort after home remedies and prevention techniques had failed, since the tooth-drawer would "draw"—that is, extract—the tooth. Patients would seek out extraction as the only permanent remedy for toothache from age, accident, or poor hygiene. Washington's first tooth was extracted in 1756, when he was twenty-four. Nearly every year after the first tooth removal, Washington suffered toothaches and frequent extractions. Indeed, by the time of his death, he had lost all his teeth to decay and extraction.

The tooth-drawer was sometimes seen as a shadowy and violent figure, as depicted in Caravaggio's painting *The Tooth-Drawer* (1607). In a dark tavern, a figure sits in the center with his head tossed back, one hand gripping a chair's armrest in pain and the other hand raised in agony. A crowd of men in dirt and shadows surround the table, watching the violent extraction with intense expressions. The men represent all ages, from a small child in the left foreground to an elderly man with hollowed cheeks, suggesting no more remaining teeth. Forced tooth extraction was part of everyone's dental history, and even a young child would experience it one day. In the center, smirking and staring at the viewer, is the tooth-drawer, holding down the patient with one strong hand while the other grasps pliers pulling out a lower molar.

Scenes like this one were not uncommon, with tooth-drawers traveling from town to town to perform extractions. In some cases, they would make a spectacle of the extraction, as in the infamous Le Grand Thomas, or "Terror of the Human Jaw," and create a larger-than-life persona with flashy and ostentatious dress and a "stage" on the marketplace to perform public tooth extractions.[12] These charlatans sold cure-alls while boasting that they could force any tooth into submission. One scholar offered this description: "His barking voice could be heard across the city. If a client's tooth resisted his assaults he would, it was said, make the individual kneel down in front of him and then, with the strength of a bull, lift him three times into the air with the hand still clenched on the recalcitrant tooth."[13] In an era of public executions and corporal punishment, tooth-drawers offered one of many public and violent forms of entertainment.

Not all extractions were public spectacles by questionable characters, though. Blacksmiths, farriers (blacksmiths who shod horses), and other artisans frequently extracted teeth in smaller communities or when the tooth-drawer was unavailable. Extracting a tooth is a violent and painful process that requires immense physical strength and ability. Thus, community members like blacksmiths were often sought out to perform extractions, owing to their tremendous strength as well as their skill in using specialized tools. As seen in James Wilson's satirical print *The Ludicrous Operator, or Blacksmith Turn'd Tooth Drawer* (1765), the burly blacksmith stands by his anvil and uses large pliers to extract an older woman's front tooth.[14] Unlike the tavern tooth-drawer scene, this is in a semi-private setting. The woman's husband watches with a scrutinizing gaze as his wife clasps her hat in pain. The frequency of artisans performing dental procedures evidently led to many craftsmen becoming full-time dentists, including Washington's dentist, John Greenwood.

The final piece of the eighteenth-century dental landscape was the home and its folksy cures, like this one, reprinted in a seventeenth-century recipe book: "Take of Gum Dragon half an ounce, mastic, and olibanum of each 3 Drams Bolcone and a half dram of Myrth seed."[15] Here, Lady Frescheville describes how to make a toothache plaster designed to help alleviate intense tooth pain. Elite White women like Lady Frescheville, as well as middling- and lower-class women, cultivated medical knowledge in order to care for their families and communities. Their recipes would frequently circulate through domestic knowledge and trade work and were most visible in elite and middling women's comprehensive recipe books. A prime example of the genre is Eliza Lucas Pinckney's recipe book, which contains recipes to "Make Snow Cream" and "Little Puddings" as well as "For A Tooth Ach" and "For the Rheumatism."[16] In this way, women's recipe books reflected the roles, responsibilities, and expectations for women and their knowledge of medicine as well as global connections for ingredients.

From elite households like Washington's to poor White and enslaved households, women practiced preventative dental care through toothpaste, powders, rinses, and pain reduction techniques for toothache, gum disease, and sensitive teeth. With the rise of printed recipe books like Eliza Smith's *The Compleat Housewife* (1753), more recipes began circulating in public channels like newspapers, leading the new class of dentists to start co-opting, making, and selling women's traditional recipes.

George Washington, however, turned to dentist John Greenwood for relief rather than to his own wife. In 1789, Washington was sworn into office as the first president of the United States of America. While he stood on the balcony of Federal Hall in New York City, he had only one tooth remaining in his head—a bicuspid on the right side of his mouth. After many misgivings, Washington had his final tooth extracted by Greenwood, who would later be hailed as the "father of modern dentistry." Between 1790 and 1799, Greenwood fashioned several sets of dentures for Washington, including the set on display at Mount Vernon.

Washington's dentures reflected the standard craftsmanship of the era. Artificial teeth, like those that John Greenwood's father, Isaac Greenwood, made, were typically carved out of ivory from Africa. Hippopotamus ivory was preferred for multiple teeth when they were needed. The ivory could be carved as a single block that could be easily inserted into the mouth and was less likely to break with normal wear and tear.[17] Similarly, elephant ivory and bone were also carved into artificial teeth, but they were considered a cheaper grade of material by medical practitioners and wearers alike: "Teeth made of ivory (the tusk of the elephant), or of bone, are very imperfect; they have no enamel, are soft, soon become discolored and begin to decay, and unavoidably render the breath offensive."[18] In other words, ivory was the most accessible artificial tooth substance available and generated repeat customers, as ivory teeth needed to be frequently replaced. However, ivory's propensity for staining and tendency to cause bad breath led to new dental technological developments and the advent of a market for human teeth. While there was a robust trade in artificial teeth, human teeth were the gold standard for live tooth transplantation and for dentures for people like Washington. They had a more natural appearance, offered greater resistance to staining, and reduced halitosis.

But a market for live human teeth? Who would donate their teeth in a world without modern anesthetics? As it turns out, plenty of people would, from all around the Atlantic world. On November 18, 1784, the French-born, English-trained dentist Jean Pierre Le Mayeur placed this advertisement in the *Pennsylvania Packet* newspaper in Philadelphia: "Any person disposed to sell their Front Teeth, or any of them may call on Dr. Le Mayeur, at his Lodging, and receive Two Guineas for each Tooth." This was far from an atypical advertisement from Le Mayeur or the scores of other dentists, quasi-dentists, and charlatans fueling the domestic and trans-Atlantic tooth trade throughout the late eighteenth and early nineteenth centuries. In the 1780s, La Mayeur and others advertised to pay for teeth for both dentures and to be transplanted directly into a patient's mouth. In fact, Le Mayeur frequently visited Mount Vernon and became a lifelong friend of the Washingtons.

Early American newspapers connected Le Mayeur and other itinerant professionals (legitimate and illegitimate alike) to clients and provided a platform to craft their identities. From 1784 to 1788, Le Mayeur purchased almost 120 newspaper advertisements throughout the United States, with the bulk occurring between 1784 and 1785 in New York City and Philadelphia. Le Mayeur's correspondence, along with newspaper posts, indicated that he traveled as far south as Charleston, with a brief international trip to San Domingo.

Print media and culture in the new republic allowed Le Mayeur to communicate beyond his social connections. Period newspapers allowed him to directly hail those in the lower classes (to purchase teeth) and speak to elites (as he developed social networks). As scholar Robert Gross outlines, reading and literacy in eighteenth-century America were surprisingly common, with one contemporary author stating in 1789, "A person of mature age, who cannot both read and write, is rarely to be found."[19] Literacy rates were not universal across the country, though. New England's population enjoyed greater literacy, owing to community schools. It is also important to note that many more people could read but not necessarily write. However, reading and oral culture combined through the circulation of newspapers that were frequently read aloud in taverns and coffeehouses.[20] As a result, even if members of the lower classes could not directly read Le Mayeur's advertisements, they still knew of and responded to them through the cultural systems already established for commercial, cultural, and political communications.

Le Mayeur's advertisements coexisted with a wide range of goods, services, and announcements typically seen in early American newspapers. Benjamin Franklin's *Pennsylvania Gazette* represented the standard period paper, with, as historian David S. Shields has described it, "timely digests of foreign news, accurate transcriptions of provincial political addresses and communications, a column for local news, a broad range of advertisements, and belletristic essays of an entertaining and useful sort."[21] The *Pennsylvania Packet and Daily Advertiser* from November 25, 1786, highlighted the consumer context for both prospective patients and potential sellers of teeth. Le Mayeur's advertisement for "those who would wish to dispose of their front teeth" appears embedded in the same column as a post for an "Assortment of Merchandize" from St. Clair & Co. Auctioneers and a notice reading, "To be sold, a Healthy Negro lad aged 18 is sober and honest." To the right of Le Mayeur's advertisement is a small illustration of a ship, with the announcements "who have for slave, Muscovado sugar, Grenada rum, Spanish hides" and "For freight or passage apply to the Captain on board" for St. Eustatius and St. Thomas in the Caribbean. The physical placement of Le Mayeur's notice on the page, situated among a wide range of goods and services, firmly places his profession and specialization within an Atlantic world consumer marketplace. In other words, the juxtaposition

FIGURE 2. *Transplanting of Teeth,* Thomas Rowlandson, 1787. (Metropolitan Museum of Art, New York)

of purchasing teeth with an auction of household furniture and the sale of an enslaved man reflects the normalization of buying teeth and the commodification of bodies.

As you would expect, the constant advertising and demand for teeth for dentures, bridges, and live tooth transplantation left thousands of people with permanent gaps in their mouths. Every human tooth embedded in Washington's mouth broke another's smile. Individuals selling teeth, like Victor Hugo's *Les Misérables* character Fantine, were in precarious economic and social positions, leaving little archival record besides a line in an account book. Literature and images provide clues, though, to help us understand the lived realities of selling teeth, albeit from a middle-class and elite perspective.

Satirical cartoonist Thomas Rowlandson captured this moment in a drawing, *Transplanting the Teeth* (1787; see fig. 2), which depicts the extraction of teeth from the poor for wealthy elites. In the center of the print, a young chimney sweep covered in soot sits with his mouth open while a dentist examines his teeth. Next to the chimney sweep sits an elegantly dressed but grotesque older woman pointing to her mouth, indicating on herself which tooth she would like extracted from the young man and embedded into her own mouth. In the background, a poor man and woman covered in soot exit the office while clutching their mouths in pain and staring at their payment. Historian Mark Blackwell argues that this print, along with other British satirical plays, novels, and prints, mock the image of the poor youth losing their teeth for the wealthy old aristocracy.[22] However, the American context did not produce the same numbers of comic images, novels, and satirical essays.

Fascination with selling teeth extended into the quasi-fictional world of memoirs throughout the nineteenth century. English novelist Laetitia Matilda Hawkins, known for her conservative *Letters on the Female Mind, Its Powers and Pursuits: Addressed to Miss H. M. Williams, with particular reference to Her Letters from France* (1793), recounted a tale of tooth-selling woe in her *Memoirs, Anecdotes, Facts, and Opinions* (1824). Hawkins narrated the cautionary tale of Emma Hart, whose "character [was] entirely gone" and made "no secret of her poverty." Emma had determined that she would "get money by selling her teeth." While going to the dentist, she encountered a friend, who exclaimed, "I am sure I would never sell my teeth, while there were such houses as I can tell you." The "houses" that Emma's friend was referring to were brothels; she convinced Emma that such work would provide her consistent, reliable income as a prostitute and would be better than selling her irreplaceable teeth.[23]

While middling and elite literary works dripped with sentimental descriptions of the poor, the reality was that poor men and women, free and enslaved, Black and White, were selling their teeth—usually for two guineas each, which was about twenty days' wages for a male laborer.[24] In other words, selling teeth could purchase temporary relief from poverty, but it was not enough to radically change poor people's social and financial status. Indeed, those who sold their teeth were permanently marked by the loss.

A moralizing story—almost certainly fictitious—published in the *Daily Advertiser* in 1789 recounted a mournful tale from the winter of 1783. A young woman supporting her aging parents "accidentally heard of a dentist who advertised that he would give 3 guineas for every sound tooth." She resolved to visit him to raise enough funds for firewood. After her arrival, "she made known the circumstances which caused her to make this sacrifice," and the dentist was "affected by her tears, refused, and presented her with 10 guineas instead."[25] The story corroborates the steady supply of individuals responding to the newspaper advertisements offering to purchase their teeth. The young woman's story, Lady Hamilton's account, and the Rowlandson print are only a few examples of sentimental tales of woe that reflect the lower classes' desperation.

While poverty existed everywhere in the Atlantic world, the domestic trade that relied on the poor to sell their teeth failed to meet the growing demand for fill-in dentures for men like George Washington. As the meaning of teeth shifted over the course of the eighteenth century, dentists like John Greenwood similarly faced a constant demand for teeth to fulfill the medical and cosmetic requests of his patients. Greenwood, along with other dentists, thus began importing human teeth.

In 1806, Greenwood, who was a Revolutionary War veteran, traveled across the Atlantic from New York City to Paris to visit, celebrate, and commemorate the fight for liberty with the Marquis de Lafayette. It was not lost on Greenwood that France, and Paris in particular, was the birthplace of modern Western dentistry, with dental care and services actively integrated into the medical and social landscape. Between sightseeing, formal ceremonies, and receiving a commemorative button from Lafayette that depicted Washington, Greenwood also visited his dental colleagues at the Imperial Lyceum. A year later, he received an unusual shipment (by today's standards) from a French surgeon-dentist, Monsieur Bosquet: 4,300 human teeth.[26]

After they met in France, Greenwood and Monsieur Bosquet continued a correspondence negotiating the sale of human teeth via a factor named Lynch. Initially, Greenwood requested 1,000 teeth, but after the shipment was delayed due to poor weather, he took the opportunity to increase his shipment by 3,000 and agreed to "pay him for them and charges on receiving them."[27] Ultimately, Bosquet agreed to sell Greenwood 4,300 human teeth for 2,628 francs or 438 pieces of silver. The human mouth contains thirty-two teeth, including wisdom teeth, so 4,300 teeth are equivalent to 135 mouthfuls or 135 people. However, Greenwood was not interested in "full mouths," as he cataloged through itemized receipts, but in specifically useful teeth, like front teeth that could be made into dentures and bridges. While itemizing his shipment, Greenwood was alarmed that he failed to receive the promised 4,300 "good teeth" but counted only 4,211 teeth—and most of those of lesser quality. He organized the shipment into "good" and "bad" teeth, with 297 good front teeth and 1,857 "rotten teeth" that he declared "good for nothing." Additionally, he noted that he received 1,057 "eye teeth," or canines, that he "seldom uses." However, Greenwood was a businessman and understood that he could still profit from the "bad teeth" by selling them to other dentists or to lower-class patients.[28]

While it is unclear where this shipment of 4,300 human teeth specifically originated, they were likely taken from battlefield dead. In the early nineteenth century, France had been ravaged by nearly a hundred years of European wars, culminating in Napoleon's wars of expansion, creating a seemingly endless supply of human teeth. Teeth were often scavenged from fallen soldiers; later, human teeth were often referred to as "Waterloo teeth" from the number of dead and, therefore, teeth taken from the 1815 battlefield.[29]

This international shipment of human teeth bore the markings of other commercial activity throughout the eighteenth and early nineteenth centuries, including negotiation, working through a factor, receiving itemized receipts, and experiencing frustration over quality control—except that the commodity traded happened to be human teeth extracted from the dead or sold by the poor.[30] This level of mercantile sophistication indicates that Greenwood's 1807 shipment of 4,211 human teeth was not an isolated event but rather part of a larger tooth trade that extended throughout the Atlantic world, a calculated business transaction no different from cases of Madeira or bolts of calico. If the trade in teeth was unique or seen as morally ambivalent, then the process would not have been so standardized. Nor would the letters between Bosquet, Lynch, and Greenwood have been so straightforward. This was just business as usual.

This trade in teeth will undoubtedly raise a particularly thorny question from students: Where did the human teeth in Washington's dentures come from? The exact origins of the human teeth in Washington's dentures are currently unknown. This question is legitimately raised, in light of both the economy of teeth outlined above and a line item in Washington's account book. In May 1784, Washington's estate manager wrote in the account book, "By Cash pd Negroes for 9 Teeth on Acct of Dr Lemoin. 6 pounds, 2 shilling."[31] Eighteenth-century enslavers often bought goods from the enslaved. Items like eggs, poultry, game, and vegetables were frequently purchased, since enslaved people, routinely undersupplied by their enslavers and thus lacking in adequate nutrition, supplemented their own diet through gardening, raising animals, foraging, and hunting. However, having physical body parts like teeth sold to enslavers is rare in account books. While it is unclear what precisely happened to those teeth, they were purchased by Jean Pierre Le Mayeur while he was visiting Mount Vernon. What is also clear is that these teeth were not placed into any set of dentures for George Washington. Le Mayeur was trained as a surgeon and specialized in tooth extraction and live tooth transplantation rather than constructing dentures. Moreover, Washington was not wearing full dentures at the time of purchase in 1784.

The iconic Greenwood dentures contain human teeth, but without invasive DNA testing, it is impossible to determine their country of origin. The teeth were likely sourced from battlefield dead in Europe or sold by the poor and desperate in New York City, where Greenwood practiced. For example, Greenwood's advertisement in the *New York Daily Gazette* from April 14, 1789, read, "LIVE TEETH. One guinea given for each," and the ad makes no comment or restriction related to race or free or enslaved status. Thus, enslaved people could have sold their teeth to Greenwood, but he would have tossed those teeth into his case with other kinds and removed them from any racialized connotations. Ultimately, dentists like John Greenwood—and clients like George Washington, by extension—constantly demanded human teeth to create dentures that, as Greenwood promised in his advertisements, "give a youthful air to the countenance, and render pronunciation more agreeable and distinct."[32] When Greenwood made Washington's dentures, determining the provenance of the teeth would never have occurred to him or to Washington. Instead, Greenwood would have selected human teeth based on size, color, and quality, just as a jeweler selects stones for a ring.

While the eighteenth-century Atlantic world made Washington's bite, it also unmade his mouth. Washington frequently complained of mouth pain, and the bulky dentures made speaking and eating difficult. The physical object thus shaped Washington's daily life and his role as a public figure. For example, it was frequently noted that Washington's favorite meal was hoecakes "swimming in butter and honey."[33] Hoecakes were cornmeal pancakes originally eaten by Indigenous North Americans that were later adopted, and adapted, by enslaved Africans and colonial settlers, becoming known as "fair Virginia's pride."[34] However, for Washington, the hoecake was also soft on pained teeth and easy to consume without dentures or teeth. Thus, the foodways that Washington followed were directly related to his physical body and the dentures he wore.

Washington's poor dental health and bulky dentures affected more than just what foods he ate. It shaped how he approached political life. Washington was known as a quiet statesman, frequently speaking little. This may, in part, have reflected his nature, but from a young age Washington was insecure about his teeth and breath. His aide allegedly wrote in 1760, "His mouth is large and generally firmly closed, but which from time to time discloses some defective teeth."[35] Nearly thirty years later, when Washington was the first president and wore heavy lead dentures in his mouth, speaking became increasingly cumbersome. Thus, the dentures, owing to their weight and their foul odor from the rotting ivory, affected Washington's speech and, therefore, his public and private personas.

As the president and then former president, Washington was expected to give public addresses and host lavish banquets with scores of toasts—a key part of the social ritual of dining in the eighteenth century. Madeira, a fortified red wine from off the coast of Portugal, was the preferred beverage of early American elites, and it constantly stained Washington's dentures. This frequent staining intensely frustrated Washington, whose dentist explained in 1798 that "the sett you sent me from Philadelphia which when I Received was very black Ocationed either by your soaking them in port wine, or by your drinking it." Greenwood advised Washington "to Either take them out After dinner and put them in cleain water and put in another scett or Cleain them with a brush and som Chalk."[36] Washington's dentures, particularly the ivory teeth, absorbed staining from tea, coffee, and Madeira, resulting in a wood-grain effect—and laying the foundation for the myth of his wooden teeth.

Stained dentures that need to be cleaned seem like a small, unimportant thing. However, the stained dentures mattered. They mattered enough to Washington to brush them—or to command enslaved valet William Lee to do so. They mattered enough that Washington frequently sought out dental services, leaving behind both written and material culture records. They mattered enough to Washington that he maintained relationships with the leading dental professionals in North America. They mattered enough that Washington's final dentist imported thousands of teeth from France and whittled countless ivory tusks from Africa. They mattered. In other words, by sitting down and writing to Greenwood complaining about his stained dentures, Washington is not just seeking dental and cosmetic care but is embodying the eighteenth-century Atlantic world in his mouth.

Coda: Teaching with Objects

George Washington's dentures tell a story—just as all objects do. The way objects are designed, made, bought, sold, and used illuminate both daily life, like Washington's preference for hoecakes, and connections across the world, like the sources for real and artificial teeth. Taken more generally, broader cultural values and economic systems come into focus through examining the everyday, the mundane, the routine, the tedious. Washington's dentures are a fascinating object with broad, revealing, and at times unsettling connections, but even a coffee cup or a tube of toothpaste tells a story, and that story begins with our asking questions.

However, when staring at an unknown object, knowing where to start can be daunting for students, educators, and scholars alike. The worksheet from George Washington's Mount Vernon contained in the appendix to this essay provides a starting place from which to walk students through the different layers of object analysis—description, historical context, materials, and use. Descriptions provide a familiar touchstone for students and will help them avoid leaping to interpretations without tangible evidence from the object to support claims and illuminate additional research inquiries. Students often feel unmoored, however, and demand more than description alone. Thus, after completing observational analysis, applying historical context—or background information—can help guide additional questions for the object. Objects like George Washington's dentures connect to a wide range of topics, and brainstorming what kinds of context should be considered can narrow the inquiry.

Likewise, identifying and tracing the origins of materials can help direct analysis. Where materials come from and how they are crafted highlight trade networks, scientific and technological innovation, occupations in society, knowledge production, and how people interact with one another. Finally, how objects are used reconnects students to vast networks and to the tangible ways in which objects shaped historical actors—and how historical actors shaped objects. Objects encourage certain kinds of use based on their design and function. Thinking about how an object is used, and how it might affect other aspects of life, demonstrates how objects live far beyond the initial purchase.

Appendix: Twenty Questions for Reading and Evaluating

Look closely at the object and draw a sketch of it. Then, briefly answer the following questions.

INQUIRY QUESTION	KEYWORD ANSWER	EXPLAIN YOUR EVIDENCE
What color is it?		
What is it made of?		
Is it big or small?		
Is it heavy or light?		
What shape is it?		
What is the pattern, or design, on the object?		
If you touched it, how would it feel?		
Does it make noise?		
Is it old or new?		
What is it used for?		
Would both adults and children use it?		
Why might someone make this?		
Do you like the way it looks?		
Has it always looked this way?		
What value does this object have?		
Will the object become more or less valuable over time?		
What happens once this object is no longer used?		
Does the object remind you of anything you use today?		
What questions do you still have about this object?		
Where would you go to learn more about this object?		

Based on your answers, write 2–3 sentences about what you can infer about this object.

Notes

Citations of Founders Online documents do not include individual links, as each source can be found by searching the site at https://founders.archives.gov/.

1. Karin Dannehl, "Object Biographies: From Production to Consumption," in *History and Material Culture: A Student's Guide to Approaching Alternative Sources,* ed. Karen Harvey (London: Routledge, 2009), 171.
2. In the eighteenth century, lead was used for a wide variety of objects, including dentures, pipe heads, drinking vessels, musket balls, and cosmetics. Concerns about lead poisoning were first raised in the twentieth century. For lead manufacturing in the eighteenth century, see D. J. Rowe, *Lead Manufacturing in Britain: A History* (London: Routledge, 1983).
3. These dentures are held at the New York Academy of Medicine.
4. *The Selected Papers of Charles Willson Peale and His Family,* vol. 2, *The Artist as Museum Keeper, 1791–1810,* ed. Lillian B. Miller et al. (New Haven, CT: Yale University Press, 1988), 693–94.
5. Mary Otto, *Teeth: The Story of Beauty, Inequality, and the Struggle for Oral Health in America* (New York: New Press, 2016), vi–x.
6. For more information, see Colin Jones, *The Smile Revolution in Eighteenth-Century Paris* (New York: Oxford University Press, 2017). Jones demonstrates that aristocratic and royal portraits often depicted elites with hollow cheeks, indicating tooth loss. However, as systems of meanings changed, portraits of toothless elites became almost extinct, suggesting a sharp change in the meaning of teeth.
7. For the consumer revolution and the body, see Jennifer Van Horn, "George Washington's Dentures: Disability, Deception, and the Republican Body," *Early American Studies* 14, no. 1 (2016): 2–47; Elizabeth Kowaleski-Wallace, *Consuming Subjects: Women, Shopping, and Business in the Eighteenth Century* (New York: Columbia University Press, 1997); Catherine E. Kelly, *Republic of Taste: Art, Politics, and Everyday Life in Early America* (Philadelphia: University of Pennsylvania Press, 2016).
8. Maurizio Valsania, *First Among Men: George Washington and the Myth of American Masculinity* (Baltimore: Johns Hopkins University Press, 2022), 209–11.
9. Charles Moore, ed., *George Washington's Rules of Civility and Decent Behaviour in Company and Conversation* (New York: Houghton Mifflin, 1926), 3–5.
10. Bernhard Weinberger, *An Introduction to the History of Dentistry in America* (St. Louis: C. V. Mosby, 1948), 257.
11. John M. Hyson Jr., Joseph W. A. Whitehorne, and John T. Greenwood, *A History of Dentistry in the U.S. Army to World War II* (Washington, DC: Borden Institute, 2008), 4.

12. Jones, *Smile Revolution*, 75–80.
13. Jones, *Smile Revolution*, 77.
14. James Wilson, *The Ludicrous Operator, or Blacksmith Turn'd Tooth Drawer*, 1765, mezzotint printmark, Wellcome Collection.
15. Ann Charlotte Frescheville, recipe book, 1669, Joseph Downs Collection of Manuscripts and Printed Ephemera, Winterthur Museum, Garden, & Library, Winterthur, DE.
16. Eliza Lucas Pinckney, *Recipe Book of Eliza Lucas Pinckney, 1756* (Charleston, SC: J. Furlong, 1956).
17. Weinberger, *Introduction*, 368.
18. Josiah Foster Flagg, *The Family Dentist: Containing a Brief Description of the Structure, Formation, Diseases, and Treatment of Human Teeth* (Boston: J. W. Ingraham, 1822), 83.
19. Jedidiah Morse, *The American Geography, or, A View of the Present Situation of the United States of America* (Elizabethtown, NJ: Shepard Kollock, 1789), 145–46, quoted in Robert Gross, "Reading for an Extensive Republic," in *A History of the Book in North America*, vol. 2, *An Extensive Republic: Print, Culture, and Society in the New Nation, 1790–1840* (Chapel Hill: University of North Carolina Press, 2010), 516.
20. Gross, "Reading for an Extensive Republic," 516–19.
21. David S. Shields, *Civil Tongues and Polite Society in British America* (Chapel Hill: University of North Carolina Press, 1997), 286.
22. Mark Blackwell, "'Extraneous Bodies': The Contagion of Live-Tooth Transplantation in Late-Eighteenth-Century England," *Eighteenth-Century Life* 28, no. 1 (2004): 21–68.
23. Laetitia Matilda Hawkins, *Memoirs, Anecdotes, Facts, and Opinions, Collected and Preserved* (London: Longman, Hurst, Rees, Orme, Brown, and Green; and C. & J. Rivington, 1824), 2:40–42.
24. Advertisement, *Massachusetts Centinel* (Boston), October 9, 1784, reprinted in Carroll D. Wright, *Comparative Wages, Prices, and Cost of Living* (Boston: Wright and Potter, 1889), 46.
25. Weinberger, *Introduction*, 173.
26. John Greenwood Correspondence, 1807–1810, Greenwood Family Papers, New York Historical.
27. John Greenwood to Lynch, December 25, 1806, Greenwood Family Papers, New York Historical.
28. John Greenwood to Bosquet, June 1807, Greenwood Family Papers, New York Historical.
29. Jones, *Smile Revolution*, 138.

30. David Hancock, *Oceans of Wine: Madeira and the Emergence of American Trade and Taste* (New Haven, CT: Yale University Press, 2009).
31. George Washington, Ledger B, 1772–1793, Founders Online.
32. Greenwood, advertisement, *New York Daily Gazette*, July 10, 1788.
33. Nelly Custis, quoted in *Dining with the Washingtons: Historic Recipes, Entertainment, and Hospitality from Mount Vernon*, ed. Stephen A. McLeod (Chapel Hill: University of North Carolina Press, 2011), 38.
34. Joel Barlow, "The Hasty Pudding," in *Selections from the American Poets*, ed. William Cullen Bryant (New York: Harper & Brothers, 1860).
35. George Mercer, quoted in Douglas Southall Freeman, *George Washington: A Biography*, vol. 3 (New York: Scribner, 1948), 6. For the full text of this description, see Resolutions of the House of Burgesses, February 26, 1759, Founders Online.
36. John Greenwood to George Washington, December 28, 1798, Founders Online.

CONTRIBUTORS

BONNIE A. BELSHE received a bachelor's degree in psychology with a minor in criminal justice from Saint Louis University. She earned an MA in teaching from the University of San Francisco and an MA in history from San José State University. She has taught US history and AP US history for more than twenty years at Monta Vista High School in Cupertino, California, and currently serves as department chair. In 2014, Belshe was named the California History Teacher of the Year by the Gilder Lehrman Institute of American History. In 2017–2018, Belshe was awarded the Life Guard Teacher Fellowship from Mount Vernon and has served as a teacher facilitator for the George Washington Teacher Institute since 2020.

KATE ELIZABETH BROWN is an associate professor of history and legal studies at Western Kentucky University, specializing in American legal and constitutional history and the early republic. She is the lead scholar for the "George Washington and the Economy of the New Nation" program at the George Washington Teacher Institute. The author of *Alexander Hamilton and the Development of American Law* (2017), she won the 2019 National Hamilton Scholar award. She has received numerous fellowships and research grants, including from the George Washington Presidential Library, New York State Archives, and American Society of Legal History.

DENVER BRUNSMAN is an associate professor and chair of the history department at George Washington University, where his courses include "George Washington and His World," taught annually at Mount Vernon. He is the author of *George Washington and His World: Enslaver, Revolutionary, President* (2026) and *The Evil Necessity: British Naval Impressment in the Eighteenth-Century Atlantic World* (2013), among other publications. He has served as the lead scholar for the "Leadership and Legacy: Lessons from George Washington" program of the George Washington Teacher Institute since its inception in 2016.

SCOTT E. CASPER is president of the American Antiquarian Society, a national research library of American history and culture in Worcester, Massachusetts. The author of *Sarah Johnson's Mount Vernon: The Forgotten History of an American*

Shrine (2008) and author or editor of eight other books, he has taught in the George Washington Teacher Institute since 2000 and advised Mount Vernon on its museum exhibition *Lives Bound Together: Slavery at George Washington's Mount Vernon.* He previously served as Foundation Professor of History at the University of Nevada, Reno, and dean of Arts, Humanities, and Social Sciences at the University of Maryland, Baltimore County.

LINDSAY M. CHERVINSKY is a presidential historian and executive director of the George Washington Presidential Library at Mount Vernon. She is the author of the award-winning books *Making the Presidency: John Adams and the Precedents That Forged the Republic* (2024) and *The Cabinet: George Washington and the Creation of an American Institution* (2020) and coeditor of *Mourning the Presidents: Loss and Legacy in American Culture* (2023). Chervinsky has published in *The Washington Post, USA Today,* CNN.com, *The Wall Street Journal,* and *Washington Monthly,* and she is a regular resource for CBS News, CNN, the BBC, *The New York Times,* and *The Washington Post.*

LORRI GLOVER is the Bannon Endowed Professor in the history department at Saint Louis University. Her books include *Founders as Fathers: The Private Lives and Politics of the American Revolutionaries* (2014), *The Fate of the Revolution: Virginians Debate the Constitution* (2016), and *Eliza Lucas Pinckney: An Independent Woman in the Age of Revolution* (2020). Glover has served as president of the Southern Association for Women Historians and the Southern Historical Association. In 2020 she joined the author team for McGraw-Hill's high school and middle school US history textbooks.

ERIC LOUÉRS-PHILLIPS is the associate superintendent of public affairs for a large public school system in the mid-Atlantic region. A native Washingtonian, he began his teaching career in 1998 with Montgomery County (Maryland) Public Schools. Over the years, he has served as an elementary and middle school teacher, assistant principal, social studies curriculum specialist, and supervisor of Accelerating Achievement and Equity. Louérs-Phillips also serves on several community-based boards. He earned degrees from Morgan State University and Hood College, where he is an adjunct professor in the education department.

JESSIE MACLEOD served on Mount Vernon's curatorial team from 2012 to 2023, first as assistant and then associate curator. She was the lead curator for the award-winning exhibition *Lives Bound Together: Slavery at George Washington's Mount Vernon* (2016–2021) and contributed to the accompanying publication. At Mount Vernon, she also curated numerous other exhibits and displays across the estate. MacLeod received a BA in history from Yale University and an MA in history, with a certificate in public history, from the University of Massachusetts, Amherst. She works as an independent museum consultant in Westchester County, New York.

ALISSA OGINSKY is director of K–12 education at George Washington's Mount Vernon. She manages a team of educators in the development and implementation of mission-aligned programming and the creation of educational resources for teachers and students in K–12 classroom settings around the United States. Oginsky is a former classroom teacher, lead teacher, curriculum contributor, and Teacher of the Year in Fairfax County (Virginia) Public Schools. She holds an MA in art museum and gallery education from Newcastle University and a BS in elementary education from York College of Pennsylvania.

SHAWNEL PADILLA, a citizen of the Mi'gmaq First Nations, is a librarian and teacher facilitator based in southcentral Alaska. She earned her BA in political science and her MA in education from the University of Alaska Southeast and holds a library certification from Montana State University with a specialization in Indigenous perspectives. Padilla's early experiences in rural Alaska shaped a lifelong commitment to mentorship, cultural continuity, and rigorous place-based education. As a fellow at Mount Vernon through the "War in Washington's World" program, she advanced her scholarship in early American history and its modern-day implications. Padilla mentors educators statewide and designs curricula that center Indigenous voices and regional histories.

LAURA J. PING is an assistant professor of US history at Bellarmine University. She received her PhD from The Graduate Center, City University of New York. Her research focuses on gender and culture. She is the coauthor of *Catharine Beecher: The Complexity of Gender in Nineteenth-Century America* (2022), which explores how social and technological changes during the nineteenth century can be understood through the life of education reformer Catharine Beecher. Ping's current book project, *Beyond the Bloomer: Fashioning Change in Nineteenth-Century Dress,* analyzes how American women used fashion as a political symbol prior to gaining the right to vote.

SARAH J. PURCELL is the L. F. Parker Professor of History at Grinnell College. She is the author of *Sealed with Blood: War, Sacrifice, and Memory in Revolutionary America* (2002) and *Spectacle of Grief: Public Funerals and Memory in Civil War America* (2022). She has written and coauthored several other books, including *American Horizons: U.S. History in a Global Perspective,* 5th ed. (2025). Purcell is the lead scholar for the annual "George Washington at War" program of the George Washington Teacher Institute.

LYNN PRICE ROBBINS holds a PhD in US history from George Mason University. She coedited *George Washington's Barbados Diary, 1751–52* (2018) and *The Papers of Martha Washington* (2022) and is the author of an essay on Martha Washington in *The Women of George Washington's World* (2022). She serves as the head of research for Primary Source Media and cohost of the podcast *2 Complicated 4 History*. Robbins previously held assistant editor positions at the University of Virginia and the Abraham Lincoln Presidential Library and Museum.

KATHRYN M. SILVA is a dean at Bunker Hill Community College. She serves as lead scholar for the George Washington Teacher Institute's "Lives Bound Together: Enslavement in George Washington's World" program and as a consultant for the George Washington exhibit at Mount Vernon. Her research centers on the skilled textile labor of African American women in plantations and mills under slavery and Jim Crow, which is the focus of her forthcoming book. She is the coeditor, with Mitali Wong, of *Perspectives on the Impact of AI in Teaching Writing and Reading* (2026). She earned her PhD in US history from the University of South Carolina.

DAVID J. SILVERMAN is professor of history at George Washington University. He is the author of several books, including *Thundersticks: Firearms and the Violent Transformation of Native America* (2016), *This Land Is Their Land: The Wampanoag Indians, Plymouth Colony, and the Troubled History of Thanksgiving* (2019), and *The Chosen and the Damned: Native Americans and the Making of Race in the United States* (2026). His essays have appeared in *The New York Times, The Washington Post, The Atlantic,* and *National Geographic.*

LUCY SMITH is a PhD candidate in the joint history and women's and gender studies program at the University of Michigan. Before graduate school, Smith worked in the museum field, most recently as the education specialist at George Washington's Mount Vernon. Her work explores the intersections of material culture, the body, and transatlantic trade.

MORGAN SMITH is the elementary social science and global studies specialist for Loudoun County (Virginia) Public Schools, where she drives curriculum development and facilitates professional development for teachers throughout the county. She specializes in creating engaging, standards-aligned resources for elementary social science instruction. Prior to her current role, Smith was an elementary educator for ten years in LCPS and served in a range of positions, including first-grade special education teacher and fourth- and fifth-grade teacher. She began her career as a special education paraprofessional in both self-contained and inclusion general education classrooms. She has also served as a teacher facilitator for three years for the "Lives Bound Together" week at the Mount Vernon Teacher Institute. Smith holds a BA in sports management with a minor in business administration from the University of Tennessee and an MA in elementary education from the University of Phoenix.

JOHN CLINTON WALSH, or Clint, teaches at Discovery Middle School in Orlando, Florida, where he was Teacher of the Year in 2022. He holds a BA in history from the University of Central Florida, an MA in instructional design and technology from Purdue University Global, and he is pursuing an MA in American history with Gilder Lehrman at Gettysburg College. He was awarded a Life Guard Teacher Fellowship in 2019 and James Madison Fellowship in 2023. In 2025, he was selected as the Florida History Teacher of the Year by the Gilder Lehrman Institute of American History.

K. ALLISON WICKENS is vice president for education at George Washington's Mount Vernon. She leads the education and guest services department at Mount Vernon and oversees the history and civics learning goals for the institution's on-site, off-site, and online efforts. She specializes in studying how young people learn at museums, historic sites, and schools and has written on this subject in articles published in the *Journal of Museum Education*. Wickens previously worked at the Smithsonian Institution and studied at the University of Colorado, Boulder, and Grinnell College.

INDEX

Italicized page numbers refer to figures and maps.

FROM PAMPHLETS TO PODCASTS

An Institute for Thomas Paine Studies Series

Creating an Informed Citizenry: Knowledge and Democracy in the Early American Republic
George D. Oberle III

Archival Communities: Constructing the Past in the Early United States
Derek Kane O'Leary

www.ingramcontent.com/pod-product-compliance
Ingram Content Group UK Ltd.
Pitfield, Milton Keynes, MK11 3LW, UK
UKHW010436220926
475848UK00005B/762

9 780813 955858